UNEP
YEAR
BOOK

NEW SCIENCE AND DEVELOPMENTS
IN OUR CHANGING ENVIRONMENT

2010

UNEP

United Nations Environment Programme

Contents

Disasters and Conflicts

Resource Efficiency

Preface

International environmental governance is likely to be a key topic on the political agenda in 2010, with an increasing number of governments interested in engaging on reform and others calling directly for it.

Governance will be a key focus of this year's UNEP Governing Council/Global Ministerial Environment Forum in Bali, providing an opportunity for reflection but also for focus as the world looks towards Rio+20 in 2012.

The UNEP Year Book 2010 underlines the way in which the international environmental architecture and machinery continues to expand, but perhaps in ways that are duplicating efforts to address environmental challenges and leading to more rather than less fragmentation.

The Year Book points out that, over the period from 1998 to 2009, 218 new multilateral environmental agreements, protocols, and amendments have emerged, in addition to existing ones.

The three chemicals and waste conventions—Basel, Rotterdam and Stockholm—are, however, spotlighting part of a possible new approach aimed at streamlining and focusing efforts towards a Green Economy. In Bali the Conferences of the Parties to the three conventions will take part in a simultaneous extraordinary conference, having agreed in early 2009 to consolidate their common functions and enhance cooperation and coordination at the administrative and programmatic levels.

The events and the outcome of the UN Climate Change Conference in Copenhagen have generated thousands of column inches and stimulated debate in the media and beyond.

The challenge of delivering the Copenhagen Accord is also fuelling the governance debate, with some world leaders calling for immediate and far-reaching action with respect to relevant UN institutions.

Where there was certainly light rather than heat was in regard to Reduced Emissions from Deforestation and Forest Degradation (REDD). Well-supported and speedily implemented, REDD will make an important contribution not only to combating climate change but also to overcoming poverty and to a successful UN International Year of Biodiversity.

The Year Book estimates that investing US$22-29 billion into REDD could cut global deforestation by 25 per cent by 2015. It also highlights a new and promising REDD project in Brazil, at the Juma Sustainable Development Reserve in Amazonas.

Here each family receives US$28 a month if the forest remains uncut, one potential way of tipping the economic balance in favour of conservation versus continued deforestation.

Only time will tell whether the overall package contained in the Copenhagen Accord—including the pledges and intentions on emissions and funding for developing countries—will genuinely move the world forward in the direction of a low carbon, resource efficient, Green Economy.

It is clear that an increasing number of countries are pressing forward on this front, and for reasons above and beyond just climate change. 2010 will be a litmus test on whether this can be accelerated nationally but also globally. The UN Climate Change Conference in Mexico may well be a defining moment in this respect.

Achim Steiner
United Nations Under-Secretary-General and Executive Director,
United Nations Environment Programme

Year Book On-line

A growing source of environmental information!

Visit our website:

www.unep.org/yearbook/2010

- Read the **press release**
- Download the **full report** for free—available in all six UN languages
- Visit the **resource database** where you can find the reference material
- Fill out the on-line **questionnaire** to give us feedback
- View the extreme water-related **environmental events map**
- Download any of the **previous** Year Books

Introduction

The UNEP Year Book 2010 reports on new environmental science and recent developments in our changing environment. It looks at progress in environmental governance; the effects of continuing degradation and loss of the world's ecosystems; impacts of climate change; how harmful substances and hazardous waste affect human health and the environment; environmentally related disasters and conflicts; and unsustainable use of resources. The chapters correspond to UNEP's six thematic priorities.

The purpose of the Year Book is to strengthen the science-policy interface. Thus, it presents recent developments and new scientific insights of particular interest to policy-makers. Consistent with the Year Book's established format and style, important issues are examined, referenced, and often illustrated. The main sources of information are peer-reviewed papers in scientific journals, results published by research institutions, news articles, and other reports. While the Year Book brings to the forefront some of the views expressed and progress made in recent months, it does not endorse particular views or indeed any scientific findings.

The Year Book's content is the product of a screening and peer-review process that involved more than 70 experts. Out of more than 100 emerging issues initially suggested by experts, less than one-third have found a place in the Year Book 2010.

Some of the issues included in the Year Book are already well-known, while others are emerging or represent years of research and continuous debate in the scientific community. It is in the nature of scientific research that there is uncertainty or disagreement about some findings. In such cases, the Year Book acknowledges that differing points of view exist.

The first chapter, on *environmental governance*, reports on the acceleration of intergovernmental efforts to reform the United Nations' system of international environmental governance. The chapter also highlights regional dimensions, and the important roles of non-governmental organizations and the private sector.

The chapter on *ecosystem management* presents emerging science on ecosystem thresholds and planetary boundaries. Concerns about how to maintain healthy ecosystems in the face of population pressures and climate change, are emphasized. Food production relies on the capacity of ecosystems to provide water, soils, climate regulation, and other benefits. The loss of these benefits, coinciding with increasing biofuel production in several parts of the world, could reduce the amount of land available for food crops.

The chapter on *harmful substances and hazardous waste* focuses on potential hazards and risks associated with nanomaterials, endocrine disrupters, brominated flame retardants, and some widely used pesticides. The impacts of international transport of hazardous and electronic waste on human health and the environment are also examined.

The *climate change* chapter discusses the effects of increasing greenhouse gas concentrations on global systems. Trends associated with climate change include decreasing Arctic sea-ice cover, ocean acidification, and the expansion of the tropical belt. This chapter looks at progress made in 'climate attribution', which demonstrates the mechanisms that are held responsible for observed changes in the climate.

The *disasters and conflicts* chapter highlights the importance of sustainable natural resource management in regard to conflict prevention and peacebuilding. It reviews the tools being used, such as threat and risk analysis and mapping that incorporate environmental indicators and local knowledge. This chapter also explores the environmental drivers of disaster risk, and how climate change is affecting disaster risk.

The final chapter, on *resource efficiency,* addresses the fundamental problem of unsustainable production and consumption, which is bringing about natural resource depletion, climate change, and material waste, as well as geo-engineered technological fixes. Although energy-related CO_2 emissions continue to increase, progress is being made in a number of areas with respect to investment in renewable energy sources.

Water is a recurrent theme in this Year Book. Each chapter considers water-related environmental changes, together with a number of challenges and opportunities:

- There are promising developments in regional cooperation to manage transboundary river basins, which cover more than 45 per cent of the planet's land surface and directly affect about 40 per cent of the world population;

- The world's densely populated, and heavily farmed, sinking deltas are receiving increasing attention. Direct human activities have significantly increased their vulnerability;

- The expansion of the tropical belt is a trend associated with climate change. The widening of the tropics will have a cascading effect on large-scale circulation systems. It will impact the patterns of precipitation on which natural ecosystems, agricultural productivity, and water resources depend. Several regions are expected to be increasingly affected by persistent drought and water scarcity;

- Amid growing concerns about water scarcity, which is projected to affect almost half of the world's population by 2030, traditional technologies are finding new applications. The karez or quanat system, traditional in some arid and semi-arid regions, collects groundwater in underground tunnels and distributes it for irrigation and domestic use;

- Wastewater has long furnished water and nutrients for agriculture. Sewage water is estimated to irrigate about half the gardens, roadside verges, and small fields where food is grown in the world's urban and peri-urban areas. A new look is being taken at how to use this traditional resource safely;

- The Year Book also includes a map of extreme water-related environmental events in 2009.

The Year Book 2010 is provided as an information document for the Eleventh Special Session of the UNEP Governing Council/Global Ministerial Environment Forum. It is also a credible source of environmental information for non-specialist audiences, research institutions, universities, and schools. Feedback on the 2010 UNEP Year Book is very welcome, as well as suggestions of emerging issues for consideration in the next edition. We invite readers to use the questionnaire form at the back, or visit www.unep.org/yearbook/2010/

Environmental Governance

In 2009, efforts to advance international environmental governance focused on defining the key objectives and functions of an improved UN architecture to address global environmental change.

The coming together of multiple stakeholders seeking solutions to environmental problems. About 15 000 representatives from governments, non-governmental organizations, and media participated in the UN Climate Change Conference in Copenhagen.
Credit: Bob Strong

INTRODUCTION

2009 was marked by the convergence of several global crises. Around the world, societies suffered the far-reaching consequences of financial and economic turmoil, fluctuating food prices and shortages, and energy market insecurity. Policy-makers put together immense economic stimulus packages. The financial, food, and energy crises did not unfold in isolation from other environmental and social challenges. They are linked in many ways to continuing biodiversity loss, ecosystem degradation, and climate change. Consequently, these crises have exacerbated existing challenges to meeting the Millennium Development Goals (UN 2009).

2009 witnessed an acceleration of inter-governmental efforts to reform the UN's system of international environmental governance (IEG). UNEP's Governing Council established a Consultative Group of Ministers or High-Level Representatives on International Environmental Governance, which has discussed the core objectives and corresponding functions of IEG in the context of the UN system.

The year will also be remembered for international efforts to create a new agreement to address climate change, which has become a quintessential long-term policy and governance issue (Giddens 2009, Hovi and others 2009, Walker and others 2009, Beck 2008).

Numerous developments in 2009 underlined the potential of regional environmental governance to help meet global environmental goals. Delegates to several multilateral environmental agreement (MEA) meetings negotiated ways to decentralize environmental governance, for example in regard to chemicals and waste management (UNEP POPs 2009). Regional initiatives were also highlighted in the context of water governance and sustainable forest management (McAlpine 2009).

Private sector involvement in various aspects of governance was also high on the international political agenda in 2009, especially following the financial crisis, which made acute demands on public finance. Public-private partnerships have experienced sustained growth, accompanied by considerable success, and some important lessons have been learned.

REFORMING THE ARCHITECTURE OF INTERNATIONAL ENVIRONMENTAL GOVERNANCE

The term 'governance' has been defined in many different ways, which vary according to the scope and locus of decision-making power (ECOSOC 2006). In recent times, many governance functions influencing individual and collective behaviour have been performed beyond the exclusive remit of governments. Accordingly, there has been a move to a definition under which "governance, at whatever level of social organization it may take place, refers to conducting the public's business—to the constellation of authoritative rules, institutions, and practices by means of which any collectivity manages its affairs" (Ruggie 2004). The most important actors in the process of IEG include national governments; intergovernmental organizations such as the UN and its specialized bodies; civil society groups; private sector associations; and a variety of partnerships between public, private, and civil society actors. The key institutions and mechanisms through which IEG is carried out include a multitude of intergovernmental, non-state, and public-private processes and initiatives that vary in format, structure, and membership.

In 2009, important deliberations centred on reforming the UN's overall system of international environmental governance. This process, which began almost a decade ago, became increasingly pressing with the momentum gathering on the road to the United Nations Climate Change Conference (COP15) in Copenhagen, negotiations of the fifth replenishment of the Global Environment Facility (GEF) in 2010, and the commencement of the preparatory process for the UN Conference on Sustainable Development to be held in Brazil in 2012.

The diverse and complex impacts of climate change highlight the importance of other related environmental and social areas, including water management, biodiversity conservation, and forest and land management. Climate change was a central concern in various MEA meetings and other gatherings in 2009 (**Box 1**). The linkages between various environmental issues emphasize the importance of developing integrated approaches to address climate change in the context of sustainable development, and in accordance with the principle of common but differentiated responsibilities and respective capabilities (CSD 2009a).

In 2009, climate change negotiations and IEG reform were linked when French President Nicolas Sarkozy and German Chancellor Angela Merkel wrote to the UN Secretary-General to outline their positions ahead of a climate change summit in New York. To reach an "effective and fair" agreement in Copenhagen, they stated that "a new institutional architecture will need to be set up to foster the development of international environmental law. Environmental governance must be overhauled. We must make use of the momentum provided by Copenhagen to make further progress towards the creation of a World Environmental Organization" (Merkel and Sarkozy 2009). Leaders of many developing countries agree. Kenyan President Mwai Kibaki, for example, has urged African leaders to support the upgrading

of UNEP into a World Environment Organization based in Nairobi, a call that was echoed in a resolution adopted at the 18th Session of the African Caribbean and Pacific-European Union Joint Parliamentary Assembly, as well as at the Glion Forum on Global Environmental Governance, which brought together academics, practitioners, and all five successive UNEP Executive Directors (ACP-EU JPA 2009, GEGP 2009).

Calls to establish and adequately fund such an organization are not new (Biermann and others 2009a, Walker and others 2009, Runge 2001, Biermann 2000, Esty 1994). An important element of IEG reform concerns the definition of the objectives and functions of the UN's work on IEG and the status to be given the environment in the context of sustainable development. Another widely discussed aspect is the extent of coherence of international environmental governance. Experts and practitioners almost universally regard the current extent of overlap, duplication, and fragmentation as a negative quality, a view echoed in the UN Joint Implementation Unit's 2008 Review of International Environmental Governance (Biermann and others 2009a, Oberthür 2009, JIU 2008). In his statement to the 2009 UNEP Governing Council/Global Ministerial Environment Forum (GC/GMEF), Marthinus van Schalkwyk, the South African Minister of Environmental Affairs and Tourism, referred to "burgeoning fragmentation and duplication in an overburdened system" as a key obstacle to the integration of environmental concerns into macro-economic policy-making, as well as an issue of "critical importance" to developing countries (Van Schalkwyk 2009). At the same time, some argue that the existing diversified system may contribute to stability, foster experimentation, promote learning, and facilitate the formation of coalitions of the willing by offering alternative venues for dialogue and action (Ansell and Balsiger 2009, Ostrom 2009, Galaz and others 2008, Dietz and others 2003).

International environmental governance in the UN system

The Joint Inspection Unit's 2008 report is one of the more recent comprehensive analyses highlighting weaknesses in international environmental governance due to institutional fragmentation and lack of a holistic approach to environmental issues and sustainable development (JIU 2008). This report, which is being considered by the UN General Assembly and the UNEP GC/GMEF, is also critical of the management framework for failing to ensure that environmental considerations and MEA compliance are integrated into development strategies. Although expressed in particularly strong terms, this review is one of several reports prepared over the years on IEG building on the Options Paper of the Co-Chairs of the General Assembly's Informal Consultations on IEG (UNGA 2007), which was established as a follow-up process to the 2005 World Summit outcome document (UNGA 2005).

In 2009, the international community continued to seek a breakthrough on IEG reform. The UNEP Governing Council established the Consultative Group of Ministers or High-Level Representatives on International Environmental Governance to present a set of options for improving international environmental governance (UNEP 2009b, UNEP 2009c). At meetings in Belgrade in June and Rome in October, the Consultative Group identified a set of options for the UN's environmental portfolio. The Group will report back at the Eleventh Special Session of the GC/GMEF in February 2010 in Bali, Indonesia. The outcomes of the Special Session on IEG are expected to feed into the General Assembly process aimed at facilitating reform of international environmental governance.

At the first meeting of the Consultative Group of Ministers or High-Level Representatives on International Environmental Governance in June 2009, held in Belgrade, the Co-chairs' summary reflected discussions that "any IEG reform should be based on the principle that form should follow function; that consultations on functions should lead to a discussion on forms that could range from incremental changes to other broader institutional reforms; that the IEG debate should be addressed in the broader context of environmental sustainability and sustainable development; that developing a set of options for improving IEG should follow from a fresh examination of multiple challenges and emerging opportunities; that incremental changes to IEG can be considered alongside other more fundamental reforms; and that the work of the Consultative Group should continue to be political in nature" (UNEP 2009d).

Proposals for IEG reform have addressed both incremental and broader reform. An example of the latter is the suggestion to create a global umbrella organization. Short of creating a World (or United Nations) Environment Organization capable of bringing all MEAs under a common institutional roof, some governance researchers have argued for less ambitious and more politically feasible clustering approaches (Oberthür 2009, Von Moltke 2001). The development of legally binding agreements has been the mainstay of international environmental governance, yet the growing number of these agreements and the observed lack of coordination between them have been the basis of many criticisms of IEG (Biermann and others 2009b). Proliferation of multilateral environmental agreements was singled out by President Sarkozy at the 17th Ambassadors Conference in Paris in August (Sarkozy 2009). It was also discussed at the June 2008 Commonwealth Heads of Government Meeting on Reform of International Institutions (Commonwealth Secretariat 2009). Although

Ministers and other high-level representatives attending the first meeting of the Consultative Group of Ministers or High-Level Representatives on International Environmental Governance, held on 27-28 June 2009 in Belgrade, Serbia. A second meeting of the Consultative Group took place on 26-29 October in Rome, Italy.
Credit: Serbian Ministry of Environmental and Spatial Planning

the annual increase in new agreements, protocols, and amendments has slowed down over the last decade or so (**Figure 1**), there is nevertheless evidence of increasing multiplicity and possibly fragmentation. A notable example of MEA clustering in 2009 occurred in the area of international chemicals and waste management. In early 2009, the signatories of three global conventions on chemicals and waste agreed to consolidate their common functions and enhance cooperation and coordination at the administrative and programmatic levels. The synergies process of the Basel Convention on the Control of Transboundary Movements of Hazardous Wastes and their Disposal, the Rotterdam Convention on the Prior Informed Consent Procedure for Certain Hazardous Chemicals and Pesticides in International Trade, and the Stockholm Convention on Persistent Organic Pollutants has been hailed as a prominent example of IEG reform (UNEP POPs 2009).

Experience with this clustering approach is expected to be reported at the Eleventh Special Session of the UNEP GC/GMEF in Bali in 2010. Progress has already been made in many areas, including joint delivery of technical assistance, joint representation at meetings, production of joint awareness materials, and establishment of a joint clearing-house mechanism (UNEP 2009g). As a sign of political support for the synergies process, the first Extraordinary Meeting of the Conference of the Parties to the three Conventions will be held back-to-back with the Special Session of the GC/GMEF in Bali.

Heading into the International Year of Biodiversity, insights gained from the synergies process will be valuable to the COPs of the six biodiversity-related conventions (Convention on Biological Diversity, Convention on International Trade in Endangered Species of Wild Fauna and Flora, Convention on the Conservation of Migratory Species of Wild Animals, International Treaty on Plant Genetic Resources for Food and Agriculture, Convention on Wetlands (popularly known as the Ramsar Convention) and the World Heritage Convention) as well as, among others, the Biodiversity Liaison Group, which has worked since 2004 to enhance coherence and cooperation in the implementation of the biodiversity-related conventions (CBD 2009a).

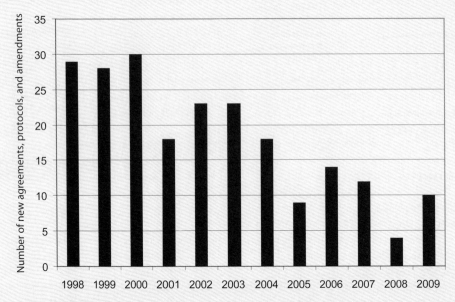

Figure 1: Number of new multilateral environmental agreements, protocols, and amendments 1998-2009

Between 1998 and 2009, there were a total of 218 new multilateral environmental agreements, protocols, and amendments.

Source: Mitchell (2009)

Scholars and practitioners alike cite fragmentation, overlap, and duplication among the main reasons for reforming the UN's system of international environmental governance (UNEP 2009c, Ivanova and Roy 2007, UNGA 2007, Biermann and Bauer 2005, Esty 2003, Charnovitz 2002, Runge 2001). At the first meeting of the Consultative Group of Ministers or High-Level Representatives on International Environmental Governance, delegates emphasized that "in addressing threats to food, energy and water security and grappling with the impacts of climate change, states are currently dealing with an array of United Nations agencies, financial institutions and mechanisms, private sector interests and civil society organizations" (UNEP 2009d). According to information on 18 MEAs compiled by the International Institute for Sustainable Development, between 1992 and 2007 there were 540 meetings, which resulted in more than 5 000 resolutions or decisions (UNEP 2009f).

Institutional overlap and fragmentation, as indicated above, are widely regarded as detrimental to efficient and effective governance.

The President's summary of the Twenty-fifth Session of the UNEP GC/GMEF pointed out that "incoherence and complexity in the international environmental governance system can lead to high transaction costs, discouraging in some cases participation in the system by developing countries and countries with economies in transition" (UNEP 2009a).

Environmental policy integration

Integration of the environmental, economic, and social dimensions of sustainability has been a key theme of the international response to the financial, food, and energy crises. High-level statements emerging from the ongoing IEG reform process have repeatedly stressed that reform should take place in the broader context of sustainable development. Proposals to integrate environmental concerns into economic recovery and socio-economic development have more generally converged around the Green New Deal elaborated by Edward Barbier and other economists and by UNEP's Green Economy Initiative. The Global Green New

Deal recommends, among other things, that a significant portion of the estimated US$3.1 trillion in economic stimulus packages be spent on energy efficiency in buildings, renewable energy technologies, sustainable transport technologies, the planet's ecosystems, and sustainable agriculture (Barbier 2010, UNEP 2009e).

Environmental policy integration is not a new concept, but the financial and climate crises have prompted scientists and others to review what has been achieved to date (Mickwitz and others 2009). At the national level, environmental policy integration can be achieved using a variety of policy instruments:

- *Communicative instruments*, such as environmental and sustainable development strategies, requirements for sectoral strategies, performance reporting, external and independent performance reviews, and inclusion of environmental goals in the national constitution;

- *Organizational instruments*, such as combining departments, green cabinets, environmental units within sectoral departments, and independent working groups; and

- *Procedural instruments*, such as veto or obligatory consultation rights for environmental departments, green budgeting, and environmental impact assessment.

An analysis of the 30 countries of the Organisation for Economic Co-operation and Development (OECD) found that most of them had introduced *communicative instruments* and many had created new organizations. However, few of these countries had developed new *procedural instruments* (Jacob and others 2008).

Environmental policy integration is of concern to both developed and developing countries. A recent review of the status of environmental policy integration in Central Asia found that inter-ministerial working groups are common, that sectoral ministries have set up specialized environmental units, and that some energy and transport policies have been subject to an environmental assessment. Nevertheless, there is still a culture of limited inter-ministerial cooperation (OECD 2009a).

What is the state of environmental policy integration at the global level? Using the same classification of policy instruments reveals a considerable diversity of instruments in use (Biermann and others 2009a). *Communicative instruments* include MEAs that require signatories to introduce relevant provisions into national legal frameworks. Moreover, various international gatherings throughout the year conclude with some sort of policy statement. There are also numerous *organizational instruments* at the international level, including the UN's Environment Management Group (EMG) at the interagency level and meetings of the G8 Environment Ministers at the intergovernmental level. An example of a *procedural instrument* at the global level is the statement endorsed by the UN System Chief Executives Board for Coordination (CEB) at its October 2007 session on moving towards a climate-neutral United Nations, and the work under the EMG supported by UNEP's Sustainable UN Facility to implement the Board's statement and promote sustainable management practices in the UN more broadly (UN 2007).

A *procedural instrument* that received increasing attention in 2009 relates to the mainstreaming of climate change adaptation in official development assistance (ODA) (Persson 2009). The important role of adaptation to climate change as an element of ODA was highlighted in several major policy guidelines published in 2008 and 2009 by the OECD, the World Bank, and the Partnership for European Environmental Research (PEER) (Mani and others 2009, Mickwitz and others 2009,

OECD 2009b). Numerous research initiatives, including the EU-funded project on Adaptation and Mitigation Strategies: Supporting European Climate Policy (ADAM), have assesed the extent to which climate change adaptation has been integrated into development assistance. ADAM concluded in July 2009, and its findings suggest that adaptation is a strongly cross-sectoral issue suitable for a mainstreaming approach, even if the extent and multidimensional character of adaptation calls for more sector-specific definitions. ADAM also found that attention to climate change adaptation in ODA projects and country strategies has been weak so far (ADAM 2009).

A recent PEER report analysed the extent of climate policy integration in Denmark, Finland, Germany, the Netherlands, Spain, and the United Kingdom (Mickwitz and others 2009). This report defines climate policy integration as "the incorporation of the aims of climate change mitigation and adaptation into all stages of policy-making in other environmental and non-environmental policy sectors, complemented by an attempt to aggregate expected consequences for climate change mitigation and adaptation into an overall evaluation of policy, and a commitment to minimize contradictions between climate policies and other policies" (Mickwitz and others 2009). The criteria used by the authors to evaluate the extent of climate policy integration are summarized in **Box 2**. The first criterion, 'Inclusion', is a prerequisite. A minimum level of integration is necessary to proceed with the analysis. The other criteria help assess the

Box 2: Criteria for assessing the extent of climate policy integration

CRITERION	KEY QUESTION
Inclusion	To what extent are direct, as well as indirect, climate change mitigation and adaptation impacts covered?
Consistency	Have the contradictions between the aims related to climate change mitigation and adaptation and other policy goals been assessed, and have there been efforts to minimize revealed contradictions?
Weighting	Have the relative priorities of climate change mitigation and adaptation impacts compared to other policy aims been decided, and if not, are there procedures for determining the relative priorities?
Reporting	Are there clearly stated evaluation and reporting requirements for climate change mitigation and adaptation impacts with deadlines ex ante, and have such evaluations and reporting happened ex post? Have indicators been defined, followed up, and used?
Resources	Is internal as well as external know-how about climate change mitigation and adaptation impacts available and used, and are resources provided?

Source: Mickwitz and others (2009)

degree to which climate change concerns are integrated into other policy sectors, such as transport or agriculture (horizontal integration), and at government levels (vertical integration). The PEER report found that while climate change is now widely recognized in strategies and programmes, there is an urgent need to intensify the incorporation of climate policy integration into specific policy instruments such as spatial planning and governmental budgeting (Mickwitz and others 2009).

REGIONAL ENVIRONMENTAL GOVERNANCE

The term 'region' can refer to a geographic area as small as a transboundary wetland or as vast as an entire continent. Regional economic integration organizations such as the EU provide many examples of regional environmental governance. In these cases, regions are defined as groups of states. Similarly, regional positions

---

Box 3: Regional dimensions of environmental governance

Climate change
The significance of regional scale climate change projections for policy-making was recognized in the IPCC's decision to include a regional focus in its upcoming Fifth Assessment Report. The Fifth Assessment Report will also look at subregions and cross-regional hotspots such as the Mediterranean and mega-deltas (IISD 2009c).

Desertification
At the Ninth Conference of the Parties to the UN Convention to Combat Desertification, delegates made progress towards the establishment of Regional Coordination Mechanisms. Even though the corresponding decision fell short of referring to "regional offices," in part because developed countries are concerned that such decentralization could set a precedent for other conventions, this was a breakthrough (UNCCD 2009).

Chemicals and waste
At its fourth meeting, the Conference of the Parties to the Stockholm Convention on Persistent Organic Pollutants endorsed eight institutions that will serve as regional and subregional centres for capacity-building and transfer of technology (UNEP POPs 2009).

Forestry
In the lead-up to the 13th World Forestry Congress, a pre-Congress workshop emphasized that regional level cooperation translates policy into practice and moves sustainable forest management forward (McAlpine 2009).

---

in intergovernmental negotiations are typically associated with groups of states.

Some environmental problems, such as climate change or depletion of the ozone layer, have been framed as global issues in need of global approaches. Others, like transboundary water management, have long been addressed through regional cooperation. Regional environmental arrangements, such as the river basin commissions for the Rhine or Danube, have a long history. Regional agreements like the regional conventions to protect the mountain areas of the Alps and the Carpathians have made significant progress in placing environmental concerns in a larger sustainable development context.

Governance experts and professionals have noted the advantages and disadvantages of regional approaches. Regional initiatives, which benefit from greater familiarity among the participants, could complement global agreements to meet region-specific needs. However, they could also undermine the effectiveness of global environmental policy by increasing administrative complexity and reducing the efficiency of economic instruments. To date, little empirical work has addressed trade-offs between regional and global architectures, but regional initiatives such as the Regional Seas Programme have been found to make important contributions to the 2002 World Summit on Sustainable Development (WSSD) global marine targets for coastal ecosystems (Sherman and Hempel 2009).

In 2009, developments in multilateral environmental negotiations on climate change, forestry, desertification, chemicals, and waste management highlighted the importance of cooperative activities at the regional level (**Box 3**). Even in the eminently global governance area of climate change, some elements are discussed from a regional perspective. For example, a UN Department of Social and Economic Affairs (UN DESA) briefing note in 2009 emphasized the potential benefits of regional mechanisms with respect to the efficient and equitable transfer of mitigation and adaptation technologies (Vera 2009). Regional mechanisms that facilitate the pooling of resources and the development of economies of scale, it argued, can help strike a politically feasible balance between what

global arrangements are able to offer and what developing countries need.

Ecoregional governance and transboundary waters management

One understanding of regions is based on their common ecological and biophysical features. Widely recognized ecoregions include river basins and mountain ranges. The practice of governance based on ecoregions is still in its infancy, although examples exist around the world (Balsiger and VanDeveer, in press). Regional cooperation on transboundary river basins is a notable example. In this context, in March 2009, Heads of State at the 5th World Water Forum in Istanbul affirmed their political will to take rapid action, bearing in mind that dialog and cooperation on transboundary waters between neighbours are key elements of success (Zukang 2009). Some 279 river basins straddle international boundaries (Bakker 2009). Transboundary river basins cover 45.3 per cent of the planet's land surface, affect about 40 per cent of the world population, and account for approximately 60 per cent of river flow (Wolf and others 1999) (**Figure 2**).

Climate change has reinforced the growing importance of transboundary waters management in governance. Spatial variations in the impacts of climate change draw attention to ecoregions, especially coastal areas (Dinar 2009, EEA 2009, WWAP 2009). In new guidelines on integrated water management, the United Nations Educational, Scientific and Cultural Organization (UNESCO) states that basin level approaches have become increasingly important as the impacts of climate change are realized through the qualitative and quantitative responses of the hydrological cycle, which in turn directly affect river basins (UNESCO 2009).

Widespread political support for transboundary waters management is somewhat tempered by scientific findings concerning the challenges of elaborating basin-level approaches and the environmental benefits these approaches can generate. A recent review of 506 international water treaties and 86 associated organizations found that the majority of international river basin institutions are limited in membership and scope (Dombrowsky 2008). Prevailing levels of water

Figure 2: Transboundary river basins

Updated map of the world's international river basins, based on Wolf and others (1999).

Source: Transboundary Freshwater Dispute Database (2010)

scarcity have been identified as one determining factor. An empirical analysis of 74 cases where rivers are shared by two states revealed that the probability of cooperation, measured in terms of international water agreements, is higher when scarcity is moderate than when it is very low or very high (Dinar 2009). This implies that when scarcity exceeds a certain threshold, cooperation may need to be encouraged by outside actors (see the chapter on Disasters and Conflicts).

In assessing the effectiveness of regional water governance, scholars in this field increasingly focus on performance rather than compliance. Compliance is the extent to which parties to an agreement meet the terms of the agreement, whereas performance is the degree to which an agreement's goals are actually reached. Parties may comply with requirements to establish new institutions and to formulate action plans, but perform poorly in reducing water pollution or flood risk. A case study of the Central Asian Naryin/Syr Darya basin, for example, shows that while compliance with a previously negotiated agreement on water releases from the Toktogul reservoir has been high, performance over time in terms of run-off has been very low and highly variable from a sustainable resource management point of view (Bernauer and Siegfried 2008).

GOVERNANCE BEYOND GOVERNMENT

Governance is overwhelmingly associated with the work of governments. Yet during the last two decades, the governmental mode of governance has been complimented by modes of governance in which non-governmental organizations and the private sector are key partners. This trend is illustrated by the sustained growth of private sector standards such as certification, and of public-private partnerships, at the local to the global level (Adger and Jordan 2009, Andonova and others 2009, Treib and others 2007).

Although governments remain the most common and authoritative source of governing activity today, non-governmental organizations and the private sector have developed a plethora of initiatives that contribute to meeting public goals such as environmental protection and sustainable development in policy formulation and implementation (O'Neill 2009). Some examples of extensive public-private partnerships are seen in forestry, such as third-party certification and labelling and power-sharing within stakeholder bodies (Chan and Pattberg 2008).

The hundreds of public-private partnerships established in the wake of the 2002 WSSD reflect the growth of private sector participation in governance activities (**Box 4**). The latest UN Secretary-General's report on partnerships for sustainable development states that "through the pooling of knowledge, skills and resources, […] collaborative initiatives are working to find innovative solutions to sustainable development challenges and to develop knowledge networks to contribute to an environment of informed decision-making" (UN 2008). Newly created partnerships included the Global Partnership on Nutrient Management, the Global Partnership for Agruculture, Food Security and Nutrition, and the Partnership for Action on Computing Equipment, a multi-stakeholder partnership for environmentally sound management of used and end-of-life computer equipment. Although there are numerous scholarly case studies of specific partnerships and their activities, systematic information about their effectiveness and aggregate impact on the environment has yet to emerge. A new overview has found that knowledge of the effectiveness of public-private partnerships in policy formulation is limited and that the effectiveness of such partnerships in policy implementation is mixed (Schäferhoff and others 2009).

The use of market-based instruments as a tool to influence behaviour by means of price and other economic signals, in combination with public-private partnerships has helped attract many advocacy and business coalitions whose interests transcend national borders. The complexity of policy coordination vertically (local-national-regional-international), and coordination across sectors and jurisdictions have also created more points of access to policy processes. In addition, the Kyoto flexibility mechanisms, which emphasize market-based instruments, have furnished significant opportunities for participation by non-state actors, including both NGOs and the private

Box 4: Partnerships for sustainable development

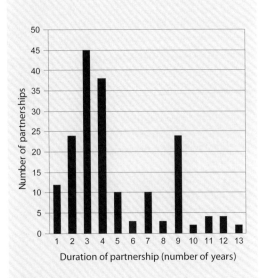

Duration of partnership (number of years)

(y-axis: Number of partnerships)

International partnerships for sustainable development bring together public, private, and non-governmental actors, yet they often emerge from intergovernmental processes. The Partnership for Action on Computing Equipment (PACE), one of the most recent initiatives, offers a case in point. The decision to launch PACE was made by delegates to the ninth meeting of the Conference of the Parties to the Basel Convention in June 2008.

This partnership was launched in recognition of the urgent need for environmentally sound management, refurbishment, recycling, and disposal of used and end-of-life computing equipment. In March 2009, a multi-stakeholder working group comprising 58 representatives of personal computer manufacturers, recyclers, international organizations, academia, environmental groups, and governments agreed on the partnership's scope of work, terms of reference, financial arrangements, and structure.

PACE has initiated work to develop guidelines, awareness raising material, and pilot projects to enhance the environmentally sound management of computing equipment. Thirty-four project partners from developing countries and countries with economies in transition have already indicated an interest in working on pilot schemes to divert end-of-life computing equipment from environmentally unsound landfills, open-pit burning, and harmful recycling operations to environmentally sound and efficient recycling operations, in a manner that is sustainable and mindful of the health and welfare of people working in the informal sector.

Source: CSD (2009b)

sector (Andonova and others 2009, Pattberg and Stripple 2008).

Market-based instruments can also help increase transparency, strengthen legitimacy, and foster broader public interest (Bartle 2009, Bled 2009, Guesnerie and Tulkens 2009, Lövbrand and others 2009). For example, Decision VIII/17 on private sector engagement, adopted by the Conference of the Parties to the CBD in 2006, seeks to raise the private sector's awareness of good practices, reporting, and certification, involve private sector actors in CBD meetings and related meetings at the national level, and ensure compliance with the Convention's objectives and implementation of its targets. A recent analysis of the Decision's impact concludes that private sector participation can indeed help strengthen the CBD's legitimacy and contribute essential business skills (Bled 2009). To ensure further positive development, it suggests involving the financial sector and carefully integrating and balancing business expertise with the social and practical experience of other stakeholders.

One of the most significant areas of private sector involvement in environmental governance is carbon emissions trading (Stern 2007). In 2007 alone, there was an estimated US$64 billion turnover in international carbon markets, up from US$30 billion the year before. At present, the largest partnership is the pan-European Emission Trading Scheme (ETS) launched in 2005. In 2008, the EU ETS was worth US$94 billion in terms of revenue (Frost & Sullivan 2009, Capoor and Ambrosi 2008, Hepburn 2007).

Carbon emissions trading and other market-based environmental governance instruments have received some criticism (Newell 2008). The EU's Emission Trading Scheme, despite serving as a model for similar schemes elsewhere (Skjærseth and Wettestad 2009), had early problems with permit over-allocation and there have been reports of widespread value-added tax fraud. Some scientists, along with Parties to the Kyoto Protocol, have expressed concern about lack of additionality in many Clean Development Mechanism (CDM) projects and what they perceive as a focus on inexpensive emissions reductions at the expense of sustainable development benefits for the host countries (Flåm 2009, Paulsson

2009, Schneider 2009, Skjærseth and Wettestad 2009). Critics have also claimed that demands for efficiency in emissions trading schemes can sideline considerations of equity, thereby exaggerating inequalities by favouring those with better access to information and resources (Baldwin 2008, Vormedal 2008).

An expanded role for the private sector in different international environmental governance activities has been sought in other areas, such as strategic planning and funding. For example, the GEF Earth Fund Board, a private sector advisory group launched in 2008, met in April 2009 to provide strategic guidance to the GEF. In addition to providing the GEF with input for decision-making, it is expected to help mobilize as much as US$150 million during its first round of financing (IISD 2009d). Regarding climate change, public finance mechanisms are being considered to scale up private sector investments and raise US$530 billion per year in the form of additionall investment, which is estimated to be required in order to avoid adverse impacts of climate change (UNEP 2009h).

LOOKING AHEAD

The convergence of several environmental, financial, and social crises, together with international efforts to reform the UN's IEG system, made 2009 a significant year for international environmental governance. The UNEP Ministerial Consultations in 2009, and the discussions of the Consultative Group of Ministers or High-Level Representatives on IEG established by UNEP's Governing Council, highlighted the urgency of IEG reform. Trends on the regional level, and involvement of the private sector, underlined that international environmental governance encompasses both multiple scales of action and multiple types of actors. Parties to several MEAs took steps to create or strengthen regional governance infrastructures; transboundary management moved up the political agenda; and new public-private partnerships and market-based instruments, especially in climate politics, allowed for more non-state involvement and investments.

The outcome of the Copenhagen conference revealed just how enormous the challenge of forging a global agreement on climate change has become. Even though no legally binding targets emerged, many countries made a commitment for the first time to decouple emissions from economic growth. The Conference of the Parties "took note" of the Copenhagen Accord, which confirms countries' willingness to limit global temperature rise to less than 2°C above pre-industrial levels, outlines support for technology transfer and capacity building for developing economies, and provides financial assistance for climate change adaptation and mitigation. Additional resources of US$30 billion, covering the period 2010-2012, will be available immediately, with developed countries supporting a "goal of mobilizing jointly US$100 billion a year by 2020 to address the needs of developing countries." The Accord also specifies the need to recognize reduced emissions from deforestation and forest degradation (REDD+) through the immediate establishment of a mechanism to enable the mobilization of financial resources from developed countries. While the Accord does not require countries to work on a new agreement, negotiations are certain to continue in 2010.

During 2010, the International Year of Biodiversity, global attention will be focused on the 2010 Biodiversity Target, which aims to achieve a significant reduction of the current rate of biodiversity loss at the global, regional, and national levels as a contribution to poverty alleviation and to benefit all life on Earth. It is unlikely that the target will be met (Gilbert 2009). The 10th Conference of the Parties to the Convention on Biological Diversity will focus on the development of a post 2010 framework. This meeting will be held in Nagoya, Japan, immediately following the 5th Meeting of the Parties to the Cartagena Protocol on Biosafety, where delegates will continue negotiations on a legally binding treaty on liability and redress.

Several important developments, assessments, and events in 2010 will be concerned with regional environmental governance. Parties to the Conventions on chemicals and waste, and desertification will take further steps to establish regional mechanisms, probing the limits of MEA decentralization. Regional policy-makers will also look to the IPCC, whose Fifth Assessment

Several generations of environmental leaders, including all five successive Executive Directors of UNEP, took part in the Global Environmental Governance Forum: Reflecting on the Past, Moving into the Future, held on 28 June-2 July 2009 in Glion, Switzerland. From left to right: The Executive Director of UNEP Achim Steiner, and former Executive Directors of UNEP Maurice Strong, Mostafa Tolba, Elizabeth Dowdeswel, and Klaus Töpfer.

Credit: Global Environmental Governance Project (www.environmentalgovernance.org)

Report is to include a regional focus. Finally, key events such as the Sixth Ministerial Conference on Environment and Development in Asia and the Pacific will generate regional perspectives in regard to pressing issues on the global environmental agenda, including green growth and climate change governance.

The IEG reform process will be a key topic during deliberations at the Eleventh Special Session of the UNEP GC/GMEF. The Consultative Group will present a set of options concerning the core objectives and functions identified for the UN's IEG work, and concrete options for incremental reforms, as well as options for moving forward with broader institutional reform. The work of the UNEP Governing Council, and the Consultative Group, on international environmental governance could help inform preparations for the UN Conference on Sustainable Development in Brazil in 2012, which will mark the 20th anniversary of the UN Conference on Environment and Development in Rio de Janeiro (UNGA 2008).

Calendar of events 2009

FEBRUARY

16-20 February Governments at Twenty-fifth Session of UNEP Governing Council/Global Ministerial Environment Forum approve launch of intergovernmental negotiations for legally binding treaty on mercury and establishment of a Consultative Group of Ministers or High-Level Representatives on International Environmental Governance.

23-27 February Group of Friends of the Co-Chairs on Liability and Redress under the Cartagena Protocol on Biosafety meeting in Mexico City produces first draft of a supplementary protocol. It includes a binding provision on civil liability for damage resulting from transboundary movements of living modified organisms.

MARCH

16-22 March UN Under-Secretary-General for Economic and Social Affairs, Sha Zukang, encourages 5th World Water Forum participants to pursue dialog with other policy communities on links between water and climate change, accelerate progress on climate change adaptation, and support human and institutional capacity with adequate financing.

APRIL

6 April European Council adopts climate-energy legislation to achieve overall EU target of 20 per cent reduction in greenhouse gas emissions, 20 per cent increase in renewable energy use, and 20 per cent energy savings by 2020.

20 April-1 May Delegates to Eighth Session of UN Forum on Forests adopt resolution on forests in a changing environment, including forests and climate change, enhanced cooperation and cross-sectoral coordination, and regional and subregional inputs. A decision on financing for sustainable forest management is postponed.

21 April Convention on International Trade in Endangered Species of Wild Fauna and Flora (CITES) Secretariat welcomes Bosnia and Herzegovina as the 175th Party to the agreement.

MAY

4-8 May More than 800 participants representing over 149 governments, intergovernmental and non-governmental organizations, and UN agencies attend the fourth COP of the Stockholm Convention on Persistent Organic Pollutants, where nine new chemicals are added to the Convention's annexes.

4-15 May At Seventeenth Session of UN Commission on Sustainable Development (CSD), Secretary-General Ban Ki-moon tells participants that sustainable agriculture can contribute to climate change mitigation. Delegates adopt policy recommendations, and discuss how CSD can better support international sectoral governance.

JUNE

1-5 June Delegates to Third Session of the Governing Body of the International Treaty on Plant Genetic Resources for Food and Agriculture, the world's first operational multilateral system of access and benefit-sharing, urge improvement of Treaty's financial situation.

16-19 June At Second Session of Global Platform for Disaster Risk Reduction (DRR), the Chair's summary stresses that DRR is increasingly driven by local leadership in developing countries, and that it should be included in climate change negotiations in Copenhagen in December.

24-26 June Political leaders at UN Conference on the World Financial and Economic Crisis and Its Impact on Development emphasize that global green initiatives should address sustainable development and environmental challenges and opportunities, including climate change mitigation and adaptation, financing, and technology transfer to developing countries.

28 June-2 July All five successive UNEP Executive Directors attend Global Environmental Governance Forum in Glion, Switzerland, where 80 participants from 26 countries discuss UNEP's past, present, and future, key functions in international environmental governance, and options for reform.

JULY

8-10 July In L'Aquila, Italy, the G8 Summit's Joint Statement on Global Food Security says effective food security actions should be combined with adaptation and mitigation measures in regard to climate change and sustainable management of water, land, soil, and other natural resources, including protection of biodiversity.

AUGUST

31 August-4 September At World Climate Conference-3 in Geneva, high-level policy-makers from more than 150 countries establish Global Framework for Climate Services to strengthen production, availability, delivery, and application of science-based climate prediction and services.

SEPTEMBER

24-25 September Political leaders of the world's 20 largest economies, gathered at the Pittsburgh G-20 summit, commit to phase out fossil fuel subsidies over the medium term while providing targeted support to help the poorest.

21 September-2 October Delegates to Ninth Conference of the Parties to UN Convention to Combat Desertification (UNCCD) call for strengthening the effectiveness and efficiency of regional coordination mechanisms to facilitate implementation of the Convention.

OCTOBER

5-9 October At Second Ad Hoc Intergovernmental and Multi-stakeholder Meeting on an Intergovernmental Science-Policy Platform on Biodiversity and Ecosystem Services (IPBES), most participants express support for a new mechanism to carry out assessments and generate and disseminate policy-relevant advice.

7-9 October More than 2 000 participants from over 73 countries travel to Léon, Mexico, for Global Renewable Energy Forum, organized to strengthen inter-regional cooperation and encourage innovative multi-stakeholder partnerships for scaling up renewable energy in Latin America and elsewhere.

26-29 October Consultative Group of Ministers or High-Level Representatives on International Environmental Governance (IEG) discusses IEG objectives and functions in the context of the UN system. Ministerial participants consider both incremental and broader institutional reform: IEG reform is to be placed in the broader context of sustainability and sustainable development.

26-29 October Delegates at Thirty-first Session of the Intergovernmental Panel on Climate Change (IPCC) agree on scope, timing, and chapter outlines of Fifth Assessment Report (AR5), to be finalized in 2013-2014. They decide that regional assessments will be central to AR5 and that the IPCC will aim to ensure the policy relevance of the report.

30 October Two initiatives on financing sustainable forest management launched at Special Session of UN Forum on Forests: an intergovernmental process to analyse all forms of forest financing, and a separate facilitative process to help countries mobilize funding from all sources.

NOVEMBER

4-8 November Twenty-first Meeting of the Parties to the Montreal Protocol results in 30 decisions. A proposal to amend the Protocol to include hydrofluorocarbons (HFCs), some of which have high global warming potential, is unsuccessful.

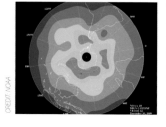

2-6 November Barcelona Climate Change Talks close just 30 days before COP15 of the United Nations Framework Convention on Climate Change begins in Copenhagen. The eyes of the world are on the climate change negotiators, but expectations are increasingly played down.

DECEMBER

7-18 December Countries attending the UN Climate Change Conference in Copenhagen agree to "take note" of the Copenhagen Accord. For the first time in the history of climate change cooperation, developing countries including Brazil, China, Indonesia, Mexico, and South Africa outline intentions to decouple emissions from economic growth.

Sources: Please go to the knowledge database at www.unep.org/yearbook/2010

Calendar of upcoming events 2010

JANUARY

6-7 January Participants at Second Curitiba Meeting on Cities and Biodiversity to draft Convention on Biological Diversity (CBD) Plan of Action on Urban Biodiversity and to prepare the 2010 City Biodiversity Summit. Meeting preceded by festivities inaugurating International Year of Biodiversity.

20-23 January 8th World General Assembly of the International Network of Basin Organizations to meet in Dakar, Senegal. Its theme is 'Adapting to the consequences of climate change in the basins: tools for action.'

FEBRUARY

8-12 February Participants at Second Meeting of Group of Friends of the Co-Chairs on Liability and Redress under the Cartagena Protocol on Biosafety will further negotiate liability and redress rules for damage resulting from transboundary movements of living modified organisms.

CREDIT: SIMONE D. MCCOURTIE/ WORLD BANK

22-24 February First Extraordinary Meeting of the Conferences of the Parties to the Basel, Rotterdam and Stockholm Conventions to be held back-to-back with the UNEP GC/ GMEF Special Session. There is high-level political support for enhancing cooperation and coordination among the three chemicals and waste conventions.

24-26 February Meeting in Bali, Eleventh Special Session of UNEP Governing Council/Global Ministerial Environment Forum (UNEP GC/ GMEF) to consider recommendations of Consultative Group of Ministers or High-Level Representatives on International Environmental Governance. The green economy, and biodiversity and ecosystems are also on the agenda.

MARCH

13-25 March Decisions at Fifteenth Conference of the Parties to the Convention on International Trade in Endangered Species of Wild Fauna and Flora (CITES) to address high-profile species including the African elephant, tiger, and polar bear. Other proposals concern trade controls for coral and shark species.

22 March Theme of World Water Day on 22 March is 'Communicating Water Quality Challenges and Opportunities.' This event seeks to raise the profile of water quality at the political level, so that it is considered alongside water quantity.

CREDIT: DOMINIC SANSONI/WORLD BANK

APRIL

21-23 April Business, government, NGO, and media leaders to meet at Business for the Environment (B4E) Global Summit in Seoul, Republic of Korea. An annual event co-hosted by UNEP, the UN Global Compact, and WWF, B4E promotes dialog and business-driven action towards a global green economy.

MAY

3-14 May Eighteenth Session of UN Commission on Sustainable Development to consider sustainable consumption and production (SCP) patterns, focusing on the Marrakech Process, a global activity that supports elaboration of a ten-year framework of programmes on SCP.

10-21 May International Year of Biodiversity to be celebrated at Fourteenth Meeting of CBD's Subsidiary Body on Scientific, Technical and Technological Advice (SBSTTA). Scientific and technical issues of relevance to the 2010 Biodiversity Target are on the agenda.

CREDIT: WWW.CBD.INT

2010 International Year of Biodiversity

CREDIT: BILL BILLCHUNG

24-28 May Fourth Global Environment Facility (GEF) Assembly to meet in Punta del Este, Uruguay, shortly before the GEF-5 replenishment period begins on 1 July.

31 May-11 June Period designated as first sessional period of the UN Framework Convention on Climate Change (UNFCCC).

SOURCE: ERIC VALENTIN

JUNE

5 June World Environment Day. The purpose of this annual event is to stimulate worldwide awareness of the environment and enhance political attention and action.

7-11 June First Session of Intergovernmental Negotiating Committee to Prepare a Global Legally Binding Instrument on Mercury to meet in Stockholm. This is expected to be the first of five intergovernmental negotiating committee meetings held to produce a legally binding instrument on mercury.

26-27 June G20 summit in Canada to mark transition from G8 summits. Brazil, China, India, the Republic of Korea, and other countries will take permanent seats alongside the G8.

AUGUST

30 August-3 September Workshop on Forest Governance,Decentralization and Reducing Emissions from Deforestation and Degradation (REDD) in Latin America.

CREDIT: ERIC VALENTIN

OCTOBER

11-15 October Delegates to 5th meeting of Conference of the Parties serving as the Meeting of the Parties to the Cartagena Protocol on Biosafety (COP-MOP 5) in Nagoya, Japan, to consider outcome of the negotiations of the Ad Hoc Open Ended Working Group of Legal and Technical Experts on Liability and Redress.

18-29 October Landmark Tenth Conference of the Parties to the UN Convention on Biological Diversity to review progress towards 2010 Biodiversity Target of significantly reducing rate of biodiversity loss, and consider international regime on Access and Benefit-Sharing.

CREDIT: MARTON BALINT/UNEP

25-29 October Twenty-second Meeting of the Parties to the Montreal Protocol in Nairobi, Kenya (dates to be confirmed).

NOVEMBER

29 November-10 December Sixteenth Conference of the Parties to UN Framework Convention on Climate Change (COP16) in Mexico to be held along with the Sixth Meeting of the Parties to the Kyoto Protocol (CMP 6) (dates to be confirmed).

CREDIT: BARBARA KESSLER

DECEMBER

11-12 December International Year of Forests to be launched in Kanazawa, Japan. UN Forum on Forests serves as focal point for the UN International Year of Forests 2011, in collaboration with governments and other partners.

CREDIT: YUKO YONEDA

Sources: Please go to the knowledge database at www.unep.org/yearbook/2010

REFERENCES

ACP-EU JPA (2009). Resolution on global governance and the reform of international institutions, adopted at the 18th Session of the African Caribbean and Pacific-European Union Joint Parliamentary Assembly (JPA), Luanda, Angola, 25 November-3 December 2009

ADAM (Adaptation and Mitigation Strategies) (2009). *Mainstreaming Climate Change Adaptation in Official Development Assistance: Issues and Early Experiences. Final Report*. Stockholm Environment Institute, Stockholm

Adger, W.N. and Jordan, A. (eds.) (2009). *Governing Sustainability*. Cambridge University Press, UK

Andonova, L.B., Betsill, M.M. and Bulkeley, H. (2009). Transnational Climate Governance. *Global Environmental Politics*, 9(2), 52-73

Ansell, C.K. and Balsiger, J. (2009). The Circuits of Regulation: Transatlantic Perspectives on Persistent Organic Pollutants and Endocrine Disrupting Chemicals. In: J. Swinnen, D. Vogel, A. Marx, H. Riss and J. Wouters (eds.), *Handling Global Challenges: Managing Biosafety and Biodiversity in a Global World – EU, US, California and Comparative Perspectives*. Leuven Centre for Global Governance Studies, Leuven, Belgium

Bakker, M.H.N. (2009). Transboundary river floods: examining countries, international river basins and continents. *Water Policy*, 11, 269-288

Baldwin, R. (2008). Regulation lite: the rise of emissions trading. *Regulation and Governance*, 2, 193-215

Balsiger, J. and VanDeveer, S.D. (in press). Regional Governance and Environmental Problems. In: R.A. Denemark (ed.), *The International Studies Compendium*. Wiley-Blackwell, Oxford, UK

Barbier, E.B. (2010, in press). *A Global Green New Deal. Rethinking the Economic Recovery*.

Bartle, I. (2009). A strategy for better climate change regulation: towards a public interest orientated regulatory regime. *Environmental Politics*, 18(5), 689-706

Beck, U. (2008). *World At Risk*. Polity Press, Cambridge, UK

Bernauer, T. and Siegfried, T. (2008). Compliance and Performance in International Water Agreements: The Case of the Naryn/Syr Darya Basin. *Global Governance*, 14, 479-501

Biermann, F. (2000). The Case for a World Environment Organization. *Environment*, 42, 22-31

Biermann, F. and Bauer, S. (eds.) (2005). *A World Environmental Organization: Solution or Threat for Effective International Environmental Governance?* Ashgate Publishing, Aldershot, UK

Biermann, F., Davies, O. and Grijp, N.M. van der (2009a). Environmental policy integration and the architecture of global environmental governance. *International Environmental Agreements*, 9, 351-369

Biermann, F., Pattberg, P., van Asselt, H. and Zelli, F. (2009b). The fragmentation of global governance architectures: A framework for analysis. *Global Environmental Politics*, 9(4), 14-40

Bled, A.J. (2009). Business to the rescue: private sector actors and global environmental regimes' legitimacy. *International Environmental Agreements*, 9, 153-171

Capoor, K. and Ambrosi, P. (2008). *State and Trends of the Carbon Market 2008*. The World Bank, Washington, D.C.

Chan, S. and Pattberg, P. (2008). Private Rule-Making and the Politics of Accountability: Analyzing Global Forest Governance. *Global Environmental Politics*, 8(3), 109-121

Charnovitz, S. (2002). A World Environment Organization. *Columbia Journal of Environmental Law*, 27(2), 323-362

Commonwealth Secretariat (2008). *Reform of International Environmental Governance: An Agenda for the Commonwealth*. Commonwealth Heads of Government Meeting on Reform of International Institutions, London, 9-10 June 2008. HGM-RII(08)2. Commonwealth Secretariat, London

CBD (Convention on Biological Diversity) (2009a). Liaison Group of Biodiversity-related Conventions. http://www.cbd.int/cooperation/related-conventions/blg.shtml

CBD (2009b). "Statement on Biological Diversity to UN General Assembly Second Committee" by the Executive Secretary Ahmed Djoglaf. Secretariat of the Convention on Biological Diversity, Montreal

CSD (Commission on Sustainable Development) (2009a). Report on the seventeenth session. E/2009/29 E/CN.17/2009/19 (16 May 2008 and 4-15 May 2009). http://daccessdds.un.org/doc/UNDOC/GEN/N09/355/72/PDF/N0935572.pdf?OpenElement

CSD (2009b). Partnerships for Sustainable Development – CSD Partnerships Database. http://webapps01.un.org/dsd/partnerships/public/welcome.do

Dietz, T., Ostrom, E. and Stern, P.C. (2003). The Struggle to Govern the Commons. *Science*, 302(5652), 1907-1912

Dinar, S. (2009). Scarcity and Cooperation Along International Rivers. *Global Environmental Politics*, 9(1), 109-135

Dombrowsky, I. (2008). Integration in the Management of International Waters: Economic Perspectives on a Global Policy Discourse. *Global Governance*, 14, 455-477

ECOSOC (UN Economic and Social Council) (2006). Definition of basic concepts and terminologies in governance and public administration. Note by the Secretariat. Committee of Experts on Public Administration, Fifth Session, New York, 27-31 March 2006. E/C.16/2006/4. United Nations, New York

EEA (European Environment Agency) (2009). *Regional climate change and adaptation. The Alps facing the challenge of changing water resources. EEA Technical Report No. 9/2009*. EEA, Copenhagen

Esty, D.C. (1994). The case for a global environmental organization. In: P.B. Kenen (ed.), *Managing the world economy: Fifty years after Bretton Woods*. Institute for International Economics, Washington, D.C.

Esty, D.C. (2003). Toward a Global Environmental Mechanism. In: J.G. Speth (ed.), *Worlds Apart: Globalization and the Environment*. Island Press, Washington, D.C.

Flåm, K.H. (2009). Restricting the import of 'emission credits' in the EU: a power struggle between states and institutions. *International Environmental Agreements*, 9, 23-38

Frost & Sullivan (2009). *Asset Management – European Emissions Trading Market*. Frost & Sullivan, London

Galaz, V., Olsson, P., Hahn, R., Folke, C. and Svedin, U. (2008). The Problem of Fit among Biophysical Systems, Environmental and Resource Regimes, and Broader Governance Systems: Insights and Emerging Challenges. In: O.R. Young, L.A. King, and H. Schroeder (eds.), *Institutions and Environmental Change*. MIT Press, Cambridge, USA

GEGP (Global Environmental Governance Project) (2009). *Global Environmental Governance in the 21st Century: Way Ahead Wide Open*. Report from the Global Environmental Governance Forum: Reflecting on the Past, Moving into the Future, Glion, Switzerland 28 June-2 July 2009

Giddens, A. (2009). *The Politics of Climate Change*. Polity Press, Cambridge, UK

Gilbert, N. (2009). Efforts to sustain biodiversity fall short. *Nature*, 462, 263

Guesnerie, R. and Tulkens, H. (eds.), *The Design of Climate Policy*. MIT Press, Cambridge, USA

Hepburn, C. (2007). Carbon Trading: A Review of the Kyoto Mechanisms. *Annual Review of Environment and Resources*, 32, 375-93

Hovi, J., Sprinz, D.F. and Underdal, A. (2009). Implementing Long-Term Climate Policy: Time Inconsistency, Domestic Politics, International Anarchy. *Global Environmental Politics*, 9(1), 20-39

IISD (International Institute for Sustainable Development) (2009a). Summary of Ninth Conference of the Parties to the UN Convention to Combat Desertification: 21 September-2 October 2009. *Earth Negotiations Bulletin*, 4(221), 5 October 2009

IISD (2009b). Summary of the 21st Meeting of the Parties to the Montreal Protocol on Substances that Deplete the Ozone layer: 4-8 November 2009. *Earth Negotiations Bulletin*, 19(73), 11 November 2009

IISD (2009c). Summary of the 31st Session of the Intergovernmental Panel on Climate Change: 26-29 October 2009. *Earth Negotiations Bulletin*, 12(441), 1 November 2009

IISD (2009d). Recent MEA Activities. *MEA Bulletin* 68, 23 April 2009

Ivanova, M. and Roy, J. (2007). The Architecture of Global Enviromental Governance: Pros and Cons of Multiplicity. http://www.centerforunreform.org/node/251

Jacob, K., Volkery, A. and Lenschow, A. (2008). Instruments for environmental policy integration in 30 OECD countries. In: A. Jordan and A. Lenschow (eds.), *Innovation in Environmental Policy? – Integrating the Environment for Sustainability*. Edward Elgar, Cheltenham, UK

JIU (Joint Inspection Unit) (2008). *Management Review of Environmental Governance Within the United Nations System*. Prepared by Tadanori Inomata. United Nations, Geneva

Lövbrand, E., Rindefjäll, T. and Nordqvist, J. (2009). Closing the Legitimacy Gap in Global Environmental Governance? Lessons from the Emerging CDM Market. *Global Environmental Politics*, 9(2), 74-100

McAlpine, J. (2009). Statement to the Workshop on Regional Forest Cooperation, Buenos Aires, 17 October 2009

McGee, J. and Taplin, R. (2009). The role of the Asia Pacific Partnership in discursive contestation of the international climate regime. *International Environmental Agreements*, 9, 213-238

Merkel and Sarkozy (2009). Letter by Angela Merkel, Bundeskanzlerin der Bundesrepublik Deutschland, and Nicolas Sarkozy, Président de la République Française, to H.E. Ban Ki-Moon, Secretary-General of the United Nations, dated 21 September 2009

Mickwitz, P., Aix, F., Beck, S., Carss, D., Ferrand, N., Görg, C., Jensen, A., Kivimaa, P., Kuhlicke, C., Kuindersma, W., Máñez, M., Melanen, M., Monni, S., Pedersen, A.B., Reinert., H. and van Bommel, S. (2009). *Climate Policy Integration, Coherence and Governance*. PEER Report No 2. Partnership for European Environmental Research, Helsinki

Mitchell, R.B. (2009). *International Environmental Agreements Database Project* (Version 2009.1). http://iea.uoregon.edu/

Newell, P. (2008). Civil Society, Corporate Accountability and the Politics of Climate Change. *Global Environmental Politics*, 8(3), 122-153

Oberthür, S. (2009). Interplay management: enhancing environmental policy integration among international institutions. *International Environmental Agreements*, 9(4), 371-391

OECD (Organisation for Economic Co-operation and Development) (2009a). *Shared Responsibility for the Environment: Brief Overview of Progress in Environmental Policy Integration in Central Asia*. Briefing Note. OECD, Paris

OECD (2009b). *Integrating Climate Change Adaptation into Development Co-operation: Policy Guidance*. OECD, Paris

O'Neill, K. (2009). *The Environment and International Relations*. Cambridge University Press, UK

Ostrom, E. (2009). *A Polycentric Approach for Coping with Climate Change*. Policy Research Working Paper 5095. World Bank, Washington, D.C.

Pattberg, P. and Stripple, J. (2008). Beyond the public and private divide: remapping transnational climate governance in the 21st century. *International Environmental Agreements*, 8, 367-388

Paulsson, E. (2009). A review of the CDM literature: from fine-tuning to critical scrutiny? *International Environmental Agreements*, 9, 63-80

Persson, A. (2009). Environmental policy integration and bilateral development assistance: challenges and opportunities with an evolving governance framework. *Econpapers*, 9(4),409-429

Purnama, B.M. (2009). Opening remarks. United Nations Forum on Forests, 8th Session, New York, 20 April-1 May 2009. United Nations, New York

Ruggie, J.G. (2004). Reconstituting the Global Public Domain: Issues, Actors and Practices. *European Journal of International Relations*, 10(4), 499-531

Runge, C.F. (2001). A Global Environmental Organization (GEO) and the World Trading System. *Journal of World Trade*, 35(4), 399-426

Sarkozy, N. (2009). Seventeenth Ambassadors Conference: Speech by Nikolas Sarkozy, President of the Republic, Paris

Schäferhoff, M., Campe, S. and Kaan, C. (2009). Transnational Public-Private Partnerships in International Relations: Making Sense of Concepts, Research Frameworks, and Results. *International Studies Review*, 11(3), 451-474

Schneider, L. (2009). A Clean Development Mechanism with global atmospheric benefits for a post-2012 climate regime. *International Environmental Agreements*, 9, 95-111

Sherman, K. and Hempel, G. (eds.) (2009). *The UNEP Large Marine Ecosystem Report: A perspective on changing conditions in LMEs of the world's Regional Seas. UNEP Regional Seas. Report and Studies No. 182*. UNEP, Nairobi

Skjærseth, J.B. and Wettestad, J. (2009). The Origin, Evolution and Consequences of the EU Emissions Trading System. *Global Environmental Politics*, 9(2), 101-122

Stern, N. (2007). *The Economics of Climate Change. The Stern Review*. Cambridge University Press, UK

Treib, O., Bahr, H. and Falkner, G. (2007). Modes of governance: towards a conceptual clarification. *Journal of European Public Policy*, 14(1), 1-20

UN (2007). *Chief Executives Board for Coordination. Report of the Second Regular Session of 2007, New York, 26 October 2007. CEB/2007/2*. United Nations, New York

UN (2008). *Partnerships for sustainable development. Report of the Secretary-General to the Commission on Sustainable Development, Sixteenth session, 5-16 May 2008*. E/CN.17/2008/10. United Nations, New York

UN (2009). *Millennium Development Goals Progress Report 2009*. United Nations, New York

UNCCD (2009). Report of the Conference of the Parties on its ninth session, held in Buenos Aires from 21 September to 2 October 2009. Part two: Action taken by the Conference of the Parties at its ninth session. UNCCD, Bonn. http://www.unccd.int/cop/officialdocs/cop9/pdf/18add1eng.pdf

UNECE (2009). Kiev Protocol on Pollutant Release and Transfer Registers. http://www.unece.org/env/pp/prtr.htm

UNEP (2009a). Twenty-fifth session of the Governing Council/Global Ministerial Environment Forum of UNEP. Ministerial consultations. President's summary. UNEP, Nairobi

UNEP (2009b). Letter from the co-chairs of the informal process of the General Assembly on the strengthening of international environmental governance. UNEP/GC.25/INF/35. UNEP, Nairobi

UNEP (2009c). Proceedings of the Governing Council/Global Ministerial Environment Forum at its twenty-fifth session. UNEP/GC.25/17. UNEP, Nairobi

UNEP (2009d). Belgrade Process. Moving Forward with Developing a Set of Options on International Environmental Governance. Co-Chairs Summary. First meeting of the Consultative Group of Ministers or High-level Representatives on International Environmental Governance, Belgrade, 27-28 June 2009. UNEP, Nairobi. http: http://www.unep.org/environmentalgovernance/LinkClick.aspx?fileticket=7RzudGTFKRI%3D&tabid=341&language=en-US

UNEP (2009e). *Global Green New Deal. Policy Brief*. UNEP, Nairobi

UNEP (2009f). *International environmental governance: help or hindrance?' – international environmental governance from a country perspective*. Background paper for the ministerial consultations. Discussion paper presented by the Executive Director. Addendum. International environmental governance and United Nations reform. UNEP/GC.25/16/Add.1. UNEP, Nairobi

UNEP (2009g). Report of the second meeting of the advisory committee on the simultaneous extraordinary meetings of the conferences of the Parties to the Basel, Rotterdam and Stockholm conventions. UNEP/FAO/AdComm.2/1. UNEP/FAO, Bangkok

UNEP (2009h). Catalyzing low-carbon growth in developing countries. Public finance mechanisms to scale up private sector investment in climate solutions. UNEP, Geneva

UNEP POPs (2009). *Report of the Conference of the Parties of the Stockholm Convention on Persistent Organic Pollutants on the work of its fourth meeting*. UNEP/POPS/COP.4/38. UNEP, Geneva

UNESCO (2009). *IWRM Guidelines at River Basin Level. Part I: Principles*. UNESCO, Paris

UNGA (2005). *2005 World Summit Outcome*. A/60/L.1. United Nations General Assembly, New York. http://www.who.int/hiv/universalaccess2010/worldsummit.pdf

UNGA (2007). Informal Consultative Process on the Institutional Framework for the United Nations' Environmental Activities: Co-Chairs' Options Paper. United Nations General Assembly, New York. http://www.un.org/ga/president/61/follow-up/environment/EG-OptionsPaper.pdf

UNGA (2008). *Implementation of Agenda 21, the Programme for the Further Implementation of Agenda 21 and the outcomes of the World Summit on Sustainable Development*. Resolution 63/212 adopted by the General Assembly at its Sixty-third session. A/RES/63/212. United Nations, New York

Van Schalkwyk, M. (2009). Keynote address by Marthinus van Schalkwyk, South African Minister of Environmental Affairs and Tourism, at the plenary Ministerial consultations on "International environmental governance: help or hindrance?" held during the UNEP Global Ministerial Environment Forum in Nairobi on 19 February 2009. UNEP, Nairobi

Vera, I. (2009). *Climate Change and Technology Transfer: The Need for a Regional Perspective*. UN-DESA Policy Brief No. 18. United Nations, New York

Von Moltke, K. (2001). *On Clustering International Environmental Agreements*. International Institute for Sustainable Development, Winnipeg, Canada

Vormedal, I. (2008). The Influence of Business and Industry NGOs in the Negotiation of the Kyoto Mechanisms: the Case of Carbon Capture and Storage in the CDM. *Global Environmental Politics*, 8(4), 36-65

Walker, B., Barrett, S., Polasky, S., Galaz, V., Folke, C., Engström, E., Ackerman, F., Arrow, K., Carpenter, S., Chopra, K., Daily, G., Ehrlich, P., Hughes, T., Kautsky, N., Levin, S., Mäler, K.-G., Shogren, J., Vincent, J., Xepapadeas, T. and de Zeeuw. A. (2009). Looming Global-Scale Failures and Missing Institutions. *Science*, 235(5946), 1345-1346

Wolf, A.T., Natharius, J.A., Danielson, J.J., Ward, B.S. and Pender, J.K. (1999). International River Basins of the World. *International Journal of Water Resources Development*, 15(4), 387-427

WWAP (World Water Assessment Programme) (2009). *The United Nations World Water Development Report 3: Water in a Changing World*. UNESCO, Paris, and Earthscan, London

Zukang, S. (2009) Statement. 5th World Water Forum, Istanbul

Ecosystem Management

Increasing pressures of human population, exploitation, pollution, and climate change have already pushed some ecosystems over critical thresholds. Other ecosystems are edging closer to thresholds beyond which a return to stable conditions could be difficult—if not impossible.

Many natural ecosystems have been converted to cropland and other uses. Agricultural workers in China.
Credit: Rob Broek

INTRODUCTION

Restoring a damaged ecosystem is a difficult and complex task, and one about which we still have much to learn (Jackson and Hobbs 2009, Scheffer and others 2009). Efforts to designate 'planetary boundaries', which are intended to define a 'safe operating space' for humanity with respect to Earth systems, have begun. These boundaries are associated with the planet's biophysical subsystems or processes (**Figure 1**). One boundary considered to have been crossed already is biodiversity loss. One hundred species per million are currently estimated to be lost per year (Rockström and others 2009a, Rockström and others 2009b).

The other boundaries considered to have been crossed are climate change and interference with the nitrogen cycle. Determining a planetary boundary for disruption of the nitrogen cycle is difficult, but scientists have proposed one based on the total amount of nitrogen removed from the atmosphere for human use. If an acceptable rate of human nitrogen fixation is 35 million tonnes per year, as they have provisionally proposed, the amount currently being converted, estimated at

about 120 million tonnes per year, is more than three times too high. Much of this nitrogen fixation is for fertilizer production. Some nitrogen is also fixed by leguminous crops, such as soybean.

Unintended releases of reactive nitrogen to the environment pollute waterways and coastal zones, accumulate in terrestrial systems, contribute several gases to the atmosphere, and ultimately undermine the resilience of critical Earth subsystems (see Harmful Substances and Hazardous Waste chapter). Scientists warn that we may also "soon be approaching the boundaries for global freshwater use, change in land use, ocean acidification, and interference with the global phosphorous cycle" (Rockström and others 2009a, Rockström and others 2009b).

Rising temperatures, shrinking supplies of freshwater, deteriorating agricultural conditions, and sea-level rise increasingly threaten global food supplies (Battisti and Naylor 2009, FAO 2009a, FAO 2009b). By 2050, East Asia will require 70 per cent more water for irrigation than today to feed its growing population; South Asia will require 57 per cent more (FAO 2009a, Mukherji and others 2009).

Figure 1: Planetary boundaries

In 2009, a team of researchers suggested that a safe operating space or boundary for human activities should be considered in order to sustain the integrity of the planet's functioning natural systems. They proposed nine components of Earth systems that show signs of global environmental change driven by human activities. As shown below, these components are climate change, disruption of biogeochemical cycling, biodiversity loss, depletion of the stratospheric ozone layer, acidification of oceans, consumption of freshwater, land use changes, aerosol loading in the atmosphere, and chemical pollution. The inner green shading represents the proposed safe operating space for the nine planetary systems. The red wedges represent an estimate of the current position for each variable. The boundaries for climate change, biodiversity loss, and interference with the nitrogen cycle have been crossed.

The interdependencies between these components are extremely complex. For example, increased concentrations of CO_2 in the atmosphere can lead to ocean acidification and increased radiative forcing. This radiative forcing, in turn, contributes to shifts in climatic zones that can exacerbate land use changes and increase consumption of freshwater. Shifts in climate zones, ocean acidification, disruptions in the nitrogen and phosphorous cycles, and chemical pollution can contribute to biodiversity loss.

Source: Rockström and others (2009a)

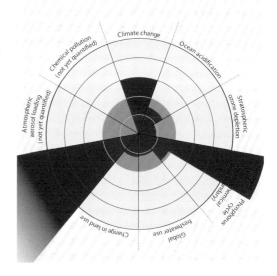

By 2025, 3.4 billion people are expected to live in countries categorized as water-scarce (Calzolaio 2009).

The health of soils and their capacity to process carbon, nutrients, wastes, toxins, and water are important factors for Earth's ability to minimize adverse environmental effects. It will be impossible to meet the planet's nutritional demands without seriously reforming agricultural, land, and ecosystem management practices (FAO 2009b, Montgomery 2008, Montgomery 2007).

The economic and financial crisis of 2008-2009 has already caused an additional 90 million people to fall into extreme poverty (UN 2009). However, a pause in the acceleration of global economic activity could provide opportunities to halt destructive practices, rein in energy use, pursue new energy sources, begin creating 'green' jobs, and concentrate on developing sustainable pathways to growth and new approaches to ecosystem restoration (Levin 2009, UK 2009, Stern 2007).

Biodiversity loss

The International Union for Conservation of Nature's (IUCN) Red List Index of Threatened Species is the most comprehensive source of information on the conservation status of plant and animal species. It is based on an objective system for assessing the risks that species will become extinct if no conservation action is taken. Not only does the Red List identify species and their designated threat category (Critically Endangered, Endangered, or Vulnerable), but it is a rich source of information on the nature of threats, ecological requirements, species distribution, and conservation actions that could prevent extinction or reduce the risk of it taking place (Walpole and others 2009).

According to the latest Red List, 17 291 species out of 47 677 assessed are under threat: 21 per cent of all known mammals, 30 per cent of all known amphibians, 12 per cent of all known birds, 28 per cent of reptiles, 37 per cent of freshwater fishes, 70 per cent of plants, and 35 per cent of invertebrates (IUCN 2009).

Biodiversity is the basis of ecosystem health and of the provision of ecosystem services (Mooney and Mace 2009). It is also a critical factor in managing ecosystems for resilience, that is, their ability to absorb and recover from disturbances.

The Conference of the Parties (COP) to the Convention on Biological Diversity called for a significant reduction in the rate of biodiversity loss by the year 2010. This target will likely not be met (Diversitas 2009, Gilbert 2009). Targets adopted to protect 10 per cent of the world's forests will not be met either, despite widespread agreement on the essential role that forests play in biodiversity conservation and climate change mitigation and adaptation (Coad and others 2009). The global set of indicators used to track progress toward the 2010 biodiversity target is underdeveloped and underinvested. To improve data reliability, global monitoring must be balanced with capacity development at the national level. In 2010, the COP will review progress towards the 2010 target. It is expected to agree on a new set of targets and a revised indicator framework (Walpole and others 2009).

ECOSYSTEM DEGRADATION

The Millennium Ecosystem Assessment (MA) was carried out between 2001 and 2005 to assess the consequences of ecosystem change. It analysed the options available to enhance the conservation and sustainable use of ecosystems, and focused on the linkages between ecosystems and human wellbeing. In particular, it looked at 'ecosystem services'; the benefits we obtain from ecosystems. The MA considered direct and indirect drivers of change in regard to ecosystems and their services, the current condition of those services, and the effects of changes in ecosystem services on human wellbeing (MA 2009).

Changes in biodiversity due to human activities have been more rapid in the past 50 years than at any other time in human history. Many of the drivers of change that lead to biodiversity loss, and to changes in ecosystem services, are growing in intensity. The extent of dead zones in the oceans has doubled every ten years since the 1960s. About 400 coastal areas are now periodically or constantly oxygen-depleted due to fertilizer run-off, sewage discharge, and combustion of fossil fuels (Diaz and Rosenberg 2008).

The scale and importance of ecosystem transformations have evoked speculation that humankind has entered a new geological epoch succeeding the 10 000-year Holocene. It has been suggested that with the Industrial Revolution we entered the 'Anthropocene', in which human activity is the main driver of environmental change. Some scientists would argue that the challenge we face today is finding a way to maintain the Holocene's more desirable environmental state (IGIP 2009, Rockström and others 2009a, Zalasiewicz and others 2008).

Threats to marine fisheries

Overexploitation, pollution, and rising temperatures threaten 63 per cent of the world's assessed fisheries stocks (Worm and others 2009) (**Box 1**).

In 2009, for the third year in a row, a major sockeye salmon run in British Columbia, Canada, was closed to fishing. Of an expected 10 million sockeye salmon, just over 1.3 million appeared, with impacts on the economy and the people and animals that rely on them for food. Some experts blamed warmer ocean and river temperatures, together with declining food supplies in the open oceans (CBC 2009, Orr 2009).

Damaged aquatic ecosystems can be successfully restored. In a two-year study on fish stocks, catch data were supplemented with information from other sources, including stock abundance and exploitation rates in ten ecosystems, ecosystem surveys from 20 regions, and ecosystem models from 30 regions, to provide a precise and accurate assessment of the state of certain fisheries. Stocks showed signs of recovery in five of the ten ecosystems studied. Regions showing the greatest improvement were in Iceland and off the coasts of

Shuswap Lake-Adams River salmon run, Canada
Credit: Hank Tweedy

The Sundarbans in Bangladesh are part of the world's largest delta, formed by the Ganges, Brahmaputra, and Meghna rivers. The mangrove forest covers about 38 000 square kilometres.
Credit: www.sundarbans.org

California and New England in the United States (Worm and others 2009). There are also positive signs in some developing countries. In Kenya and Tanzania, for example, scientists, managers, and local communities are cooperating to restrict some types of fishing equipment and close certain areas to fishing (Nyandwi 2009).

Combining traditional control measures like catch quotas and community management with closures, equipment restrictions, ocean zoning, and economic incentives is a promising approach. The study concluded that when fishery industries, scientists, and conservation biologists work together, sharing the best available data and bridging disciplinary divisions, ecosystem management can be effective (Worm and others 2009).

Half of all fish consumed globally are produced by aquaculture. This does not necessarily relieve pressures on wild species since much of the feed for farmed fish is made from these species. Up to five kilograms of wild fish is required to produce one kilogram of aquaculture salmon (Dewailly and Rouja 2009, Naylor and others 2009). Expansion of fish farming in coastal areas has contributed to the loss of over 50 per cent of the world's mangrove forests compared with the early 20th century. Shrimp farming accounts for almost three-quarters of this loss (Bosire and others 2008).

Coastal areas

Almost half of the world's largest cities lie within 50 kilometres of a coast. Rich coastal areas provide food, recreation, and transportation, and serve as huge biogeochemical processors (Vörösmarty and others 2009). These areas are experiencing increasing pressures from the land side, as populations grow and coastal wetlands are lost to agriculture and urban expansion. At the same time, creeping inundation is eroding coastlines on the ocean side (Vörösmarty and others 2009).

Many of the world's largest deltas are densely populated and heavily farmed. Nevertheless, they are increasingly vulnerable to flooding and conversion of land to sea. A recent study found that 24 of the 33 largest deltas are sinking and that all but five have experienced temporary flooding in the last decade. Tens of millions of people have been affected and a total of 250 000 square kilometres has been inundated (Syvitski and others 2009). Deltas are at risk from sea-level rise, and direct human activities have significantly increased the vulnerability of deltas. Dams and reservoirs, for example, interrupt the natural flow of rivers and keep sediments from reaching the deltas.

In the next 40 years, it is estimated that the total amount of land vulnerable to flooding will increase by as much as 50 per cent globally (Syvitski and others 2009). Thousands of lives have already been lost as a result of recurrent flooding in the deltas of the Irrawaddy River in Myanmar and the Ganges-Brahmaputra in India and Bangladesh.

Mangrove forests provide valuable ecosystem services, not only functioning as essential spawning grounds, but also stabilizing coastal areas (Alongi 2008). They shelter these areas from storms and help prevent flooding, and upstream and underground salinization. They also furnish fuel, food, and medicines to local communities, in some cases contributing to biodiversity conservation (Pritchard 2009, Walters and others 2008).

Mangrove forests, like coral reefs and tidal flats, attenuate wave energy and contribute to coastal defences far more cost-effectively than 'hard' defences. During the 2004 Asian tsunami, areas protected by intact mangrove forests and coral reefs were less affected than areas without such natural barriers (Pritchard 2009, Wetlands International 2008). The need to maintain and restore 'blue carbon sinks' in the oceans, seas, and marine ecosystems to combat climate change was a focus of international attention in 2009. Of all the biological carbon captured in the world, over half ('blue carbon') is captured by marine living organisms (Nellemann and others 2009, UNEP 2009).

ECOSYSTEM MANAGEMENT MODELS

Policy-makers need the capacity to create and implement policies for social-ecological systems, foresee consequences, and evaluate outcomes. Relevant research should bridge disciplines effectively and create the areas of knowledge required to build systems that are resilient.

Ecosystems that have high biodiversity are more resilient than those that do not. Management and policy formulation need to be based on an understanding of how biodiversity enhances ecosystem resilience. In a biosphere shaped by human actions, managing for resilience is critical in order to cope with uncertainty (Resilience Alliance 2007, Elmqvist 2003).

By quantifying social-ecological connections and the associated trade-offs of different actions over relevant time frames, managers can better anticipate the impacts of their actions (Carpenter and others 2009). Ecosystems respond to stressors and drivers in complex, non-linear, and sometimes even abrupt ways. Moreover, ecosystem services are affected by the interactions of multiple drivers, the varying spatial extents and time lags of processes, and conflicting connections between and among various services. Changes in one ecosystem service invariably impact another (Kellner and Hastings 2009, Mitchell and others 2009).

The recommendations of the Millennium Ecosystem Assessment some five years ago have proven difficult to apply. Balancing human needs with ecosystem health is particularly challenging. In view of the complex interactions between multiple drivers and human feedback, policy decisions designed to manage and improve ecosystems can be exceedingly hard to make, and even more problematic to evaluate. These concerns are illustrated by an analysis of World Bank projects between 1998 and 2006 that had the dual goals of promoting biodiversity and alleviating poverty. Only 16 per cent of the projects were considered successful in both areas (Tallis and others 2008).

How to quantify the trade-offs that occur when ecosystem services interact with human needs remains poorly understood. Researchers have suggested that a conceptual framework needs to be developed for assessing changes in social-ecological systems through the use of a suite of broadly accepted metrics and indicators that can be collected consistently and compared across a range of cases (Carpenter and others 2009). Only then can there be an accurate analysis of policies and management practices intended to increase ecosystem resilience and improve ecosystem services (**Figure 2**).

Some scientists believe that future research should focus on controls of ecosystem services themselves, addressing the effects of multiple drivers. Such research would directly address the need for information about how drivers and management interventions change ecosystem services. It would evaluate not only the direct effects of biodiversity, but also biodiversity's role in modifying the effects of drivers on ecosystem services. New, integrated models need to be developed to identify conceptual frameworks for ecosystem assessment, and to address scales and drivers for specific situations. Changes in ecosystem services could then evoke feedback through human responses (Carpenter and others 2009).

There are significant gaps in long-term observation and monitoring programmes, particularly in regard to data and interactions between drivers of change, ecosystems, and human wellbeing. Data collection needs to be consistent, rigorous, and available through searchable databases, on-line virtual libraries, and training programmes. Local and traditional knowledge also needs to be collected and considered. The development of tools that can help model or analyse the responses of biodiversity and ecosystem services to drivers of change and, in turn, help predict how those responses would affect human wellbeing are key. The different scientific disciplines need to work together to create a common, credible, replicable, and scalable framework (Connelley and others 2009, Daily 2009, Ostrom 2009, UNEP IPBES 2009a).

The Intergovernmental Platform on Biodiversity and Ecosystem Services (IPBES) is designed to serve as an international mechanism to deliver scientific expertise on biodiversity and to follow up on the MA's global strategy to address problems presented in its findings (UNEP IPBES 2009b). International cooperation aimed at halting biodiversity loss focus on the importance of these efforts to human wellbeing and poverty eradication. To emphasize the importance of biodiversity among scientists, governments, and the general public, the UN has declared 2010 the International Year of Biodiversity.

Figure 2: Expansion of ecosystem services for human use

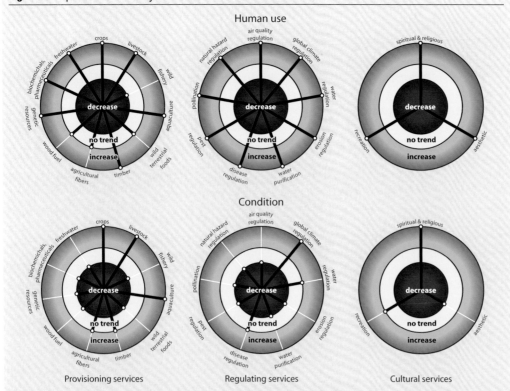

Trends in human use (upper diagrams) vs. condition of ecosystem services (lower diagrams). Provisioning, regulating, or cultural ecosystem services are shown at left, centre, and right. The length of the black radial lines indicates the degree of change in human use or condition of the service.

Source: Carpenter and others (2009)

Agricultural ecosystems

The world food crisis has resulted from the combined effects of competition for cropland, weather conditions, crop disease, and export restrictions (Battisti and Naylor 2009). Food production relies entirely on ecosystems' ability to provide water, nutrient-rich soils, climate regulation, pollinators, and to help control infestations. These factors, along with the conversion of cropland to biofuel production, may reduce the amount of cropland available for growing food crops by 8-20 per cent by 2050 (Ericksen 2008). Environmental degradation will be a major constraint on future world production, affecting both food prices and food security. Soil erosion has already led to a 40 per cent global decline in agricultural productivity (Ericksen 2008).

Maintaining and building efficient food systems in the face of growing population pressures and climate change is one of the most serious challenges the world faces. In the tropics and sub-tropics, the temperatures of the growing season at the end of the 21st century are expected to surpass the highest temperatures recorded in the last 100 years (Battisi and Naylor 2009), with profound effects on crop and livestock production. In addition, to secure supplies of agricultural produce some countries are making investments in other developing countries to grow crops (**Box 2**). The food price spike in the first half of 2008 has increased concerns about the global food supply in in the future. Although technically it seems possible to feed the 9 billion people expected to inhabit the planet by mid-century, diminishing returns, rising input prices, and the difficulties of logisitics, institutional arrangements, and security constraints in some areas mean that the world food economy is likely to reach a ceiling long before this technical potential is realized.

Based on an analysis of the literature, researchers argue that if the long-term decline in food prices in the 20th century changes, the short-time horizons of private and public actors are likely to pose special risks since they could prevent timely investments in increasing world capacity for food production. Governments can exercise a number of options to mitigate this risk, such as influencing supply and demand for farm products, investing in research and infrastructure, and reducing price instability in agricultural markets (Koning and Van Ittersum 2009).

Box 2: Foreign land acquisition

Countries that export capital, but lack sufficient land or water to grow their own crops, have triggered a powerful and contentious investment trend in the developing world, mainly in Africa. According to a recent FAO study, leasing of farmland by foreign companies, investment funds, and foreign governments has become a worldwide phenomenon. Abu Dhabi has leased 28 000 hectares in Sudan to produce maize, beans, and potatoes for the United Arab Emirates (UAE). China is producing palm oil for biofuel on 2.8 million hectares in the Democratic Republic of the Congo. India has invested US$4 billion in Ethiopian cropland to grow sugarcane and flowers.

Outsourcing agricultural production to countries in need of capital is nothing new, but these land acquisitions are different in kind and scale. Major food importers including China, India, the Republic of Korea, Qatar, Saudi Arabia, and the UAE are leasing or purchasing vast tracts of farmland, as much as 15-20 million hectares, in developing countries. According to the International Food Policy Research Institute, the value of these transactions is estimated at US$20 to US$30 billion.

These large-scale land acquisitions followed, in particular, the food crisis of 2007-2008, when wheat, rice, and cereal prices skyrocketed. Food market turmoil and concerns about the cost of imports, coupled with the threat of climate change and ongoing water shortages, have provided an impetus for this surge in land transactions. Some countries are also looking for opportunities to make a profit on food and on products such as biofuels.

Advocates point out that these transactions provide income to struggling countries, and that local communities could benefit from access to new crop varieties and technologies. Critics warn that local populations could be pushed off their land. Moreover, countries in which millions of people are starving will be exporting food. This practice has been described as 'neo-colonial'.

In 2009, there were riots in Madagascar when the Korean company Daewoo Logistics attempted to lease 1.3 million hectares (nearly half the island's total arable land) to produce maize and palm oil.

Criticism of such transactions has continued to grow. In response, a number of organizations, including the FAO, the UN Conference on Trade and Development (UNCTAD), and the World Bank, are developing guidelines to regulate this practice.

The land rush appears to have slowed down. As Jean-Philippe Audinet, Acting Director of the Policy Division of the UN International Fund for Agricultural Development (IFAD), says, "some don't want to take this political risk, reputational risk and economic risk." However, there are concerns that once food prices start to climb, such acquisitions will again begin to increase.

Hectares obtained by key investors, 2006-2009

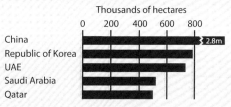

Source: International Food Policy Research Institute

Since 2006, 15 to 20 million hectares of farmland in developing countries—in size, about one-fifth of all that in the European Union—has been subject to transactions or talks involving foreigners, according to the International Food Policy Research Institute.

Sources: BBC (2009), Coluta and others (2009), Economist (2009), FAO (2009c), Viana and others (2009), Rice (2008)

Expanding Africa's genetic resource base

Most of Africa's population experiences climate-related stress and shocks on a regular basis as a result of climate variability. The scale and nature of these impacts, however, will change dramatically as climate changes (Conway 2009).

Food security issues have become increasingly prominent since the food price crisis of 2007-2008. Vulnerability to fluctuations in food supplies has been of particular concern (Mittal 2009). Recent studies call for concerted adaptation efforts to build resilience in African agricultural systems in the face of climate change (Burke and others 2009, Conway 2009, Lobell and others 2008). In adapting to climate change, African farmers could benefit from wider experience available in other parts of the continent and from access to genetic resources available elsewhere (Burke and others 2009).

Knowledge about the potential speed and magnitude of shifts in climate conditions is also required (**Figure 3**). Donor and research institutions must understand how rapid and how extreme these changes will be so they can prioritize the collection, evaluation, and conservation of genetic resources. Arican crop diversity may not be sufficient to allow the adaptation of crop production to climate change. While great strides have been made in the collection of plant genetic resources for seed banks over the last half-century, collections in key areas of African crop diversity are largely unavailable for a variety of reasons (Burke and others 2009).

Figure 3: Percentage crop overlap in African countries 2002-2050

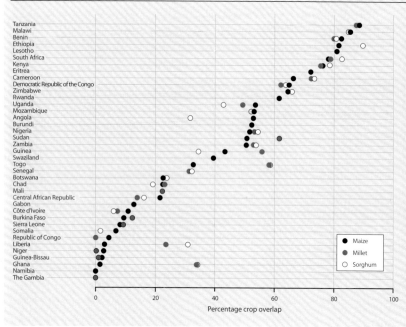

The figure shows the percentage overlap between the current (1993-2002 average) distribution of growing season temperatures within a country and the simulated 2050 distribution of temperatures in the same country for three crops: maize, millet, and sorghum. For the majority of the countries, current growing season temperatures in maize, millet and sorghum areas within the country will represent less than half the range of expected 2050 growing season temperatures in the same areas.

Legend:
- ● Maize
- ● Millet
- ○ Sorghum

Source: Burke and others (2009)

Investments in the collection and conservation of crop diversity in countries, including Cameroon, Nigeria, Sudan, and Tanzania, would be promising initial activities.

Many African countries could benefit from the genetic resources of other countries on the continent if these resources were effectively managed and shared. Interdependence among countries in regard to plant genetic resources has led to the development of collaborative mechanisms such as the Multilateral System for access and benefit sharing of the International Treaty on Plant Genetic Resources for Food and Agriculture, sometimes referred to as the 'Seed Treaty'. This interdependence will clearly increase with climate change, as will the need for international collaboration in the conservation and use of crop genetic diversity (Burke and others 2009).

ECOSYSTEM-CLIMATE INTERACTIONS
Ecosystems' capacity to deliver essential services to society is already under pressure. The additional stresses imposed by climate change in the coming years will require extraordinary adaptation. It will be necessary to track the changing status of ecosystems, deepen our understanding of the biological underpinnings of ecosystem service

delivery, and develop new tools and techniques to maintain and restore resilient biological and social systems, building on an ecosystem foundation that has been radically altered during the past half century. Most rivers have been totally restructured; water bodies are severely polluted and fish stocks are depleted; coral reefs are near a tipping point and may disappear as functional ecosystems due to warming, pollution, and acidification; and over half the planet's land surface is devoted to livestock and crop agriculture, with little consideration given to the ecosystem services that are being lost as a consequence (Fagre and others 2009, Smol and Douglas 2007).

Climate change, mainly caused by anthropogenic GHG emissions, will disrupt our ecosystem base in new ways. Already we see widespread signs of change. Species behaviour is being altered, disrupting longstanding mutualisms. We are seeing extinctions within vulnerable habitats, and conditions in which migrations are necessary for survival. This represents an extraordinary threat and calls for urgent attention by the scientific community (Mooney and others 2009).

Scientists and conservation managers are re-examining ecosystem management approaches in

relation to climate change, including looking at how ecosystems influence climate and how climate drives changes in ecosystems (Glick and others 2009, Chapin and others 2008, Hoegh-Guldberg and others 2008, Campbell and others 2008, MacLachlan and others 2007).

Considering multiple interactions and feedbacks between climate and ecosystem management could lead to innovative climate mitigation strategies to reduce at the same time, for example, GHG emissions and rates of land degradation and deforestation. Achieving each of these objectives would result in multiple ecological and societal benefits. Assessing such strategies' effectiveness requires a good understanding of interactions among feedback processes, their consequences at the local and global levels, and the ways that changes on various scales in different regions are linked (Chapin and others 2008).

Oceans' role in climate mitigation is being explored through the attention being given to 'blue carbon' sequestration. A recent UNEP publication, produced in collaboration with FAO and UNESCO, reports that an estimated 50 per cent of the carbon in the atmosphere that becomes sequestered in natural systems is cycled in seas and oceans (Nellemann and others 2009). Seventy per cent of the carbon stored permanently in marine areas is found in mangrove, seagrass, and salt marsh ecosystems. Yet these critical ecosystems are disappearing more rapidly than land ecosystems and urgently need to receive greater attention.

An essential tool for ecosystem-based responses to climate change is active adaptive management, in which systems are closely monitored and management strategies are altered to address expected and ongoing changes (Lawler and others 2009). A global mean warming of 2°C by 2100 could have catastrophic effects–although the precise nature of these effects is still being debated. The 2007 IPCC Fourth Assessment Report predicted that drought, higher temperatures, and severe weather would affect food productivity, threaten up to 30 per cent of species with extinction, and cause the bleaching of much of the world's coral reefs (IPCC 2007a, IPPC 2007b). Many scientists are now convinced that temperature rises and the impacts in the 21st century will exceed those projected in the 2007 IPCC report (Le Quéré and others 2009, Rockström and others 2009a, Rockström and others 2009b, Smith and others 2009, UNEP 2009).

Managing ecosystems in a way that ignores the probable impacts of climate change would fail to meet the most basic management objectives. Therefore, the uncertainty of these impacts is one of the greatest challenges facing ecosystem managers. Successful management strategies need to take account of the uncertainty inherent in projections of impacts on climate, and how these uncertainties will affect the outcomes of management activities.

Progress on REDD

The active protection of tropical forests is now widely perceived as a crucial ecosystem management priority and a cost-effective way to reduce global carbon emissions. Formalizing the concept of 'reducing emissions from deforestation and forest degradation' (REDD) while building consensus, knowledge, and awareness concerning the importance of including a REDD mechanism in a post-2012 climate change treaty is the aim of the new collaborative UN-REDD Programme.

REDD is an ambitious, innovative payment scheme for ecosystem services. It recognizes forests as a major mitigating factor with respect to climate change; it also offers financial incentives to keep tropical forests standing and growing. Roughly 25 per cent of terrestrial carbon is stored in forests. Deforestation accounts for about 20 per cent of man-made greenhouse gas emissions, more than those produced by the entire transport sector. REDD assigns a monetary value to standing forests in developing countries and allows developed countries to offset their CO_2 emissions by reimbursing local landowners, including indigenous people, for protecting the forests instead of cutting them down. For example, Brazil's first REDD project is in the state of Amazonas at the Juma Sustainable Development Reserve, where each family receives US$28 a month if the forest remains uncut (Viana 2009).

There are challenges related to ensuring that this programme operates effectively and has a maximum impact, for example monitoring. Today, satellite imagery is the main tool being used to track forest forest destruction and degradation (**Box 3**).

Box 3: Using satellite imagery to track forest destruction and degradation

Over one per cent of all tropical humid forests was lost between 2000 and 2005. NASA's Moderate Resolution Imaging Spectroradiometer (MODIS) is able to capture images of large-scale deforestation. Clear-cut areas of 15-25 hectares can be identified. Brazil has a well-established satellite imaging programme, the Amazon Deforestation Monitoring Project (PRODES), which monitors the world's largest tropical rainforest. This is just one of the tools being used to try to halt the illegal logging and rainforest destruction that contribute 30 per cent of global carbon emissions. A joint pilot project with Japan (the Daichi satellite) has made it possible to see beneath cloud cover, a frequent challenge in imaging tropical forests.

These satellites are part of the Global Earth Observation System of Systems (GEOSS). Launched in response to a call for action by the 2002 World Summit on Sustainable Development and by the G8, this initiative, involving 80 governments and the European Union, links all existing Earth observation systems and organizations for the purpose of obtaining a complete picture of the planet. Its GEO Portal is a single internet access point where imagery, data, and analytical software packages relevant to all areas of the globe can be found. This project is designed to help understand and predict climate change, improve water management, and make the management and protection of terrestrial, coastal, and marine resources more effective.

A new initiative focusing on biodiversity has been established within GEOSS, as the Group on Earth Observations Biodiversity Observation Network (GEO BON) has been added to the GEO family.

While satellites can track the destruction and degradation of forests, they are unable to evaluate carbon content, a parameter that would be required for an accurate REDD assessment. Determining carbon content and monitoring carbon emissions from forests is currently time-consuming and difficult. Calculating the biomass and ultimately the amount of carbon sequestered in a forest often requires manual measurement of trees' diameter and height. This is performed plot by plot, tree by tree. However, new software will allow users to map and monitor forest degradation and deforestation using a personal computer.

The Carnegie Landsat Analysis System - Lite (CLASLite) uses images from Earth observation satellites like Landsat, in combination with LiDAR (the Light Detection and Ranging system), to estimate how much carbon is contained in a forest. This will be an especially important monitoring tool for large and remote tropical forests. Data are based on remote sensing technologies that can map 10 000 square kilometres per hour, yet CLASLite is as accurate as more traditional data collection techniques.

Sources: Asner (2009), GEOSS (2009), Tollefson (2009)

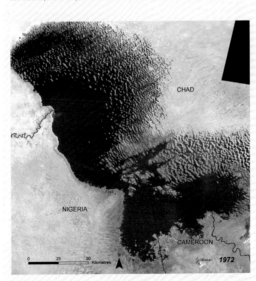 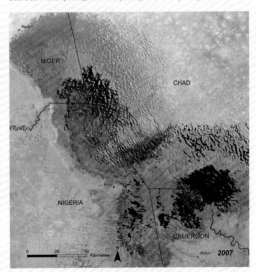

The Lake Chad drainage basin, a 2 500 000 km² hydrologically closed catchment, extends to eight countries: Algeria, Cameroon, the Central African Republic, Chad, Libyan Arab Jamahiriya, Niger, Nigeria, and Sudan. It is home to over 20 million people, who derive direct or indirect livelihoods from the lake. Most of the region's rainfall occurs in the southern one-third of the drainage basin, contributing about 90 per cent of the basin's run-off. The northern two-thirds is dominated by arid conditions.

As these satellite images from 1972 and 2007 show, the surface area of the lake has been reduced dramatically over time despite a recent increase in its water levels. Less rainfall and increased water consumption by the area's inhabitants have changed the water balance within the drainage basin and are continuing to do so. The lake is especially susceptible to climatic variability since it is rather shallow, with an average depth of 4.11 metres. As a result of lower rainfall and greater water usage, the extent of Lake Chad has decreased by 95 per cent over roughly 35 years.

Credit: Atlas of Our Changing Environment (http://na.unep.net/digital_atlas2/google.php)

In order to have an effect on atmospheric CO_2 concentrations, trees must be protected against any kind of degradation, fire, or logging for at least 100 years (Shrope 2009).

A second, even more difficult challenge is how to determine the 'reference levels' against which future greenhouse gas abatement would be measured. The problem is how to find a way to ensure that REDD mechanisms do not perversely reward countries with high deforestation rates while discriminating against those with low ones. Furthermore, countries that receive funding should have effective accountable governance to ensure that payments received are redistributed to communities and individual landowners to compensate them for not cutting down trees. Land ownership needs to be clear, and special efforts should be made to involve and protect indigenous populations (Cotula and Meyers 2009, Viana 2009). Local communities that depend on these ecosystems for their livelihood will be impacted the most.

REDD initiatives are most likely to succeed where they build on the interests of indigenous people and forest communities. Attention must be paid to the balance of incentives, benefits, rights, and political participation across levels of decision-making, interest groups, and administration. Incentives can include payments or other benefits for good practices, development of alternative livelihoods, formalizing of land tenure and local resource rights, and intensification of productivity on non-forest lands. The pressure to reduce deforestation should be spread across many levels to aleviate the burden on forest communities.

A healthy standing forest provides many benefits beyond carbon sequestration and mitigation of climate change. Forests also protect biodiversity, halt soil erosion, and maintain water quality. Critics of REDD would like to see these other benefits be given greater recognition than they are at present.

It has been estimated that putting US$22-29 billion into REDD would cut global deforestation by 25 per cent by 2015 (IWG-IFR 2009). Transaction costs are likely to be very high, although lower than those associated with almost any other mitigation vehicle with similar impacts. REDD provides a useful mechanism for offsetting developed countries' CO_2 emissions, as long as

these countries do not use it as a comparatively easy way out to avoid reducing their own emissions (Wollenberg and Springate-Baginski 2009).

Assisted colonization

Climate change has already forced changes in distributions of many plants and animals at the local level, some of which have led to severe range contractions and even the potential extinction of some species. The geographic ranges of many species are moving to higher latitudes and altitudes, in response to shifts in the habitats to which they have adapted over long periods. Some species are unable to disperse or adapt rapidly enough to keep up with changes in climatic conditions. Not only do these species face increased risks of extinction, but entire ecosystems, such as cloud forests and coral reefs, may cease to function in their current form due to a lack of options to migrate or adapt in time (Hoegh-Guldberg and others 2008).

Discussions of conservation responses to climate change consider 'assisted colonization', the translocation and succesful colonization of species that are threatened with extinction by climate change, to be one option (McLachlan and others 2007). Researchers have proposed the adoption of a risk assessment and management framework to help identify circumstances that require moderate action, such as enhancement of conventional conservation measures, and those calling for a more extreme response, such as assisted colonization.

There are many socio-economic as well as biophysical considerations. For example, moving threatened large carnivores into livestock grazing areas is controversial. In some cases, until more suitable habitats can be found or developed, the use of gene banks could be a practical option for the conservation of species. Existing gene banks for agriculturally significant seeds have been established with a view to conservation in a warming world. This approach could be a useful alternative for many more plants and animals that may not now be of economic significance, and could prove invaluable in an uncertain future (Swaminathan 2009, Hoegh-Guldberg and others 2008).

Assisted colonization entails some risks, particularly when translocated species become invasive, but these must be weighed against the possibility of extinction and ecosystem loss. Already some regions, including the Arctic, are experiencing higher temperatures. Others are likely to experience unprecedented warming within the next 100 years, as well as altered precipitation patterns and increasing ocean acidity. The future for some species and ecosystems is so uncertain that assisted colonization could be their best chance. The relevant management decisions will require careful thought, supported by solid scientific understanding (Running and Mills 2009, Hoegh-Guldberg and others 2008).

LOOKING AHEAD

Many questions about the health, functions, and resilience of ecosystems remain to be answered. It is clear, however, that ecosystem management has an important role to play in mitigating and adapting to the impacts of climate change. If managed properly, ecosystems can provide a cost-efficient and effective way to reduce these impacts. Managing ecosystems for resilience, and protecting biodiversity to support this resilience, is critical both to meet development objectives and to address the challenges of climate change.

There are interventions that can mitigate or facilitate adaptation to climate change. They consist of *technology-based* adaptation, such as a new seawall; *direct ecosystem management* concerned with specific ecosystems or ecosystem services, such as constructed wetlands; or longer-term *indirect ecosystem management* related to ecosystem resilience and functions, which will have a range of ecosystem co-benefits. These benefits directly enhance priority ecosystem services. Maintaining healthy, resilient ecosystems is therefore key to the mitigation of, and adaptation to, climate change (**Figure 4**).

Figure 4: Coastal ecosystem management adaptation options

Adaptation option	Climate stressors addressed	Other management goals addressed	Benefits	Constraints
Allow coastal wetlands to migrate inland, for example through setback, density restrictions, land purchases	Sea level rise	Preserve habitat for vulnerable species; preserve coastal land/development	Maintains species habitats; maintains protection for inland ecosystems	In highly developed areas, there is often no land available for wetlands to migrate, or it can be costly to landowners
Incorporate wetland protection into infrastructure planning, for example for sewer utilities	Sea level rise; changes in precipitation	Maintain water quality; preserve habitat for vulnerable species	Protects valuable and important infrastruture	
Preserve and restore the structural complexity and biodiversity of tidal marshes, seagrass meadows, and mangroves	Increases in water temperatures; changes in precipitation	Maintain water quality; maintain shorelines; invasive species management	Vegetation protects against erosion, protects mainland shorelines from tidal energy, storm surge, and wave forces, filters pollutants, and absorbs atmospheric CO_2	
Identify and protect ecologically signicant areas such as nursery grounds, spawning grounds, and areas of high diversity	Altered timing of seasonal changes; increases in air and water temperatures	Invasive species management; preserve habitat for vulnerable species	Protecting critical areas will promote biodiversity and ecosystem services (for example, producing and adding nutrients for coastal systems, serving as refuges and nurseries for species)	May require federal or state protection
Integrated Coastal Zone Management approaches to achieve sustainability	Changes in precipitation; sea level rise; increase in air and water temperatures; changes in storm intensity	Preserve habitat for vulnerable species; maintain/restore wetlands; maintain water availability; maintain water quality; maintain sediment transport; maintain shorelines	Considers all stakeholders in planning, balancing objectives; addresses all aspects of climate change	Stakeholders must be willing to compromise; requires much more effort in planning
Incorporate consideration of climate change impacts into planning for new infrastructure	Sea level rise; changes in precipitation; changes in storm intensity	Preserve habitat for vulnerable species; maintain/restore wetlands	Engineering could be modified to account for changes in precipitation or seasonal timing of flows; siting decisions could take sea level rise into account	Land owners will likely resist relocation away from prime coastal locations
Create marshland by planting the appropriate species–typically grasses, sedges, or rushes–in the existing substrate	Sea level rise	Maintain water quality; maintain/restore wetlands; preserve habitat for vulnerable species; invasive species management	Provides protective barrier; maintains and often increases habitat	Conditions must be right for marsh to survive, for example sunlight for grasses and calm water; can be affected by seasonal changes
Use natural oyster breakwaters or other natural breakwaters to dissipate wave action and protect shorelines	Increases in water temperatures; sea level rise; changes in precipitation; changes in storm intensity	Preserve coastal land/development; maintain water quality; invasive species management	Naturally protects shorelines and marshes and inhibits erosion inshore of the reef; will induce sediment deposition	May not be sustainable in the long term because breakwaters are unlikely to provide reliable protection against erosion in major storms
Replace shoreline amouring with living ones through beach nourishment and planting of vegetation	Sea level rise; changes in storm intensity	Maintain/restore wetlands; preserve habitat for vulnerable species; preserve coastal land/development	Reduces negative effects of armouring, such as downdrift erosion; maintains beach habitat	Can be costly; requires more planning and materials then armouring
Remove shoreline hardening structures like bulkheads and dikes to allow shoreline migration	Sea level rise	Maintain sediment transport	Allows shoreline migration	Costly for, and destructive to, shorelines property
Plant submerged aquatic vegetation (SAV) such as seagrasses to stabilize sediment and reduce erosion	Changes in precipitation; sea level rise	Maintain/restore wetlands; preserve habitat for vulnerable species; preserve coastal land/development	Stabilizes sediment; does not require costly construction procedures	Seasonality: grasses diminish in winter months, when wave activity is often more severe because of storms; light availability is essential

Source: Adapted from Hale and others (2009)

REFERENCES

Alongi, M.D. (2008). Mangrove forests: Resilience, protection from tsunamis, and responses to global climate change. Estuarine, Coastal and Shelf Science 76, 1-13

Asner, G.P. (2009). Tropical forest carbon assessment: Integrating satellite and airborne mapping approaches. *Environmental Research Letters,* 7 September 2009

Battisti, D.S. and Naylor, R.L. (2009). Historical Warnings of Future Food Insecurity with Unprecedented Seasonal Heat. *Science*, 323(5911), 240-244

BBC (2009). Madagascar leader axes land deal. BBC News. http://news.bbc.co.uk/2/hi/africa/7952628.stm

Bosire, J.O., Dahdouh-Guebas, F., Walton, M., Crona, B.I., Lewis III, R.R., Field, C., Kairo, J.G. and Koe-dam, M. (2008). Functionality of restored mangroves: a review. *Aquatic Botany* 89(2), 251-259

Burke, M., Lobell, D. and Guarino, L. (2009). Shifts in African crop climates by 2050, and the implications for crop improvement and genetic resources conservation. *Global Environmental Change*, 19(3), 317-325

Calzolaio, V. (2009). Securing water resources for water scarce ecosystems. United Nations Convention to Combat Desertification (UNCCD) Secretariat, Bonn

Campbell, A., Kapos, V., Chenery, A., Kahn, S.I., Rashid, M., Scharlemann, J.P.W. and Dickson, B. (2008). *The linkages between biodiversity and climate change mitigation*. UNEP World Conservation Monitoring Centre

Carpenter, S.R., Mooney, H.A., Agard, J., Capistrano, D., Defries, R.S., Díaz, S., Dietz, T., Duraiappah, A.K., Oteng-Yeboah, A., Pereira, H.M., Perrings, C., Reid, W.V., Sarukhan, J., Scholes, R.J. and Whyte, A. (2009). Science for managing ecosystem services: Beyond the Millennium Ecosystem Assessment. *Proceedings of the National Academy of Sciences*, 106, 1305-1312

CBC (2009) Fraser River sockeye salmon fishery closed again. Canadian Broadcasting Corporation, 13 August 2009.
http:www.cbc.ca/canada/british-columbia/story/2009/08/12/bc-fraser-river-sockeye-salmon-closure.html

Chapin III, F.S., Randerson, J.T., McGuire, A.D., Foley, J.A. and Field, C.B. (2008). Changing feedbacks in the climate-biosphere system. *Frontiers in Ecology and the Environment*, 6(6), 313-320

Coad, L., Burgess, N.D., Bomhard, B. and Besançon, C. (2009). *Progress towards the Convention on Biological Diversity's 2010 and 2012 Targets for Protected Area Coverage. A technical report for the IUCN international workshop 'Looking to the Future of the CBD Programme of Work on Protected Areas,' Jeju Island, Republic of Korea, 14-17 September 2009*. UNEP World Conservation Monitoring Centre (WCMC), Cambridge, UK

Connelly, S., Pringle, C.M., Bixby, R.J., Brenes, R., Whiles, M.R., Lips, K.R., Kilham, S. and Huryn, A.D. (2008). Changes in Stream Primary Producer Communities Resulting from Large-Scale Catastrophic Amphibian Declines: Can Small-Scale Experiments Predict Effects of Tadpole Loss? *Ecosystems*, 11, 1262-1276

Conway, G. (2009). *The science of climate change in Africa: impacts and adaptation. Grantham Institute for Climate Change, Discussion paper No. 1*. Imperial College, London

Cotula, L. and Mayers, J. (2009). *Tenure in REDD: Start-point or afterthought? Natural Resource Issues No. 15*. International Institute for Environment and Development, London

Cotula, L., Vermeulen, S., Leonard, R. and Keeley, J. (2009). *Land Grab or Development Opportunity? Agricultural Investment and International Land Deals in Africa*. International Institute for Environment and Development (IIED)/FAO/International Fund for Agricultural Development (IFAD).
ftp://ftp.fao.org/docrep/fao/011/ak241e/ak241e.pdf

Daily, G.C., Polaskya, S., Goldstein, J., Kareivas, P.M., Mooney, H.A., Pejchara, L., Ricketts, T.H., Salzman, J. and Shallenberger, R. (2009). Ecosystem services in decision making: time to deliver. *Front. Ecol. Environ.*, 7(1), 21–28

Dewailly, E. and Rouja, P. (2009). Think Big, Eat Small. *Science*, 326(5949), 44

Diaz, R.J. and Rosenberg, R. (2008). Spreading Dead Zones and Consequences for Marine Ecosystems. *Science*, 321(5891), 926-929

Diversitas (2009). Open Science Conference II, 2009. World won't meet 2010 Biodiversity targets.
http://owl.english.purdue.edu/owl/resource/560/10/

Economist (2009). Buying farmland abroad: Outsourcing's third wave. *The Economist*, 21 May 2009.

Elmqvist, T., Folke, C., Nyström, M., Peterson, G., Bengtsson, J., Walker, B. and Norberg, J. (2003). Response diversity, ecosystem change, and resilience. *Frontiers in Ecology and the Environment*, 1(9), 488-494

Ericksen, P.J. (2008). What is the vulnerability of a food system to global environmental change? *Ecology and Society*, 13(2), 14

Fagre, D.B., Charles, C.W., Allen, C.D., Birkeland, C., Chapin III, F.S., Groffman, P.M., Guntenspergen, G.R., Knapp, A.K., McGuire, A.D., Mulholland, P.J., Peters, D.P.C., Roby, D.D. and Sugihara, G. (2009). *CCSP, 2009: Thresholds of Climate Change in Ecosystems. A Report by the U.S. Climate Change Science Program and the Subcommittee on Global Change Research*. US Geological Survey, Washington, D.C.

FAO (2009a). 1.02 Billion People Hungry. Food and Agriculture Organization of the United Nations.
http://www.fao.org/news/story/en/item/20568/icode/

FAO (2009b). *Feeding the World, Eradicating Hunger: Executive Summary of the World Summit on Food Security. WSFS 2009/INF/2*. Food and Agriculture Organization of the United Nations. http://www.fao.org/fileadmin/templates/wsfs/Summit/WSFS_Issues_papers/WSFS_Background_paper_Feeding_the_world.pdf

FAO (2009c). *From Land Grab to Win-Win: Seizing the Opportunities of International Investments in Agriculture. Economic and Social Perspectives, Policy Brief 4*. Food and Agriculture Organization of the United Nations. ftp://ftp.fao.org/docrep/fao/011/ak357e/ak357e00.pdf

GEOSS (2009) Earth Observation in Support of Climate Monitoring within the GEO International Initiative. Global Earth Observation System of Systems. European Commission.
http://www.earthobservations.org/meetings/20091207_18_cop15_leaflet_geo.pdf

Gilbert, N. (2009) Efforts to sustain biodiversity fall short. *Nature*, 462, 263

Glick, P., Staudt, A. and Stein, B. A New Era for Conservation: Review of Climate Change Adaptation Literature. Discussion Draft. 2009. National Wildlife Federation

Hale, Z.L., Maliane, I., Davidson, S., Sandwith, T., Beck, M., Hoekstra, J., Spalding, M., Murawski, S., Cyr, N., Osgood, K. Hayiolos, M., Eijk, van P., Davidson, N., Eichbaum, W., Dreus, C., Obure, D., Tamelander, J., Herr, D., McClennen, C., and Marshall, P. (2009). Ecosystem-based Adaptation in Marine and Coastal Ecosystems. *Renewable Resources Journal*, 25, 4

Hoegh-Guldberg, O., Hughes, L., McIntyre, S., Lindenmayer, D.B., Parmesan, C., Possingham, H.P. and Thomas, C.D. (2008). Ecology: Assisted Colonization and Rapid Climate Change. *Science*, 321 (5887), 345-346

IGIP (2009). Welcome to the Anthropocene. International Geosphere and Biosphere Programme.
http://www.igbp.net/page.php?pid=293

IPCC (2007a). *Climate Change 2007: The Physical Science Basis. Contribution of Working Group I to the Fourth Assessment Report of the Intergovernmental Panel on Climate Change* (eds. S. Solomon, D. Qin, M. Manning, Z. Chen, M. Marquis, K.B. Averyt, M. Tignor and H.L. Miller). Cambridge University Press, UK

IPPC (2007b). Summary for Policymakers. In: *Climate Change 2007: Impacts, Adaptation and Vulnerability. Contribution of Working Group II to the Fourth Assessment Report of the Intergovernmental Panel on Climate Change* (eds. M.L. Parry, O.F. Canziani, J.P. Palutikof, P.J. van der Linden and C.E. Hanson). Cambridge University Press, UK

IUCN (2009). Extinction crisis continues apace. International Union for Conservation of Nature.
http://www.iucn.org/about/work/programmes/species/red_list/?4143/Extinction-crisis-continues-apace

IWG-IFR (2009). Putting $22-29 Billion into REDD cuts deforestation by 25% by 2015. Informal Working Group on Interim Finance for REDD+. http://www.un-redd.org/NewsCentre/NewsUnitedNationseventonforestsandclimate/tabid/1530/language/en-US/Default.aspx

Jackson, S.T. and Hobbs, R.J. (2009). Ecological Restoration in the Light of Ecological History. *Science*, 325(5940), 567-569

Kellner, J.B. and Hastings, A. (2009). A reserve paradox: introduced heterogeneity may increase regional invisibility. *Conservation Letters*, 2, 115-122

Koning, N. and Van Ittersum, M.K. (2009). Will the world have enough to eat?
Current Opinion in Environmental Sustainability, 1, 77-82

Lawler, J.J., Shafer, S.L., White, D., Kareiva, P., Maurer, E.P., Blaustein, A.R. and Bartlein, P.J. (2009). Projected climate-induced faunal change in the Western Hemisphere. *Ecology*, 90(3), 588-597

Le Quéré, C., Raupach, M.R., Canadell, J.G., Marland, G., Bopp, L., Ciais, P., Conway, T.J., Doney, S.C., Feely, R.A., Foster, P., Friedlingstein, P., Gurney, K., Houghton, R.A., House, J.I., Huntingford, C., Levy, P.E., Lomas, M.R., Majkut, J., Metzl, N., Ometto, J.P., Peters, G.P., Prentice, I.C., Randerson, J.T., Running, S.W., Sarmiento, J.L., Schuster, U., Sitch, S., Takahashi, T., Viovy, N., van der Werf, G.R. and Woodward, F.I. (2009). Trends in the sources and sinks of carbon dioxide. *Nature Geoscience*, 2, 831-836

Levin, P.S., Fogarty, M.J., Murawski, S.A. and Fluharty, D. (2009). Integrated Ecosystem Assessments: Developing the Scientific Basis for Ecosystem-Based Management of the Ocean. Public Library of Sciences, *Biology* 7(1), 23-28

Lobell, D., Burke, M.B., Tebaldi, C., Mastrandrea, M.D., Falcon, W.P. and Naylor, R.L. (2008). Prioritizing Climate Change Adaptation Needs for Food Security in 2030. *Science*, 319 (5863), 607-610

MA (2009). Millennium Ecosystem Assessment web site. http://www.millenniumassessment.org/en/Index.aspx

McLachlan, J.S., Hellmann, J.J. and Schwartz. M.W. (2007). A framework for debate of assisted migration in an era of climate change. *Conservation Biology*, 21, 297-302

Mitchell, S.R., Harmon, M.E. and O'Connell, K.E.B. (2009). Forest fuel reduction alters fire severity and long-term carbon storage in three Pacific Northwest ecosystems. *Ecological Applications*, 19(3), 643

Mittal, A. (2009). *The 2008 Food Price Crisis: Rethinking Food Security Policies, G-24 Discussion Paper Series, No. 56*. UN Conference on Trade and Development (UNCTAD)

Montgomery, R.D. (2007). Why We Need Another Agricultural Revolution. *Chronicle of Higher Education*, 13 April 2007

Montgomery, R.D. (2008). *Dirt: The Erosion of Civilizations*. University of California Press

Mooney, H., Larigauderie, A., Cesario, M., Elmquist, T., Hoegh-Guldberg, O., Lavorel, S., Mace, G.M., Palmer, M., Scholes, R. and Yahara, T. (2009). Biodiversity, climate change, and ecosystem services. *Current Opinion in Environmental Sustainability*, 1, 46–54

Mooney, H. and Mace, G. (2009). Biodiversity Policy Challenges. *Science*, 325(5947), 1474

Mukherji, A., Facon, T., Burke, J., de Fraiture, C., Faurès, J.-M., Füleki, B., Giordano, M., Molden, D. and Shah, T. (2009). *Revitalizing Asia's irrigation: to sustainably meet tomorrow's food needs*. International Water Management Institute (IWMI) and FAO

Naylor, R.L, Hardy, R.W., Bureau, D.P., Chiu, A., Elliott, M., Farrell, A.P., Forster, I., Gatlin, D.M., Goldburg, R.J., Hua, K. and Nichols, P.D. (2009). Feeding aquaculture in an era of finite resources. *Proceedings of the National Academy of Sciences*, 106,15103-15110

Nellemann, C., Corcoran, E., Duarte, C.M., Valdes, L., DeYoung, C. Fonseca, L., Grimsditch, G. (eds.) (2009). *Blue Carbon. A Rapid Response Assessment*. United Nations Environment Programme, in collaboration with the Food and Agriculture Organization and UNESCO. GRID-Arendal

Nyandwi, N. (2009). Protection of the coelacanth: A primitive fish in the coastal waters of Tanzania. *Ocean & Coastal Management*, 52(12), 655-659

Orr, C. (2009). A call to action on B.C. sockeye salmon. Watershed Watch Salmon Society, 30 December 2009

Ostrom, E. (2009). A General Framework for Analyzing Sustainability of Social-Ecological Systems. *Science*, 325(5939), 419-422

Pritchard, D. (2009). Reducing Emissions from Deforestation and Forest Degradation in developing countries (REDD)–the link with wetlands. A background paper for FIELD. Foundation for International Law and Development. http://ccsl.iccip.net/wetlands.pdf

Resilience Alliance (2007). Assessing and managing resilience in social-ecological systems: A practitioners workbook. Volume 1, version 1.0. http://www.resalliance.org/3871.php
Rice, X. (2008). Qatar looks to grow food in Kenya. *The Guardian*.
http://www.guardian.co.uk/environment/2008/dec/02/land-for-food-qatar-kenya [Accessed 23 November 2009]

Rockström, J., Steffen, W., Noone, K., Person, Å., Chapin III, S.F., Lambin, E.F., Lenton, T.M., Scheffer, M., Folke, C., Schellnhuber, H.J., Nykvist, B., Wit, C.A., Hughes, T., Leeuw, S., Rodhe, H., Sörlin, S., Snyder, P.K., Costanza, R., Svedin, U., Falkenmark, M., Karlberg, L., Corell, R.W., Fabry, V.J., Hansen, J., Wlaker, B., Liverman, D., Richardson, K., Crutzen, P. and Foley, J.A. (2009a). A safe operating space for humanity. *Nature*, 461, 472-475

Rockström, J., Steffen, W., Noone, K., Person, Å., Chapin III, S.F., Lambin, E.F., Lenton, T.M., Scheffer, M., Folke, C., Schellnhuber, H.J., Nykvist, B., Wit, C.A., Hughes, T., Leeuw, S., Rodhe, H., Sörlin, S., Snyder, P.K., Costanza, R., Svedin, U., Falkenmark, M., Karlberg, L., Corell, R.W., Fabry, V.J., Hansen, J., Wlaker, B., Liverman, D., Richardson, K., Crutzen, P. and Foley, J.A. (2009b). Planetery Boundaries: Exploring the safe operating space for humanity. *Ecology and Society*, 14, 2 (issue in progress: this is a longer version 2009a, above). http://www.ecologyandsociety.org/vol14/iss2/art32/

Running, S.W. and Mills, L.S. (2009). Terrestrial Ecosystem Adaptation. Resources for the Future report.
http://www.rff.org/rff/documents/RFF-Rpt-Adaptation-RunningMills.pdf

Scheffer, M., Bascompte, J., Brock, W.A., Brovkin, V., Carpenter, S.R., Dakos, V., Held, H., van Nes, E.H., Rietkerk, M. and Sugihara, G. (2009). Early-warning signals for critical transitions. *Nature*, 461, 53-59

Schrope, M. (2009). When money grows on trees: Protecting forests offers a quick and cost-effective way of reducing emissions, but agreeing a means to do so won't be easy. *Nature Reports Climate Change*, 14 August 2009

Smith, J.B., Schneider, S.H., Oppenheimer, M., Yohee, W., Hare, W., Mastrandrea, M.D., Patwardhan, A., Burton, I., Corfee-Morloti, J., Magadza, C.H.D., Fussel, H-M., Pittock, A.B., Rahman, A., Suarez, A. and Ypersele, J-P. (2009). Assessing dangerous climate change through an update of the Intergovernmental Panel on Climate Change (IPCC) "reasons for concern". *Proceedings of the National Academy of Sciences*, 106(11), 4133-4137

Smol, J.P. and Douglas, M.S.V. (2007). Crossing the final ecological threshold in high Arctic ponds. *Proceedings of the National Academy of Sciences, 104*(30), 12395-12397

Stern, N. (2007). *The Economics of Climate Change: The Stern Review*. Cambridge University Press, UK

Swaminathan, M.S. (2009). Gene Banks for a Warming Planet. *Science*, 325(5940), 517

Syvitski, J.P.M., Kettner, A.J., Overeem, I., Hutton, E.W.H., Hannon, M.T., Brakenridge, G.R., Day, J., Vörösmarty, C., Saito, Y., Giosan, L. and Nicholls, R.J. (2009). Sinking Deltas due to Human Activities. *Nature Geoscience*, 2, 681-686

Tallis, H., Kareiva, P., Marvier, M. and Chang, A. (2008). An ecosystem services framework to support both practical conservation and economic development. *Proceedings of the National Academy of Sciences*, 105(28), 9457-9464

Tolefson, J. (2009). Climate: Counting the Carbon in the Amazon. *Nature*, 461, 7261

UN (2009). The Millennium Development Goals Report 2009. United Nations, New York.
http://www.un.org/millenniumgoals/pdf/MDG_Report_2009_ENG.pdf

UNEP (2009). *Climate Change Science Compendium 2009*. Earthprint, Nairobi

UNEP IOC-UNESCO (2009). *An Assessment of Assessments, Findings of the Group of Experts. Start-up Phase of a Regular Process for Global Reporting and Assessment of the State of the Marine Environment including Socio-economic Aspects*. UNEP/Intergovernmental Oceanographic Commission (IOC)-UNESCO

UNEP IIPBES (2009a). *Second ad hoc intergovernmental and multi-stakeholder meeting on an intergovernmental science-policy platform on biodiversity and ecosystem services, Nairobi, 5–9 October 2009. Summary of perspectives from the scientific community and broader civil society*. UNEP/Intergovernmental Platform on Biodiversity and Ecosystem Services (IPBES)

UNEP IPBES (2009b). *Gap analysis for the purpose of facilitating the discussions on how to improve and strengthen the science-policy interface on biodiversity and ecosystem services. Information document*. UNEP/Intergovernmental Platform on Biodiversity and Ecosystem Services (IPBES)

Viana, V. (2009). Seeing REDD in the Amazon: a win for people, trees and climate. International Institute for Environment and Development (IIED). http://www.iied.org/pubs/pdfs/17052IIED.pdf

Vörösmarty, C.J., Syvitski, J., Day, J., de Sherbinin, A., Giosan, L. and Paola, C. (2009). Battling to save the world's river deltas. *Bulletin of the Atomic Scientists*, 65(2), 31-43

Walpole, M., Almond, R.E.A, Besançon, C., Butchart, S.H.M., Campbell-Lendrum, D., Carr, G.M., Collen, B., Collette, B., Davidson, N.C., Dulloo, E., Fazel, A.M., Galloway, J.N., Gill, M., Goverse, T., Hockings, M., Leaman, D.J., Morgan, D.H.W., Revenga, C., Rickwood, C.J., Schutyser, F., Simons, S., Stattersfield, A.J., Tyrrell, T.D., Vié, J-C, and Zimsky, M. (2009). Tracking Progress Toward the 2010 Biodiversity Target and Beyond. *Science*, 325(5947), 1503-1504

Walters, B.B., Rönnbäck, P., Kovacs, J.M., Crona, B., Hussain, S.A., Badola, R., Primavera, J.H., Barbier, E. and Dahdouh-Guebas, F. (2008). Ethnobiology, socio-economics and management of mangrove forests: A review. *Aquatic Botany*, 89, 220-236

Wetlands International (2008). Wetlands and climate change adaptation. Sustaining and restoring wetlands: an effective climate change response.
http://www.wetlands.org/Default.aspx?TabId=56&articleType=ArticleView&articleId=1953

Wollenberg, E. and Springate-Baginski, O. (2009). *Incentives + How can REDD improve well-being in forest communities*? Info-Brief, Center for International Forestry Research (CIFOR)

Worm, B., Hilborn, R., Baum, J.K., Branch, T.A., Collie, J.S., Costello, C., Fogarty, M.J. Fulton, E.A., Hutchings, J.A., Jennings, S., Jensen, O.P., Lotze, H.K., Mace, P.M., McClanahan, T.R., Minto, C., Palumbi, S.R., Parma, A.M., Ricard, D., Rosenberg, A.A., Watson, R. and Zeller, D. (2009). Rebuilding Global Fisheries. *Science*, 325(5940), 578-585

Zalasiewicz, J., Williams, M., Smith, A., Barry, T.L., Coe, A.L., Bown, P.R., Brenchley, P., Cantrill, D., Gale, A., Gibbard, P., Gregory, F.J., Hounslow, M.W., Kerr, A.C., Pearson, P., Knox, R., Powell, J., Waters, C., Marshall, J., Oates, M., Rawson, P., Rawson, P. and Stone, P. (2008). Are we now living in the Anthropocene? *GSA Today*, 18(2), 4-8

Harmful Substances and Hazardous Waste

Much work remains to be done to understand and find ways to reduce and mitigate the effects of harmful substances and hazardous waste on human health and the environment. There are increasing concerns about exposure and, above all, the exposure of children to harmful substances.

An agricultual worker without a mask sprays chemical pesticides on a bean field in Ecuador. The use of methods for safe storage, handling, and use of pesticides is far less widespread in developing countries. Consequently, pesticides can pose serious health hazards to farm workers.
Credit: Philippe Henry / Biosphoto

INTRODUCTION

New potential environmental hazards and risks are emerging. Perhaps most notably, nanomaterials present policy-makers in a number of countries with the problem of how to assess their hazards and risks and regulate them. Science is also advancing our understanding of the subtle and often hidden hazards of existing and widely used chemicals that act as endocrine disruptors, interfering with hormone systems. Policy-makers face new challenges here, too, not least in interpreting the emerging science and deciding when and how to act.

Control of hazardous materials is an important aspect of international cooperation. The Stockholm Convention on Persistent Organic Pollutants (POPs) lists a growing number of harmful substances. In 2009, several brominated flame retardants (BFRs) were added to the list of substances whose release to the environment is to be eliminated or reduced under the Stockholm Convention. In the case of two commonly used pesticides, endosulfan and atrazine, the science remains unclear and regulation is scattered.

Waste streams have a profound impact on health and the environment. In 2009, there was increased international transport of hazardous and electronic waste, highlighting the need for international cooperation on this problem. Properly handled, much waste can be turned into valuable raw resources. This may even include urban sewage water, which, once it has been treated, can be an important source of irrigation water and agricultural nutrients.

Many countries will face the challenge of handling hazardous materials safely in the years ahead. In rapidly industrializing developing countries, activities ranging from mining and minerals processing to manufacturing and waste recycling are cause for concern to local citizens and foreign consumers alike. Growing awareness of the threats to human health and the environment arising from these activities is informing policy choices.

Some health and environmental problems persist, seemingly no matter how much is known about them or how accessible the solutions appear to be. Indoor air pollution caused by smoke from open fires, which poses serious health risks to millions of people, could be significantly reduced if a few low-cost behavioural changes were made.

CONTINUING CONCERNS
Unanswered questions about nanomaterials

In 2009, researchers logged the appearance of the thousandth consumer product containing nanomaterials (Nanotechproject 2009a). It is estimated that revenues from nanotechnology and its many applications, such as nanoelectronics and nanobiotechnology, could increase a hundredfold in the next decade, from around US$32 billion today. Millions of new jobs could be created (Kelly 2009, Lux 2009, Palmberg and others 2009).

A recent report by the Organisation for Economic Co-operation and Development (OECD) points out that while nanotechnology is generally considered to offer "considerable promise extending from business opportunities throughout various industries to broader socio-economic benefits, especially in the context of energy, health care, clean water and climate change," monitoring of investments and of companies' involvement in nanotechnology development needs to be improved. Just as there is still some debate among scientists concerning the definition of nanoparticles, it can be hard to define a nanotechnology company. Surveys on the difficulties such companies face in commercializing nanotechnology show that "high processing costs, problems in the scalability of research and development (R&D) for prototype and industrial production, the basic research orientation of the related sciences, and concerns about environment, health and safety…emerge as the key challenges" (Palmberg and others 2009).

Nanotechnology R&D programmes exist in dozens of countries, including Brazil, China, India, and other developing economies. President Medvedev announced in 2009 that Russia intends to become a nanotechnology leader (PRIME-TASS 2009). As more workers and consumers worldwide are exposed to nanomaterials, the need to understand the potential health and environmental risks associated with their manufacture, use, distribution, and disposal is receiving increasing attention (**Figure 1**).

In 2008, a US National Research Council (NRC) report identified what the authors considered to be serious weaknesses in the government's plans for research on potential health and environmental risks. Asked to evaluate the US National Nanotechnology Initiative (NNI), which coordinates nanotechnology R&D funding among 25 federal departments and agencies, they found that some

important types of research were not adequately covered. Moreover, several lead agencies, such as the National Institutes of Health, the Environmental Protection Agency (EPA), and the Food and Drug Administration, have roles in overseeing research, but no single government entity is responsible for the strategy's successful implementation (NRC 2009).

Some nanomaterials are considered 'chemical substances' under the US Toxic Substances Control Act (TSCA) and are therefore regulated by the Environmental Protection Agency. Research on nanomaterials by EPA's Office of Research and Development is guided by the Nanomaterials Research Strategy (US EPA 2009a), in which some of the issues raised by the NRC report are addressed.

Governments, industry, and research institutions use information obtained internationally to develop their policies and guidance on nanotechnology safety concerns. Government agencies in a number of countries take part in cooperative activities with international bodies, including the International Organization for Standardization (ISO), the OECD, and the United Nations, for the purpose of identifying and addressing nanotechnology research needs and agreeing on international standards. This also enables information sharing on national regulatory mechanisms (OECD 2009a, OECD 2009b, ISO 2008a, ISO 2008b, OECD 2008).

A study carried out in 2008 by the European Commission's independent Scientific Committee

on Emerging and Newly Identified Health Risks (SCENIHR) surveyed recent developments in nanomaterials risk assessment for both humans and the environment. SCENHIR concluded that one of the main limitations on risk assessment is a general lack of high-quality exposure data. Some specific human health hazards have been identified, including the possibility that nanotubes (one type of nanomaterial) could pose the same risks as asbestos fibres if inhaled. The possibility of toxic effects on organisms has been pointed out, as well as the potential to transfer across species, indicating a risk that nanomaterials could bioaccumulate.

Since there is no generally available paradigm for hazard identification in regard to nanomaterials, SCENHIR cautioned that risk assessment needs to be carried out on a case-by-case basis. Like other types of substances, some nanomaterials may prove toxic while others do not. SCENHIR called for coordinated research strategies to obtain the comparable, reliable human and environmental risk assessment data that are currently lacking (SCENIHR 2009).

Nanoparticles have been defined as having at least one dimension less than 100 nanometres (one billionth of a metre, or 1/80 000 the width of a human hair). At nanoscale, the characteristics of materials—such as their colour, strength, and reactivity—often change. Innumerable nanotechnology applications have been introduced or are envisioned. Nano-engineered coatings can make textiles stain-proof or static-

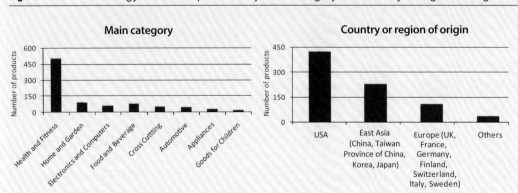

Figure 1: Nanotechnology consumer products by main category and country or region of origin

Main category

Country or region of origin

The Project on Emerging Nanotechnologies Consumer Product Inventory contains information on the manufacturer of each product, its country of origin, and category. The graphs show the distribution of these products by main category and country or region, based on 2008 data. Altogether, 21 countries were involved at the time this inventory was compiled. The dominance of US companies was clear, with 426 products, followed by East Asian countries with 227 and Europe with 108.

Source: Woodrow Wilson International Center for Scholars (2008) (http://www.nanotechproject.org)

free. Nanosilver is added to medical and consumer products because of its antimicrobial properties. There are, however, concerns that nanomaterials are being used in consumer goods for relatively trivial purposes (Dowling and others 2004). Manufacturers of sun protection products add titanium dioxide and zinc oxide nanoparticles. Leading environmental NGOs have condemned such uses (FoE 2009).

Deliberate releases of nanoparticles to remediate contaminated soil and groundwater have occurred in the US and Europe (Karn and others 2009, Nanotechproject 2009b) despite the findings of prestigious independent scientific bodies, including the Science Council of Japan and the Royal Society in the UK, that research should first be carried out to assess the health and environmental effects (Maynard 2009, Royal Society 2005). As an example of a remediation technique under development made possible by 'tiny technology', US EPA scientists have synthesized activated carbon with nanoparticles of iron/palladium bimetallic to produce a new nano-scale treatment that could be more successful than conventional methods in detecting, treating, and removing dangerous pollutants (US EPA 2009b).

Brominated flame retardants to be phased out

Combustible products are frequently treated with flame retardants. The most widely used chemical flame retardants are the brominated flame retardants (BFRs). Evidence of some BFRs' toxicity, widespread persistence in the environment, and potential to bioaccumulate has increased pressure for this type of chemical to be banned from production and use, and for safer alternatives to be developed.

The total amount of BFRs manufactured each year is in excess of 200 000 tonnes. In addition to the factories where they are made, BFRs are found in household dust, at waste sites specializing in electronic waste, in landfills, and in river sediments. BFRs have even been found on the ocean floor (Kimbrough and others 2008, Alaee and others 2003).

The greatest consumer of BFRs is the electronics industry. Electronic waste recycling sites in developing countries are among the most significant sources of BFR releases to the environment. Soil near the well-known Guiyu recycling site in southern China contains up to 3 parts per million (ppm) of BFRs and ash from fires at this site contains up to 60 ppm, some of the highest levels ever recorded (Luo and others 2009, Leung and others 2007).

There are three broad classes of BFRs: tetra-bromobisphenol A (TBBPA), hexa-bromocyclododecane (HBCD), and poly-brominated diphenyl ethers (PBDEs). Concern is greatest about PBDEs, partly because they degrade slowly and are known to build up in air and soils in urban source regions. PBDEs also migrate widely to non-urban areas (Law and others 2008). A recent US National Oceanic and Atmospheric Administration (NOAA) study found that there are PBDEs "throughout the US coastal zone, including the Great Lakes," with especially high levels in molluscs and sediments near Los Angeles and New York (Kimbrough and others 2008).

PBDEs are toxic and can affect brain development. They accumulate in the body fat of mammals that consume them, including humans. One study detected them in mothers' milk in a number of countries, with the highest concentrations in the US (Kotz and others 2005). Another study found that concentrations of PBDEs in human blood and tissue had doubled every five years starting in the 1970s (Hites 2004). In China, extremely high levels (above 3 ppm) have been found in the body fat of electronic waste dismantlers (Wen and others 2008).

Two types of PBDEs (penta-BDE and octa-BDE) are banned in many countries. In 2009, they were added to the list of POPs to be phased out under the Stockholm Convention (Stockholm Convention 2009a). While the Convention calls for halting new production of these chemicals, both the recycling and reuse of products containing them are allowed until 2030. This means some of the people who are most at risk will continue to be exposed to them (ChemSec 2009).

Deca-BDE, a third type of PBDE, is not covered by the Stockholm Convention although it is banned in much of Europe and in some US states. When assessments of deca-BDE were completed in 2004, there was less scientific evidence than today concerning its potential to bioaccumulate and its human health effects. Some animal studies have found that deca-BDE damages the liver and neurological systems, and is carcinogenic. Since 2004, studies on Norwegian polar bears, Chinese birds of prey, and other animals have also shown that deca-BDE bioaccumulates (Chen and others 2007, Verreault and others 2005).

There is growing evidence that deca-BDE degrades in sunlight into other forms of PBDEs, including those already banned under the Stockholm Convention. One modelling study has estimated that 13 per cent of penta-BDE in the environment arises from the degradation of deca-BDE (Schenker 2008). Partly in response to such concerns, some manufacturers of furniture and electronic goods have voluntarily stopped using deca-BDE and have switched to using alternatives posing fewer risks (Gue and MacDonald 2007).

Growing attention to endocrine disrupters

Many environmental toxins disrupt mammalian development processes in the womb, leaving foetuses and young children particularly at risk. At the G8 Environment Ministers' Meeting in Italy in April 2009, this issue was discussed in depth. In Japan, for example, rates of congenital abnormalities such as spina bifida and Down's syndrome have doubled in the past quarter century, while impairment of children's immune system, associated with diseases including asthma, has tripled over 20 years (Saito 2009). Japanese studies also suggest that rising obesity levels may be a result of disrupted hormone systems in young people (Takimoto and Tamura 2006).

The G8 Ministerial Meeting agreed that countries should work together to identify the environmental drivers of common childhood diseases (G8 2009). Such concerns are reflected in a number of national initiatives. In 2009, the US government began a series of studies in which some 60 000 pregnant women will participate. Their children will be observed from the foetal stage to age 12, in order to identify environmental influences on their health and development. In Italy, evaluations of prenatal and perinatal exposure to persistent toxic substances have begun.

Some of the chemicals causing the greatest concern are endocrine disrupters. These chemicals damage animals' hormone systems, with actual and potential effects on reproductive systems. They include BFRs, PCBs and other industrial chemicals; pesticides like atrazine and DDT; plasticizers like phthalates and bisphenol A, which is found in many plastic products and beverage cans; and anabolic steroids. While production of some of these chemicals is banned in many countries, they continue to be found in products, waste streams, and the wider environment (Connolly 2009) (**Box 1**).

Endocrine disrupters behave similarly to natural hormones in the human body, disrupting the chemical signalling systems that guide development of the brain and reproductive systems (**Figure 2**). There is particular concern that endocrine disrupters and their breakdown products can mimic the female hormone oestrogen and block male androgen hormones. These chemicals' effects may be most damaging if the foetus is exposed to them in the womb. The discovery of hermaphrodite polar bear cubs in the Arctic has been linked to PCBs once used in nuclear submarines (Steiner 2009). Testicular cancer in humans has been linked to perinatal exposure to endocrine-disrupting POPs (Hardell and others 2006).

The number of such chemicals found in everyday consumer products and in the environment means that, even if they pose little threat individually at doses to which most people are exposed, they could constitute a collective threat. This 'cocktail effect' of cumulative small doses could create synergies and complex interactions that are impossible to predict based on studies of individual compounds (Connolly 2009).

WASTE STREAMS AND NITROGEN CYCLING
International toxic waste trafficking

Waste trafficking is a global business, driven in part by more stringent rules for handling hazardous waste in some countries—especially in Europe. Far from eliminating illegal and dangerous waste disposal, the new rules have often merely succeeded in offshoring it. There are concerns that the Basel Convention on the Control of Transboundary Movements of Hazardous Wastes and their Disposal is failing to prevent an explosion in illegal waste trafficking.

Box 1: Two hazardous but widely used pesticides

Pesticides are designed to kill plant and animal pests. Ensuring that they kill the right organisms–and that they do more good than harm–is a constant challenge, especially when the science on which health and safety evaluations are based is unclear. Two widely used pesticides, endosulfan and atrazine, are allowed to be applied in many countries despite their known hazards.

Endosulfan is applied to kill insects on crops. Its use has increased since similar substances, such as aldrin and heptachlor, were added to the Stockholm Convention list. Endosulfan is cheap and highly effective, especially when used to control insects that are becoming resistant to other pesticides. It is banned in more than 60 countries, including in the European Union. Endosulfan is responsible for the deaths of thousands of farm workers, especially in developing countries. Five school children in Jharkhand, eastern India, died in late 2008 after drinking endosulfan-contaminated milk. Endosulfan is also an endocrine disrupter. In the state of Kerala, southwest India, boys in villages exposed to aerial spraying of cashew nut plantations over a period of 20 years were found to suffer from delayed sexual maturity, low testosterone levels, and cryptorchidism–the failure of the testes to descend during foetal development. A rash of such cases resulted in endosulfan being banned by the state government.

While a 2007 study in the US found that women living near fields sprayed with endosulfan were more likely to give birth to autistic children, recent research has questioned these findings. In 2010, the Stockholm Convention will review the case for adding endosulfan to its list of persistent organic pollutants (POPs) to be phased out.

Atrazine is probably the world's most commonly used herbicide. Applied to plants in more than 80 countries, mostly in Asia and Africa, it is widely present in agricultural run-off, rivers, and wetlands, as well as in rainfall. Atrazine can be carried as much as 1 000 kilometres through the atmosphere and has been found in the Arctic.

Atrazine is the second most popular herbicide in the United States, where it is used on maize and other crops, pastureland, golf courses, and domestic lawns. In 2009, 43 water supply systems in Illinois and five other states joined a class action suit against atrazine's main manufacturer, Monsanto, demanding that it pay for the installation of carbon filters to remove this chemical.

After being widely detected in underground drinking water supplies, atrazine was banned in the European Union in 2004. Using a precautionary approach, the EU concluded that there was insufficient evidence to demonstrate its safety.

In September 2009, an independent review of more than 100 research studies concluded that there is 'consistent' data showing widespread non-lethal threats to animals, including altered gonad function and reduced sperm production. Atrazine has been implicated in birth defects in humans and low sperm levels in men. It may be carcinogenic, with particular concerns raised about lung and bladder cancers, non-Hodgkin lymphoma and multiple myeloma.

Sources: Duhigg 2009, Rohr and McCoy 2009, Silva and Gammon 2009, Stockholm Convention 2009b, Roberts and others 2007, Rusiecki and others 2004, Saiyed and others 2004, US EPA 2009c

Plant response to controlled application of atrazine. While this herbicide provides a higher margin of crop safety than many of its possible replacements, there are concerns about its widespread use. Atrazine has been detected in both surface and groundwater.

Credit: James L. Griffin

The effect of the European Union's Waste Electrical and Electronic Equipment (WEEE) Directive, which came into force in 2007, is also under scrutiny. The WEEE Directive is intended to encourage those involved in the design and production of electrical and electronic equipment to take into account and facilitate reuse, recycling, and recovery. A 2009 study by the European Environment Agency (EEA) found that this has not always been its effect (EEA 2009).

While the WEEE Directive bans e-waste exports, it allows functional equipment to be exported for reuse. There is a large, legitimate, and valuable market for electronic equipment

Figure 2: The endocrine system and effects of endocrine disruptors

For more than a decade, scientists have recognized that chemicals in the environment are able to disrupt the body's normal functions. Some chemicals are known to mimic hormones, while others are known to block their effects. Researchers are particularly concerned about the effects these chemicals have on developing foetuses and children who rely on messages from hormones for proper organ, brain, and sexual development. A growing number of scientists are concerned that spikes in cancer, reproductive abnormalities, infertility, and behavioural disorders are the result of these chemicals interfering with critical messages in the development of foetuses and children.

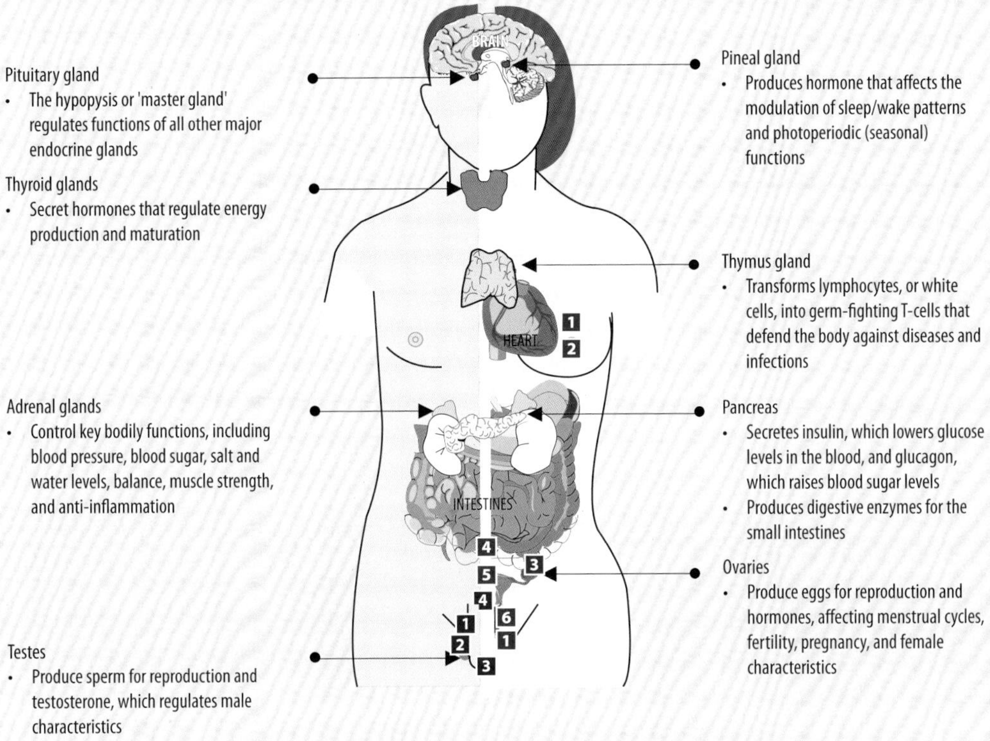

Pituitary gland
- The hypopysis or 'master gland' regulates functions of all other major endocrine glands

Thyroid glands
- Secret hormones that regulate energy production and maturation

Adrenal glands
- Control key bodily functions, including blood pressure, blood sugar, salt and water levels, balance, muscle strength, and anti-inflammation

Testes
- Produce sperm for reproduction and testosterone, which regulates male characteristics

Pineal gland
- Produces hormone that affects the modulation of sleep/wake patterns and photoperiodic (seasonal) functions

Thymus gland
- Transforms lymphocytes, or white cells, into germ-fighting T-cells that defend the body against diseases and infections

Pancreas
- Secretes insulin, which lowers glucose levels in the blood, and glucagon, which raises blood sugar levels
- Produces digestive enzymes for the small intestines

Ovaries
- Produce eggs for reproduction and hormones, affecting menstrual cycles, fertility, pregnancy, and female characteristics

Potential effects of endocrine disruptors on men and women

Men

1 Poor semen quality — low sperm counts, low ejaculate volume, high number of abnormal sperm, low number of mobile sperm

2 Testicular cancer

3 Malformed reproductive tissue — undescended testes, small penis size

4 Prostrate disease and other abnormalities of the male tissues

Women

1 Breast and reproductive tissue cancers

2 Fibrocystic disease of the breast

3 Polycystic ovarian syndrome

4 Endometriosis

5 Uterine fibroids and pelvic inflammatory diseases

6 Declining sex ratio (fewer women)

Other potential effects on both men and women

- Impaired behavioural/mental, immune, and thyroid functions in developing children
- Osteoporosis
- Advanced puberty

Source: Adapted from Atlas of Anatomy

that can be reused in developing countries. For example, a British-based charity that has shipped 150 000 refurbished computers over a period of ten years, mostly to Africa, reports that it could find new homes for ten times as many (CAI 2009).

However, this represents only a small fraction of the estimated 4 million computers thrown away in the UK alone each year. Much of the rest, it is widely if anecdotally reported, becomes part of the illegal trade in e-waste. In Europe, the illegal exportation of e-waste costs only one-quarter as much as disposing of it legally (Rosenthal 2009). The EEA estimates that 20 million waste containers are shipped from Europe—legally and illegally—every year, half of them through Rotterdam. The difficulty for port and customs authorities is that even when paperwork appears to be in order, distinguishing between material fit for reuse and that destined for disposal is not always easy. Equipment described as being shipped for reuse may be dismantled and processed in extremely dangerous ways in a receiving country (EEA 2009, Greenpeace 2009).

Toxic waste scandals

A number of toxic waste scandals occurred in 2009. In September it was reported that Italian criminals had sunk up to 30 ships containing radioactive and toxic cargoes off the coast of Calabria. An informer directed investigators to one, which he said had been scuttled by the Mafia in 1992 along with 120 barrels of radioactive sludge originating from European pharmaceutical companies. There is still considerable uncertainty about what the ships were carrying, but Calabria's environment agency has warned that the contamination could be widespread and that clean-up and removal could be complex and expensive (Day 2009).

In the same month, Brazil returned a consignment of 2 000 tonnes of British domestic and hospital waste, claiming that the waste had been mislabelled as recyclable plastic in contravention of the Basel Convention and Brazilian law. President Lula da Silva accused Britain of treating his country as "the world's rubbish bin", but it emerged that this waste came from companies set up by Brazilian nationals in the British city of Swindon (Milmo 2009).

An earlier case in Côte d'Ivoire received renewed media attention in 2009. In 2006, the government of Côte d'Ivoire fell in the aftermath of a highly publicized scandal concerning 500 tonnes of toxic sludge unloaded from a cargo ship and distributed to local landfills, where toxic fumes were alleged to have caused 15 deaths and hospitalization of 69 people. The sludge began as a by-product from a Mexican oil refinery. A Dutch-based oil trading company, Trafigura, bought dirty sulphur-rich oil called 'coker naptha' in hopes of cleaning it up and making a profit. Aboard the cargo ship *Probo Koala*, it was mixed with caustic soda to remove the sulphur and this 'caustic washing' left sulphurous toxic slops behind. After the *Probo Koala* failed to offload the slops in the Netherlands for treatment and disposal, it travelled to Côte d'Ivoire, where a local contractor was paid to dispose of them. The contractor, who did not have toxic waste treatment facilities, disposed of the slops in local landfills. Trafigura has repeatedly denied any wrongdoing, stating that it complied with local laws and that the waste could not have caused the reported deaths and injuries (UN 2009).

The nitrogen cycle in hyperdrive

A major study in 2009 identified human interference in biogeochemicle cycles, particularly the nitrogen cycle, as one of three key areas where 'planetary boundaries' have been crossed, threatening Earth's habitability. The others are climate change and the rate of biodiversity loss (Rockström and others 2009).

An estimated 120 million tonnes of atmospheric nitrogen per year is converted into reactive forms through human processes, mainly the manufacturing of fertilizers and the cultivation of leguminous crops such as soybeans. Manufactured fertilizers are used to grow crops that currently feed an estimated 3 billion people. Half of all manufactured fertilizer applications have occurred in the past 20 years (Erisman and others 2008, UNESCO 2007).

Many agricultural systems receive far more nitrogen than they need (Vitousek and others 2009). Less than half the nitrogen applied to fields worldwide is used by crops. Nitrogen

losses are particularly great in China, where application rates are among the highest in the world. Since many high-yielding crop varieties use nitrogen very inefficiently, there is considerable scope for improvement. It is estimated that better nitrogen management in China could cut nitrogen emissions to the environment by 25 per cent without affecting agricultural output (Ermolieva and others 2009).

Most of the world's biodiversity hotspots receive nitrogen from air and water at levels known to affect many species (Phoenix and others 2006). Studies have shown that nitrogen-saturated rivers are losing their ability to reduce nitrates from fertilizer and sewage through denitrification, the natural process of converting biologically available nitrogen compounds into nitrogen oxides and, ultimately, inert nitrogen (Mulholland 2008).

In the coastal waters, where most excess nitrogen from agricultural run-off and urban sewage ends up, blooms of sometimes toxic algae are being formed. It was reported in 2009 that the main neurotoxin in algal blooms, the shellfish-killing domoic acid, does not, as previously thought, degrade as rapidly as the blooms themselves. Instead, it sinks with the dead algae and persists for weeks on the seabed. Researchers found this toxin on the seabed, and accumulating in the food chain, after it had been eaten by worms and commercially important species such as crabs and flatfish (Sekula-Wood 2009).

The impacts of excess nitrogen in the oceans are increasing. Euthrophification has lead to dead zones in coastal waters, which are caused when algae die and decay, using up available oxygen in the process. A recent study found that there are more than 400 dead zones in the world's coastal areas, most of them formed in the past half century. These dead zones, which cover a quarter of a million square kilometres, are usually found where rivers discharge large amounts of fertilizers and sewage into relatively enclosed ocean areas (Diaz and Rosenberg 2008). Examples are the 20 000 square kilometre dead zone in the Gulf of Mexico; the partly enclosed waters between Japan and Korea; and areas in the Black Sea, off the tourist beaches of the northern Adriatic Sea, and in the Baltic Sea, which has the world's

largest dead zone. The safe limit for the amount of nitrogen fixation from the atmosphere by humans has been estimated at 35 million tonnes, less than one-third of current levels. Global nitrogen use in agriculture will however double to some 220 million tonnes a year by 2050 if present trends continue (Pearce 2009, Rockström and others 2009).

Reducing the world's nitrogen use will be difficult. The transformation in agriculture will need to be as profound as that soon required in other sectors to meet targets for greenhouse gas emission reductions. It is essential, however, to keep ecosystems from becoming so over-enriched with nitrogen that they become terrestrial equivalents of the oceans' dead zones (INI 2009).

Taking another look at urban sewage water use in agriculture

Urban wastewater has been used in agriculture for centuries. It continues to be widely accepted in some parts of the world as an inexpensive source of irrigation water and nutrients. Although pervasive, this use of sewage water poses health and environmental risks. Untreated sewage can contain pathogenic bacteria, worms, viruses, heavy metals, and hazardous human-made organic compounds. Based on a 53-city study of urban agriculture in developing countries, the International Water Management Institute (IWMI) estimates that half the gardens, roadside verges, and small fields where food is grown in the world's urban and peri-urban areas are irrigated and fertilized with wastewater. Most green and perishable vegetables, in particular, are grown this way (Raschid-Sally and Jayakody 2008). IWMI also estimates that about 20 million hectares of the world's farms are irrigated with sewage, although the practice is theoretically banned in many countries. In Pakistan, where one-quarter of vegetables may be so irrigated, IWMI researchers discovered that city authorities in Faisalabad auction untreated sewage to farmers during droughts (Scott and others 2004). More land is irrigated with sewage water in Ghana than with clean water. In Accra, 200 000 people a day are estimated to consume sewage-irrigated vegetables (IWMI 2006).

Figure 3: Nitrogen cycle

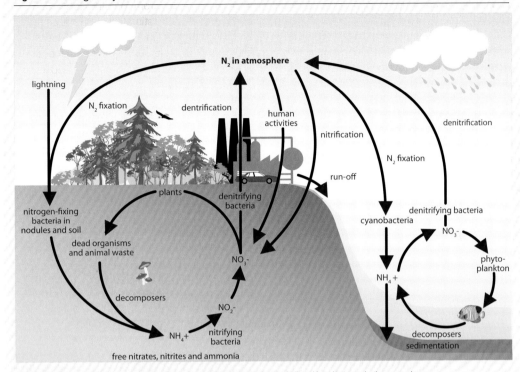

Atmospheric nitrogen is converted ('fixed') in various forms that can be assimilated by plants and other organisms.

Source: Adapted from Michigan Water Research Center

Recent research suggests that the health risks could in some cases be exaggerated. A study of crops irrigated with wastewater along the Musi River, which flows through the Indian city of Hyderabad, found lower than expected risk indicators. The Musi receives a million litres of waste per day, mostly untreated. Six villages downstream that use this water to irrigate most of their fields were studied. Low rates of hookworm and other parasitic infections were found; the water contained lead and cadmium, but most of the soils tested did not contain high levels of these heavy metals and plant uptake was low. The study concluded that "contrary to common perception, wastewater can be regarded as a valuable resource" (Weckenbrock and others 2009).

Risks may change over time, particularly when pollutants tend to accumulate. Potential health risks also depend on soil makeup and the effluent content. In Iran, a study of crops irrigated with wastewater along the Khoshk River in Shiraz City found that while soils contained more organic matter as a result, there was also a marked build-up of cadmium, lead, and other heavy metals (Salati and Moore 2009).

According to IWMI, efforts should be made to help farmers use sewage water more safely, while also trying to make the wastewater itself safer. This approach is supported by the World Health Organization and others in the Hyderabad Declaration (IWMI 2002).

Low-tech safety measures in this regard could include storing sewage water in ponds for a few days so that solids, including the eggs of intestinal worms, settle out. Washing vegetables in clean water before they are sold in markets should be encouraged.

The long-term solution is likely to be more centralized sewage treatment, of the kind already adopted in countries where irrigation with treated sewage water is an accepted practice, including Israel, Jordan, and Mexico. Even with more advanced technology, treatment may not remove viruses, complex organic compounds, hormones, and heavy metals. A study of Israeli fields irrigated with treated sewage also found that microbes showed higher microbial activity, resulting in increased depletion of soil organic matter, which could have negative long-term effects on soil quality (Juschke and others 2009).

HEAVY METAL POLLUTION

Managing hazardous waste is a challenge faced by many rapidly industrializing countries. As the world's fastest growing economy, China is confronted with the health and environmental risks associated with industrialization. While chemicals play an important economic role and contribute to improving living standards in China, it is acknowledged that this needs to be balanced with recognition of potential health risks. In 2009, there was widespread public concern over heavy metal pollution near mining and industrial installations. The following cases from China are by no means exceptional among industrializing countries, but illustrate the issues of heavy metal pollution.

In September, 121 children out of 287 tested in the Jiaoyang, Tangxia, and Chongtou communities in the Fujian Province were found to have lead poisoning. The children's blood lead levels exceeded the danger level of 100 micrograms per litre, apparently as a result of exposure to pollution from a lead-acid battery factory (Zhu and Wang 2009). The Fujian case was one of several metal poisoning scandals during the year. In August, authorities in Hunan Province closed a metals plant near Wugang and detained two managers after parents protested. More than 1 300 children had fallen ill as a result of lead poisoning and some were losing their hair. The plant had been in operation for 15 months, reportedly without the approval of the local environmental protection bureau (BBC 2009a).

In Shaanxi Province a few days earlier, parents broke into the Dongling lead and zinc smelting works in Changqing town. A reported 615 local children, out of 731 examined, had been diagnosed with lead poisoning, and 166 were hospitalized. All the children lived near the plant. Although this plant appeared to meet national environmental safety standards, it had emitted 1.11 tonnes of lead to the air and to local watercourses during the previous year. This plant, too, was closed. To help remove lead from the children's bodies, the authorities distributed laver, garlic, wulong tea, and seaweed (Bristow 2009, Li 2009).

In another case in Hunan Province, doctors diagnosed 500 inhabitants of Zhentou township, in Liuyang city, with cadmium poisoning. This incident came to light after two residents died. The nearby Changsha Xianghe plant, which opened in 2003, manufactures zinc sulphate, an animal feed additive. Cadmium is frequently found in zinc ores. According to media reports, the Changsha plant discharged industrial waste containing cadmium into watercourses used by villagers to irrigate their crops (BBC 2009b, Xinhua 2009).

Lead, cadmium, zinc, and other heavy metals are increasingly recognized as a human health threat in China's mining areas. The state-owned Dabaoshan mine, in operation since 1958, was targeted for criticism in 2009. The mine discharges large amounts of acidic water containing metals, including cadmium, which have killed most aquatic life in the Hengshihe River. The villagers drink well water contaminated with cadmium and zinc and use this water to irrigate their rice crops. A study published in 2009 revealed that the metals present in paddy soils are above Chinese permissible levels, and local diets also exceed health limits (Zhuang and others 2009). Another study has found high levels of lead, cadmium, and zinc in children downstream of the mine. Their symptoms include significantly increased anxiety, depression, social problems, somatic complaints, and difficulty in concentrating (Bao and others 2009).

Concerned by the scale and possible number of such cases, China has begun the ambitious task of surveying major pollution sources. Tens of thousands of companies have been asked to report their emissions. The government says it will evaluate emissions and take legal action if companies provide false data (Bristow 2008).

Plant in a contaminated lake near the Dabaoshan mine in Shangba, Guangdong Province, China. The lake's waters are polluted by cadmium, lead, zinc, and other heavy metals.
Credit: Dreamcatcher

Box 2: Tackling health and environmental problems by changing people's behaviour

Some health and environmental problems appear to persist no matter how much is known about them, or how simple the solutions seem to be. Indoor air pollution caused by smoke from open fires used for cooking and heating is, according to most estimates, one of the worst environmental killers in the developing world. Wherever people burn firewood, cow dung, and other types of biomass in confined spaces, the impact on the lungs is catastrophic. Yet researchers have discovered that those most affected can be extremely reluctant to adopt behavioural changes which, to outsiders, seem very reasonable.

According to the World Health Organization, up to 3 billion people cook over indoor fires that fill their homes with smoke, carbon monoxide, and other poisons. Typically, the women and young children spend three to five hours a day near a fire. Three-quarters of women in South Asia live this way. Even in rapidly industrializing countries, the problem is serious. In Mexico, for example, one in four households cooks with biomass fuel. Better cooking stoves have been designed and manufactured, featuring improved ventilation and more efficient burning, which reduce pollution. Dozens of models exist, many developed by indigenous NGOs. Studies show that most such stoves reduce symptoms like wheezing, eye discomfort, and headaches and improve lung function in the women who use them. In the longer term, these stoves are also likely to reduce the risk of serious lung disease.

The rate of take-up of improved stoves often remains low. In a study conducted in Mexico and published in 2009, women were given new, vented Patsari stoves which typically reduce indoor air pollution by 70 per cent. A year later, only 30 per cent of them used these stoves for most of their cooking. One-fifth used them occasionally, and most of the rest had returned to cooking over an open fire. The same study showed that women who used the new stoves had markedly better health, with only half the loss of lung function observed in the control group that cooked over open fires.

A skilled craftsman can build a Patsari stove in 40 minutes. Since these stoves were introduced, the health of women who use them for household cooking has improved significantly. Use of the stoves has also reduced air pollution and wood consumption.
Credit: The Ashden Awards for Sustainable Energy (http://www.ashdenawards.org)

Researchers are trying to understand this reluctance. In 2009, a team from Stanford University in California found that women in villages in Bangladesh were well aware of the health benefits of better stoves, but were extremely conservative about adopting any new technology. They did not want to be 'early adopters' and felt constrained by what their families, neighbours, friends, and community leaders did. They also told researchers they were afraid a new stove could change their husbands' opinion of their cooking.

Sources: McCann (2009), Romieu and others (2009)

The head of the National Population and Family Planning Commission warned in 2009 that birth defects have risen by 40 per cent in China since 2001. This is partly blamed on emissions from the mining and chemical industries. A new screening programme has been announced for the worst affected areas (BBC 2009c).

Many such concerns emerging in China and other rapidly industrializing countries resemble those in Europe and North America several years ago, and some of these problems are more persistent than others. In regard to poisoning by heavy metals such as lead and cadmium, for example, China is far from alone in facing problems related to heavy metal exposures. The International Atomic Energy Agency estimates that approximately 120 million people in the world are exposed to potentially hazardous lead concentrations in air, soil, and water. Dangerous blood lead levels are found in children in some 80 countries. Most of this lead is associated with illegal or poorly regulated smelting of lead-acid batteries (IAEA 2009) (**Box 2**).

LOOKING AHEAD

The rapid industrialization of many developing economies in recent years has had a major impact on where harmful substances turn up and what happens to hazardous waste. Toxic materials and waste streams that were once localized in a handful of industrialized countries are now found much more widely.

Critics compare the rapid introduction of nanomaterials, including in food products and food containers, to that of genetically modified organisms (GMOs) in the 1990s. As in the case of GMOs, hazard and risk assessments and governmental regulation are perceived by many people to have been inadequate so far (EFSA 2009, Nanoproject 2009c, Sutcliffe 2009, Taylor 2008). Analysing the "differences and similarities between bio- and nanotechnologies and other emerging technologies could be insightful, especially in light of the cross-pollination and possible convergence between these fields" (Palmberg and others 2009). In the future, information exchange and debate among those engaged in nanotechnology in all kinds of ways, worldwide, will be crucial to addressing both known and potential risks.

Box 3: Remote sensing landfills

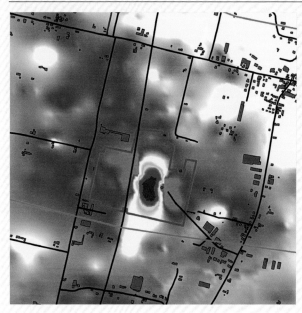

Credit: Sonia Silvestri

Toxic waste in landfills can leach to water and soil. Nobody knows how many such toxic time bombs there are in the world. A new technology can help discover hidden landfills without digging them up. Studies published in 2009 demonstrate that illegally buried waste can be spotted from the surface, or even the air, using ground-penetrating radar techniques in which electric and magnetic fields are inducted into the ground by a coil carried in a helicopter.

In northeast Italy, near Padua, this method has been used to trace the source of toxic liquids leaching to drinking water supplies from a landfill. A researcher in Northern Ireland has reported finding four hazardous waste burial sites in peat bogs.

Sources: Biotto and others (2009), Ruffel and Kulessa (2009), Silvestri (2009)

Governments and civil society will continue to call for more detailed and wider access to information (**Box 3**). In September 2009, for example, the US Environmental Protection Agency incorporated the principle of 'green chemistry' in its new Essential Principles for the Reform of Chemicals Management Legislation. This principle acknowledges that provisions assuring transparency and public access to information should be strengthened.

In 2010, the Stockholm Convention will review the case for adding endosulfan to its list of persistent organic pollutants (POPs) to be phased out (Stockholm 2009b). Also at the global level, the first Extraordinary Meeting of the Conferences of the Parties to the Basel, Rotterdam, and Stockholm Conventions will be held back-to-back with the Eleventh Special Session of the UNEP Governing Council/Global Ministerial Environment Forum in 2010. There is high-level political support for enhancing cooperation and coordination among these three conventions on chemicals and waste (see the Environmental Governance chapter).

The International Nitrogen Initiative, a network of scientists, plans a major meeting in Delhi in late 2010 to address the challenge of reducing nitrogen flows to the natural environment (INI 2009). More scrutiny of waste regulations to deal with waste trafficking is also expected in 2010. Properly handled, much waste can be turned into valuable raw resources. This includes urban sewage water, a vital source of irrigation water and fertilizer in some countries. As water becomes scarcer in many parts of the world, there will be an increasing need to take a look at this centuries-old practice and how to make it as safe as possible.

REFERENCES

Alaee, M., Arias, P., Sjödin, A. and Bergman, A. (2003). An overview of commercially used brominated flame retardants, their applications, their use patterns in different countries/regions and possible modes of release. *Environment International,* 29(6), 683-689

Bao, Q.S Q. S., Lu, C-Y., Song, H., Wang, M., Ling, W., Chen, W-Q., Deng, X-Q., Hao Y-T. and Rao, S. (2009). Behavioural development of school aged children who live around a multi-metal sulphide mine in Guangdong province, China: a cross-sectional study. *BMC Public Health*, 9, 217

BBC (2009a). Hundreds ill near China smelter. BBC News Online, 20 August 2009

BBC (2009b). Chinese factory poisons hundreds. BBC News Online, 3 August 2009

BBC (2009c). China birth defects up sharply. BBC News Online, 1 February 2009

Biotto, G., Silvestri, S., Gobbo, L., Furlan, E., Valenti, S. and Rosselli, R. (2009). GIS, multi-criteria and multi-factor spatial analysis for the probability assessment of the existence of illegal landfills. *International Journal of Geographical Information Science*, 23, 1233-1244

Bristow, M. (2008). China to log its worst polluters. BBC News Online, 29 February 2008

Bristow, M. (2009). China villagers storm lead plant. BBC News Online, 17 August 2009

CAI (2009). Computer Aid International web site

ChemSec (2009). Stockholm Convention on Persistent Organic Pollutants press release: Mixed results from Geneva Conference. International Chemical Secretariat. Göteborg, Sweden, 11 May 2009

Chen, D., Mai, B., Song, J., Sun, Q., Luo, Y., Luo, X., Zeng, E.Y. and Hale, R.C. (2007). Polybrominated Diphenyl Ethers in Birds of Prey from Northern China. *Environmental Science and Technology*, 41(6), 1828-1833

Connolly, L. (2009). Endocrine disrupting toxins. Queen's University Belfast web site

Day, M. (2009). Skulls found on Mafia ship laden with toxic waste. *The Independent*, 26 September 2009

Diaz, R.J. and Rosenberg, R. (2008). Spreading dead zones and consequences for marine ecosystems. *Science*, 321(5891), 926-9

Dowling, A., Clift, R., Grobert, N., Hutton, D.D., Oliver, R., O'Neill, B.O., Pethica, J., Pidgeon, N., Porritt, J., Ryan, J., Seaton, A., Tendler, S., Welland, M. and Whatmore, R. (2004). *Nanoscience and nanotechnologies: opportunities and uncertainties*. Royal Society and Royal Academy of Engineering, London

Duhigg, C. (2009). Debating how much weed killer is safe in your water glass. *The New York Times*, 23 August 2009

EEA (2009). *Waste without borders in the EU? Transboundary shipment of waste*. European Environment Agency, Report No 1/2009

EFSA (2009) The Potential Risks Arising from Nanoscience and Nanotechnologies on Food and Food Safety. European Food Safety Authority web site

Erisman, J.W, Sutton, M.A., Galloway, J., Kilmont, Z. and Winiwater, W. (2008). How a century of ammonia synthesis changed the world. *Nature Geoscience*, 1, 636-639

Ermolieva, T., Winiwater, W., Fischer, G., Cao, G.-Y., Kilmont, Z., Schöpp, W., Li, Y. and Asman, W.A.H. (2009). Integrated nitrogen management in China. International Institute for Applied Systems Analysis, Interim report 09-005, August 2009

Estrada, R. (2009). California sticks toe in green chemistry pond. *Science and Environment*, 27 July 2009

FoE (2009). Fact Sheet: Brief Background Information on Nanoparticles in Sunscreens and Cosmetics. Friends of the Earth web site, March 2009

G8 (2009). Ministerial Statement: Children's Health and the Environment. Syracuse Environment Ministerial Meeting, 24 April 2009

Greenpeace (2009). Where does e-waste end up? Greenpeace web site

Gue, L. and MacDonald, E. (2007). *Issue Backgrounder: Proposed PBDE regulations, DecaBDE, and Notice of Objection*. Sierra Legal and David Suzuki Foundation, May 2007

Hardell, L., van Bavel, B., Lindström, G., Eriksson, M. and Carlberg, M. (2006). In utero exposure to organic pollutants in relation to testicular cancer risk. *International Journal of Andrology,* 29, 228-234

Hites, R.A. (2004). Polybrominated dophenyl ethers in the environment and in people: a meta-analysis of concentrations. *Environmental Science & Technology*, 38, 945-956

IAEA (2009). IAEA Helps Developing Countries Tackle Lead and other Heavy Metal Pollution, International Atomic Energy Agency press release

INI (2009). N2010: *Reactive Nitrogen: Management for Sustainable Development Science, Technology and Policy*. International Nitrogen Initiative Conference web site

ISO (2008a) ISO/TR 12885:2008 Nanotechnologies–Health and safety practices in occupational settings relevant to nanotechnologies. International Organization for Standardization, Geneva

ISO (2008b) ISO/TS 27687:2008 Nanotechnologies–Terminology and definitions for nano-objects–Nanoparticle, nanofibre and nanoplate. International Organization for Standardization, Geneva

IWMI (2002). Reuse of Wastewater for Agriculture: The Hyderabad Declaration on Wastewater Use in Agriculture. Hyderabad, India, 14 November 2002. International Water Management Institute web site

IWMI (2006). *Recycling Realities: managing health risks to make wastewater an asset*. International Water Management Institute. Water Policy Briefing 17

Juschke, E., Marschner, B., Chen, Y. and Tarchitzky, J. (2009). Effects of treated wastewater irrigation on contents and dynamics of soil organic carbon and microbial activity. *Geophysical Research Abstracts*, 11, EGU2009-4780

Karn, B., Kuiken, T. and Otto, M. (2009). Nanotechnology and In situ Remediation: A Review of the Benefits and Potential Risks. *Environmental Health Perspectives* online, 23 June

Kelly, B. (2009) Small concerns: nanotech regulations and risk management. SPIE newsletter, 2 December 2009

Kimbrough, K.L., Lauenstein, G.G., Christensen, J.D. and Apeti, D.A. (2008). *An Assessment of Two Decades of Contaminant Monitoring in the Nation's Coastal Zone. National Status and Trends: Mussel Watch Program*. US National Oceanic and Atmospheric Administration, Technical Memorandum NOS NCCOS 74

Kotz, A. , Malisch, R., Kypke, K. and Oehme, M. (2005). PBDE, PBDD/F and mixed chlorinated-brominated PXDD/F in pooled human milk samples from different countries. *Organohalogen Compd*., 67, 1540-1544

Law, R.J., Herzke, D., Harrad, S., Morris, S., Bersuder, P., Allchin, C. R. (2008). Levels and trends of HBCD and BDEs in the European and Asian environments. *Chemosphere*, 73, 223-241

Leung, A.O.W., Luksemburg, W.J., Wong, A.S. and Wong, M.H. (2007). Spatial distribution of polybrominated diphenyl ethers and polychlorinated dibenxo-p-dioxins and dibenzofurans in soil and combustion residue at Guiyu. *Environmental Science and Technology,* 41, 2730-2737

Li, S. (2009). Lead poisoning highlights development dilemma in China. China.org, 20 August

Luo, Y., Luo, X.J., Lin, Z., Chen, S.J., Liu, J., Mai, B.X., Yang, Z.Y. (2009). Polybrominated diphenyl ethers in road and farmland soils from an e-waste recycling region in Southern China. *Science of the Total Environment,* 407(3), 1105-1113

Lux (2009). Overhyped Technology Starts to Reach Potential: Nanotech to Impact $3.1 Trillion in Manufactured Goods in 2015. Lux Research, New York

Maynard, A. (2009). A Beacon or Just a Landmark, The Responsible Nano Forum, London

McCann, A. (2009). *Combatting indoor air pollution in Bangladesh*. Stanford University, 25 September

Milmo, C. (2009). How a cargo of rubbish became a crime scene that shames Britain. *The Independent*, 23 September 2009

Mulholland, P.J., Helton, A.M., Poople, G.C., Hall, R.O., Hamilton, S.K., Peterson, B.J., Tank, J.L., Ashkenas, L.R., Cooper, L.W., Dahm, C.N., Dodds, W.K., Findlay, S.E.G., Gregory, S.V., Grimm, N.B., Johnson, S.L., McDowell, W.H., Meyer, J.L., Valett, H.M., Webster, J.R., Arango, C.P., Beaulieu, J.J., Bernot, M.J., Burgin, A.J., Crenshaw, C.L., Johnson, L.T., Niederlehner, B.R., O'Brien, J.M., Potter, J.D., Sheibley, R.W., Sobota, D.J. and Thomas, M.S. (2008). Stream denitrification across biomes and its response to anthropogenic nitrate loading. *Nature*, 452, 202-205

Nanotechproject (2009a). The Project on Emerging Nanotechnologies: Consumer Products: An inventory of nanotechnology-based consumer products currently on the market

Nanotechproject (2009b). The Project on Emerging Nanotechnologies: Nanoremediation Map

Nanotechproject (2009c). The Project on Emerging Nanotechnologies: Agriculture and food

NRC (2009). *Review of Federal Strategy for Nanotechnology-Related Environmental, Health and Safety Research*. National Research Council, Washington, D.C.

OECD (2008) *Current Developments/Activities on the Safety of Manufactured Nanomaterials/ Nanotechnologies*. Organisation for Economic Cooperation and Development web site

OECD (2009a). *Conference on Potential Benefits of Nanotechnology: Fostering Safe Innovation-Led Growth*. Background Paper. Organisation for Economic Cooperation and Development web site

OECD (2009b). Organisation for Economic Cooperation and Development, Safety of Manufactured Materials web site

Palmberg, C., Dernis, H. and Miguet, C. (2009). *Nanotechnology: An overview based on indicators and statistics*. STI Working Paper 2009/7 Statistical Analysis of Science, Technology and Industry. Directorate for Science, Technology and Industry, Organisation for Economic Co-operation and Development

Pearce, F. (2009) The Nitrogen Fix: Breaking a Costly Addiction. Yale Environment 360 web site, 5 November 2009

Phoenix, G.K., Hicks, W.K., Cinderby, S., Kuylenstierna, J.C.I., Stock, W.D., Dentener, F.J., Giller, K.E., Austin, A.T., Lefroy, R.D.B., Gimeno, B.S., Ashmore, M.R. and Ineson, P. (2006). Atmospheric nitrogen deposition in world biodiversity hotspots. *Global Change Biology*, 12, 1-7

PRIME-TASS (2009). Medvedev says Russia should become leader in nanotechnologies. PRIME-TASS, 6 October 2009

Raschid-Sally, L. and Jayakody, P. (2008). *Drivers and characteristics of wastewater agriculture in developing countries: results from a global assessment*. International Water Management Institute Research Report 127

Roberts, E.M., English, P.B., Grether, J.K., Windham, G.C., Somberg, L. and Wolff, C. (2007). Maternal residence near agricultural pesticide applications and autism spectrum disorders among children in the California Central Valley. *Environmental Health. Perspectives*, 115, 1482-9

Rockström, J., Steffen, W., Noone, K., Persson, A., Chapin III, F.S., Lambin, E.F., Lenton, T.M., Scheffer, M., Folke, C., Schellnhuber, H.J., Nykvist, B., de Wit, C.A., Hughes, T., van der Leeuw, S., Rodhe, H., Sörlin, S., Snyder, P.K., Costanza, R., Svedin, U., Falkenmark, M., Karlberg, L., Corell, R.W., Fabry, V.J., Hansen, J., Walker, B., Liverman, D., Richardson, K., Crutzen, P. and Foley, J.A. (2009). A safe operating space for humanity. *Nature*, 461, 472-5

Rohr, J.R. and McCoy, K.A. (2009). A qualitative meta-analysis reveals consistent effects of atrazine on freshwater fish and amphibians. National Institute of Environmental Health Sciences. *Environmental Health Perspectives,* 23 Sept. 2009

Romieu, I., Riojas-Rodríguez, H., Marrón-Mares, A.T., Schilmann, A., Perez-Padilla, R. and Masera, O. (2009). Improved biomass stove intervention in rural Mexico. *American Journal of Respiratory and Critical Care Medicine*, 180, 649-656

Rosenthal, E. (2009). Smuggling Europe's waste to poorer countries. *The New York Times*, 26 Sept. 2009

Royal Society (2005) *Report of workshop on potential health, environmental, and societal impacts of nanotechnologies*. London, 25 November 2005

Ruffell, A. and Kulessa, B. (2009). Application of geophysical techniques in identifying illegally buried toxic waste. *Environmental Forensics*, 10, 196-207

Rusiecki, J.A., De Roos, A., Lee, W.J., Dosemeci, M., Lubin, J.H., Hoppin, J.A., Blair, A. and Alavanja, M.C.R. (2004). Cancer incidence among pesticide applicators exposed to atrazine in the agricultural health study. *Journal of the National Cancer Institute*, 96,1375

Saito, T. (2009). *Children's Health and the Environment*. Syracuse Environment Ministerial Meeting, April 2009

Silvestri, S., Viezzoli, A., Edsen, A., Auken, E. and Giada, M. (2009). *The use of remote and proximal sensing for the identification of contaminated landfill sites*. Proceedings Sardinia 2009, Twelfth International Waste Management and Landfill Symposium

Saiyed, H., Dewan, A., Bhatnagar, V., Shenoy, U., Shenoy, R., Rajmohan, H., Patel, K., Kashyap, R., Kulkarni, P., Rajan, B. and Lakkad, B. (2004). Effect of endosulfan on male reproductive development. *Environmental Health Perspectives*, 111, 1958-1962

Salati, S. and Moore, F. (2009). Assessment of heavy metal concentration in the Khoshk River water and sediment, Shiraz, Southwest Iran. *Environmental Monitoring and Assessment,* 7 May 2009

SCENIHR (2009). *Risk Assessment of Products of Nanotechnologies*. Scientific Committee on Emerging and Newly Identified Health Risks. 19 January 2009

Schenker, U., Soltermann, F., Scheringer, M. and Hungerbühler, K. (2008). Modeling the environmental fate of polybrominated diphenyl ethers (PBDEs): The importance of photolysis for the formation of lighter PBDEs. *Environmental Science and Technology*, 42, 9244-9249

Scott, C., Faruqui, N.I. and Raschid, L. (eds.) (2004). *Wastewater use in irrigated agriculture: confronting the livelihood and environmental realities*. International Development Research Centre

Sekula-Wood, E. (2009). Rapid downward transport of the neurotoxin domoic acid in coastal waters. *Nature Geoscience*, 2, 272-275

Silva, M.H. and Gammon, D. (2009). An assessment of the developmental, reproductive and neurotoxicity of endosulfan. *Birth Defects Res. B. Dev. Reprod. Toxicol*., 86, 1-28

Steiner, A. (2009). Speech by Achim Steiner, UN Environment Programme (UNEP) Executive Director at the Helsinki Chemicals Forum, 28 May 2009

Stockholm Convention (2009a). Stockholm Convention press release: Governments unite to step-up reduction on global DDT reliance and add nine new chemicals under international treaty, 9 May 2009

Stockholm Convention (2009b). Stockholm Convention press release: Endosulfan and other chemicals being assessed for listing under the Stockholm Convention, 16 October 2009

Sutcliffe, H. (2009). A Beacon or Just a Landmark, Responsible Nano Forum, London

Takimoto, H. and Tamura, T. (2006). Increasing trend of spina bifida and decreasing birth weight in relation to declining body mass index of young women in Japan. *Medical Hypotheses*, 67, 1023-1026

Taylor, Michael J. (2008). *Assuring the Safety of Nanomatrials in Food Packaging: The Regulation Process and Key Issues*. Woodrow Wilson International Center for Scholars, Association of Food, Beverage and Consumer Products Companies, and Project on Emerging Nanotechnologies

UN (2009). Toxic wastes caused deaths, illnesses in Côte d'Ivoire – UN expert. United Nations press release, 16 September 2009

UNESCO (2007). *Human alteration of the nitrogen cycle*. United Nations Educational, Scientific and Cultural Organization UNESCO/SCOPE Policy Brief No. 4, April 2007

US EPA (2009a). *Nanomaterials Research Strategy*. US Environmental Protection Agency. EPA 620/K-09/011

US EPA (2009b). Research Development: Very Small Offers Big Cleanup Potential (news story). US Environmental Protection Agency

US EPA (2009c). Atrazine Updates. US Environmental Protection Agency

US EPA (2009d). Essential Principles for Reform of Chemicals Management Legislation. US Environmental Protection Agency

Verreault, J., Gabrielsen, G.W., Chu, S., Muir, D.C.G., Andersen, M., Hamaed, A. and Letcher, R.J. (2005). Flame Retardants and Methoxylated and Hydroxylated Polybrominated Diphenylethers in Two Norwegian Arctic Top Predators. *Environ. Sci. and Technol*., 39, 6021-6028

Vitousek, P.M., Naylor, R., Crews, T., David, M.B., Drinkwater, L.E., Holland, E., Johnes, P.J., Katzenberger, J., Martinelli, L.A., Matson, P.A., Nziguheba, G., Ojima, D., Palm, C.A., Robertson, G.P., Sanchez, P.A., Townsend, A.R. and Zhang, F.S. (2009). Nutrient imbalances in agricultural development. *Science*, 324(5934), 1519-1520

Weckenbrock, P., Prof. Dr. Drescher, A., Dr. Amerasinghe, P., Dr. Simmons, R.W. and Jacobi, J. (2009). Lower than expected risks of wastewater irrigated agriculture along the Musi River, India. Second German-Indian Conference on Research for Sustainability, April. United Nations University, Bonn

Wen, S., Yang, F-X., Gong, Y., Zhang, X-L., Hui, Y., Li, J-G., Lui, A-L., Wu, Y-N., Lu, W-Q. and Xu, Y. (2008). Elevated Levels of Urinary 8-Hydroxy-2'-deoxyguanosine in Male Electrical and Electronic Equipment Dismantling Workers. *Environ. Sci. and Technol*., 42, 4202-4207

Woodrow Wilson International Center for Scholars (2008). Project on Emerging Nanotechnologies Consumer Product Inventory

Xinhua (2009). 509 sickened in chemical plant pollution in central China city. Xinhua Online, 3 August 2009

Zhu, X. and Wang, Q. (2009). Tests confirm widespread lead poisoning. *China Daily*, 28 September 2009

Zhuang, P., Zou, B., Li, N.Y. and Li, Z.A. (2009). Heavy metal contamination in soils and food crops around Dabaoshan mine in Guangdong, China: implications for human health. *Environmental Geochemistry and Health 31(6)*, 707-715

Climate Change

The effects of increasing atmospheric greenhouse gas concentrations on Earth systems are better understood due to the attention being given to their regional impacts, as well as to international monitoring results. Of particular concern are the implications of melting ice for sea-level rise, the signficance of ocean acidification for marine ecosystems, and the risks to global agriculture and water supply posed by the expanding tropical belt.

Many glaciers in the margins of the ice sheets of Greenland and Antarctica have begun to flow more rapidly. For this reason, their contribution to global sea-level rise is growing.
Credit: Lisa Ross

INTRODUCTION

The global mean surface air temperature is continuing its long-term increasing trend (**Figure 1**). The years 2000-2009 constitute the warmest decade since instrumental records for global temperatures were established in the mid-19th century, and 2009 is likely to be the fifth warmest year ever recorded (NCDC 2009, WMO 2009). The warmest year on record remains 2005, according to analyses by the Goddard Institute for Space Studies. 2009 was tied as the second warmest year with a cluster of other years—1998, 2002, 2003, 2006, and 2007—and the end of the warmest decade (GISS 2009a). In 2009, the cooling effects attributed to La Niña cycle were weakening while an El Niño system was maturing in the eastern Pacific (NCDC 2009) (**Box 1**).

Figure 1: Global surface air temperature change

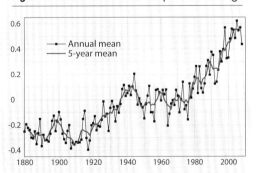

The global surface air mean temperature rose between 1951 and 1980. The period 1951-1980 is used as the baseline in the figure.

Source: GISS (2009b)

MELTING ICE

Warmer temperatures in the oceans cause thermal expansion of their volume. Recent estimates suggest that thermal expansion in the oceans' top 700-metre layer account for an average global sea-level rise of about 0.52 millimetres (mm) per year between 1961 and 2003, or 2.1 centimetres (cm) during this 42-year period (Domingues and others 2008).

Another process that results in rising sea levels is the addition of water mass from land ice. Melting glaciers and ice caps, as well as the vast ice sheets of Greenland and Antarctica, raise sea-levels if their water mass enters the ocean as meltwater or icebergs (Pritchard and others 2009, Steig and others 2009, Velicogna 2009). Loss of land-based ice to the ocean can occur through the melting of glaciers and ice sheets due to direct temperature forcing. Ice can also enter the ocean through changes in the patterns and rates of glacier and ice sheet motion that deliver the ice straight into the ocean as icebergs (Holland and others 2008). Glacier and ice sheet dynamics could produce rapid sea-level rise since increasing glacier flow and iceberg calving do not track temperature increases in a linear way. Instead, they may respond to climate change by abruptly and irreversibly accelerating discharges into the ocean (Bamber and others 2009, Pfeffer and others 2008).

Geologic evidence suggests that dynamic changes in ice sheets have contributed to phases of significant sea-level rise in the past. Most research on dynamic changes, including accelerated iceberg discharges, has focused on glaciers and ice caps. However, in recent years, and especially in connection with the International Polar Year, research on the dynamics of ice

Box 1: Attribution

Policy-makers are increasingly looking for answers to explain why the climate is evolving as it is—in other words, to provide an attribution of the causes for observed climate variations and change. To establish attributions, scientists rely on various types of evidence and methods, including data sets and modelling (NOAA 2009).

There are a number of possible explanations for climate change. External forces—including solar variability, volcanic eruptions, and human interference with carbon sinks and sources or with reflectivity—introduce new energy or material from outside the climate system. Internal forces include processes due primarily to interactions within the atmosphere, as well as processes involving various components of the climate system such as the El Niño and La Niña cycle. Before attributing a climate condition to human interference, it is necessary to determine whether this condition is likely to have resulted from natural external forcing or from internal variations alone (NOAA 2009).

Scientists divide the human-induced activities that influence climate change into three related and overlapping types: greenhouse gas emissions, aerosol emissions, and land use changes.

Greenhouse gases (GHGs) are emitted by the transport, industrial, agriculture, and other sectors. They account for about two-thirds of radiative forcing, or influences on changes in Earth's energy balance, during the 20th century and earlier. GHGs, which persist from decades to centuries, include carbon dioxide (CO_2), methane (CH_4), nitrous oxide (N_2O), and a number of man-made compounds such as hydrofluorocarbons (HFCs), perfluorocarbons (PFCs), and sulphur hexafluoride (SF_6). More than half of GHG emissions currently come from power stations, fossil fuel production and use, cement production, waste disposal, and the building sector (IPCC 2007).

Aerosols are suspensions of tiny solid and liquid particles that enter the atmosphere from slash and burn agriculture, the use of diesel and biomass fuels, and other sources, often producing black carbon or soot. Aerosols and dust can accumulate in the atmosphere and form clouds that keep radiation from reaching Earth's surface. They can also enhance radiative forcing, depending on the size of the particles, their physical attributes, and their location in the atmosphere or on the surface of the planet (IPCC 2007).

Land use changes include deforestation and forest fires, the destruction of wetlands, and changes in the reflectance of the land surface. Agriculture, particularly livestock and irrigated rice production, is responsible for significant methane emissions (IPCC 2007).

Confidence in attributing global warming to the cumulative effects of these activities has grown over the last two decades. This can be shown by comparing the conclusions of the successive Assessment Reports of the Intergovernmental Panel on Climate Change (IPCC). In 1990, the First Assessment Report cautiously stated: "The size of this warming is broadly consistent with predictions of climate models, but it is also of the same magnitude as natural climate variability. Thus the observed increase could be largely due to this natural variability; alternatively this variability and other human factors could have offset a still larger human-induced greenhouse warming. The unequivocal detection of the enhanced greenhouse effect is not likely for a decade or more" (IPCC 1990).

The Second Assessment Report in 1995 went somewhat further: "Our ability to quantify the human influence on global climate is currently limited because the expected signal is still emerging from the noise of natural variability, and because there are uncertainties in key factors. These include the magnitude and patterns of long term natural variability and the time evolving pattern of forcing by, and response to, changes in concentrations of greenhouse gases and aerosols, and land surface changes. Nevertheless, the balance of evidence suggests that there is a discernible human influence on global climate" (IPCC 1995).

In 2001, the Third Assessment Report demonstrated an advance in confidence: "In the light of new evidence and taking into account the remaining uncertainties, most of the observed warming over the last 50 years is likely to have been due to the increase in greenhouse gas concentrations". This report defined "likely" as having over 66 per cent probability (IPCC 2001).

The Fourth Assessment Report in 2007 declared that "Most of the observed increase in global average temperatures since the mid-20th century is very likely due to the observed increase in anthropogenic greenhouse gas concentrations." It defined "very likely" as having over 90 per cent probability (IPCC 2007).

Attribution studies are currently focusing on consistencies, at the regional and ecosystem levels, between anthropogenic influences and the changes in climate associated with temperature and precipitation. Recently, anthropogenic influences have been proposed to account for shifts in polar temperature trends; in sea surface temperatures in cyclone-producing ocean basins; in habitat shifts; in hydrology in the western United States; and in physical and biological systems, such as glacier loss or budburst patterns (Barnett and others 2008, Gillett and others 2008a, Gillett and others 2008b, Kelly and Goulden 2008, Rosenzweig and others 2008).

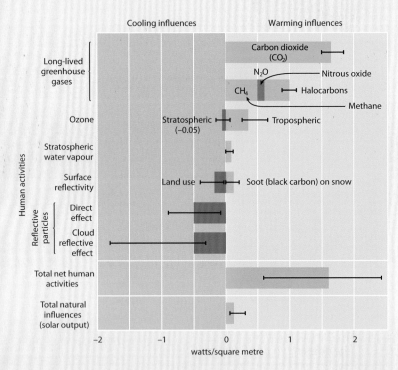

The figure shows the warming influences (orange bars) or cooling influences (blue bars) that various factors have had on Earth's climate from the beginning of the industrial age, around 1750, to the present expressed in watts per square metre. The thin black line overlaid on each bar represents an estimate of the range of uncertainty. Factors considered include all the major human-induced factors and the sun, the only major natural factor that has a long-term effect on climate. The cooling effect of individual volcanoes is also natural, but is a relatively short-lived factor lasting two to three years. Thus, its influence is not included in the figure. There is a total net warming effect of human activities and a relatively smaller total warming effect of natural influences.

Source: Adapted from Karl and others (2009) and from IPCC (2007)

sheets, as well as those of glaciers and ice caps, has increased sharply (Briner and others 2009, IPY 2009, Pritchard and others 2009, Bell 2008, Howat and others 2008, Pfeffer and others 2008, Rignot and others 2008) (**Box 2**). Understanding the mechanisms of, and controls on, the contribution of rapid dynamic changes in glaciers, ice caps, and ice sheets to sea-level rise is among the goals being pursued most urgently in glaciology and sea-level investigations (Bamber and others 2009, Cazenave and others 2009, Fletcher 2009, Milne and others 2009, Meier and others 2007, Pfeffer and others 2008).

Currently, global estimates put the contribution of ice melt to sea-level rise at about 1.8 to 2.0 mm per year. This contribution could increase if shrinking ice shelves and tidewater glaciers release grounded ice or initiate the large-scale collapse of vulnerable parts of the ice sheets

(Bamber and others 2009, Cazenave and others 2009, Meier and others 2007).

Dynamic thinning—ice loss resulting from accelerated flow—is not well understood and its potential contribution to sea-level rise has not yet been determined. The dynamic thinning of continent-scale ice sheets has been monitored by repeat satellite altimetry observations to track changes in surface elevation, but until recently there were few systematic observations at finer scales (Pritchard and others 2009, IPCC 2007). The application of new analytical capabilities has demonstrated that dynamic thinning at the edges of these large ice sheets can be tracked. A high-resolution analysis in 2009, based on 43 million satellite-based measurements of Antarctica and 7 million of Greenland between 2003 and 2007, demonstrates that substantial changes in ice sheets result from glacier dynamics at ocean margins (Pritchard and others 2009). Dynamic thinning of ice shelves and tidewater glaciers is underway; it has reached all latitudes in Greenland and intensified on key Antarctic grounding lines. This dynamic thinning has lasted for decades after ice-shelf collapse, penetrated far into the interior of each ice sheet, and is spreading as ice shelves are thinned by ocean-driven melt (Pritchard and others 2009, Van den Broeke and others 2009).

Arctic transformations

Arctic Ocean ice cover has decreased significantly in the last decade. The minimum covered area thus far was found in 2007 and the minimum volume in 2008 (NSIDC 2009). The area of sea-ice cover in 2009 was the third smallest recorded. It recovered slowly. On some days in November 2009, the ice cover was the smallest ever recorded for that date (IJIS 2010, NSIDC 2009) (**Figure 2**).

The nature of Arctic sea-ice cover has changed dramatically in the last few decades. The sea-ice has become thinner and more prone to rapid melting, with growing proportions of one- and two-year-old ice. In 1987, 57 per cent of Arctic basin ice was five or more years old and at least 14 per cent was nine or more years old. By 2007, only 7 per cent was five or more years old; none was as much as nine years old (Haas and others 2008, Maslanik and others 2007). As warm, moist air feeds into sub-Arctic weather systems, the change to thinner and more vulnerable Arctic sea ice will have significant implications for the global climate system (Serreze and others 2007).

Since newer and thinner ice melts more quickly, larger areas of open water are exposed to solar radiation earlier in the year and are warmed over a longer season. Greater heat transfer from the ocean to the atmosphere—the maritime effect—is expected to help moderate cold autumn and winter temperatures (Serreze and others 2007).

Figure 2: Extent of Arctic sea ice 2002-2009

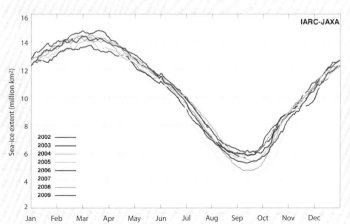

Sea-ice extent is calculated as the areal sum of sea ice covering the ocean where sea-ice concentration exceeds 15 per cent. In 2009, it was at its greatest in the spring of 2009, when it covered about 14.41 million km^2 or approximately 9.67 per cent of the planet's surface area. Sea-ice cover is usually at its minimum in September. The 2009 September minimum was 5.36 million km^2.

Source: IJIS (2010)

As ice retreats from shorelines, winds gain a longer fetch over open water, resulting in stronger waves and increased shore erosion (Perovich and Richter-Menge 2009, Mars and Houseknecht 2007).

Considerable changes have been observed in cyclone behaviour and atmospheric circulation over the Arctic in recent years. New research suggests that the changes are related to variability in September ice coverage (Simmonds and Keay 2009). This reinforces suggestions that the shrinking and thinning of Arctic ice leaves the region vulnerable to future anomalous cyclonic activity and atmospheric forcing (Simmonds and Keay 2009).

The weather at lower latitudes can be affected by these changes high in the Arctic basin (Serreze and others 2007). Combining satellite measurements of the extent of sea-ice with conventional atmospheric observations, researchers have found that summer ice variability is associated with large-scale atmospheric features during the following autumn and winter well below the Arctic Circle. These may include warming and destabilization of the lower troposphere, increased cloudiness, and slackening of the poleward thickness gradient that weakens the polar jetstream (Francis and others 2009). The rapid retreat of Arctic sea-ice could accelerate warming up to 1 500 kilometres inland, affecting considerable portions of Greenland, Scandinavia, Russia, Alaska, and Canada. During rapid ice retreat, inland warming could have dramatic effects on ecosystems and the human populations that depend on them (Jones and others 2009, Lawrence and others 2009).

The consequences of persistent climate warming of the Arctic and subarctic terrestrial ecosystems, and associated processes, are worrying. Releases of CO_2, CH_4, and, more recently, N_2O in these regions have accelerated in recent decades (Tarnocai and others 2009). Arctic permafrost soils store enormous amounts of carbon. Including all the northern circumpolar regions, these ecosystems are estimated to store twice as much carbon as is currently present in the atmosphere in the form of CO_2 (Tarnocai and others 2009, Schuur and others 2008). Warming in the Arctic is already causing increased emissions of CO_2 and CH_4, suggesting that feedback processes may have begun (Walter and others 2007). Evidence is also

accumulating that submarine methane deposits in the North Atlantic are degassing (Westbrook and others 2009) (**Figure 3**).

Most of the carbon released from thawing soils results from the decomposition of organic matter—plant, animal, and microbial remains—accumulated over thousands of years. This organic matter has remained relatively stable because of the low temperatures in the permafrost where it is trapped. As the permafrost thaws, thermokarst is created, a landscape of collapsed and subsiding ground with new or enlarged lakes, wetlands, and craters on the surface (Walter and others 2007). In this newly thawing landscape, upland areas with good drainage and oxygen available for microbial activity are usually sources of CO_2 emissions. In waterlogged areas and in lakes where anaerobic microbes decompose the organic matter, methane becomes the dominant emission. Carbon emissions from Arctic terrestrial ecosystems are increasing with the longer warm seasons and higher temperatures. Warming also supports extended and vigorous plant growth, which increases consumption of carbon dioxide. The effect of emissions from the Arctic will be determined by the interactions of these climate-related processes on land and in the sea (Tarnocai and others 2009, Schuur and others 2008).

OCEAN ACIDIFICATION

Emissions resulting from the use of fossil fuels increased by 29 per cent between 2000 and 2008 (Le Quéré and others 2009). A very important consequence of higher CO_2 concentrations in the atmosphere is the acidification of the oceans. Since anthropogenic carbon dioxide emissions began to increase, the oceans have functioned as a carbon sink, absorbing more than 450 billion tonnes of CO_2 from the atmosphere or about one-third of total carbon emissions since 1750 (Doney and others 2009). When CO_2 is absorbed by seawater, chemical changes occur that reduce both seawater pH and the concentration of carbonate ion. This process is commonly referred to as ocean acidification.

Acidification is affecting shellfish and corals in the surface layer of the oceans. The decrease in carbonate ions makes calcium carbonate ($CaCO_3$) structures vulnerable to dissolution. Ocean habitats conducive to organisms that incorporate calcium carbonate into their shells and skeletons—called marine clacifiers—have contracted (Doney 2009, Fabry and others 2008). Projections suggest that by 2070 water considered suitable for coral growth will vanish as a result of corrosive acidification (IPCC 2007). The processes that mix ocean layers and distribute CO_2 at different levels are not clearly

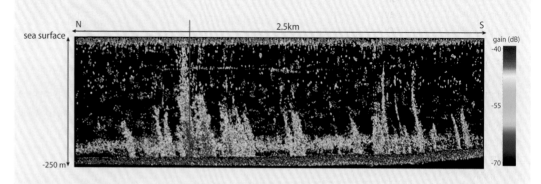

Figure 3: Distribution of methane bubbles escaping from the Arctic sea-bed

The figure shows an extract from a sonor acoustic survey and examples of observed plumes of methane bubbles escaping from the Arctic seabed. The intensity of the acoustic response is indicated by the colour of the 'bubbles'. All plumes show a deflection towards the north, caused by the West Svalbard Current. The brown line indicates the seabed at a depth of about 240 metres.

Source: Westbrook and others (2009)

understood. Future rates of CO_2 absorption by the oceans are uncertain and acidification may occur even more rapidly than recently forecast (Raupach and others 2007). Important questions remain about how much CO_2 the oceans can absorb (Khatiwala and others 2009, Le Quéré and others 2009).

Seasonal acidification events are occurring, but the ocean uptake of anthropogenic CO_2 is extending the affected area. Water that can corrode aragonite, the softest form of $CaCO_3$, is welling up in the summer onto large portions of the North American continental shelf (Feely and others 2008). Researchers anticipate that corrosive water will be found in some polar and subpolar locations by 2020 (Steinacher and others 2009).

Ongoing ocean acidification may harm a wide range of marine organisms and the food webs that depend on them, eventually degrading entire marine ecosystems (Doney and others 2009, Fabry and others 2008). Laboratory studies suggest that molluscs, including commercially valuable species like mussels and oysters, and especially their juveniles, are particularly sensitive to these changes (Cohen and others 2009, Kurihara and others 2009). Societies whose economies depend on marine calcifiers could experience significant financial losses and even social disruptions in the next several decades (Cooley and Doney 2009).

The total effect of ocean acidification on the marine environment will depend on ecosystem responses. Even if calcifying organisms succeed in forming shells and skeletons under elevated CO_2 conditions, they may have to expend more energy to do so, possibly reducing survival and reproduction rates (Wood and others 2008). Losses of plankton, juvenile shellfish, and other organisms at the bottom of marine food chains will affect harvests of economically important predator species (Cooley and Doney 2009). At the same time, acidic conditions will damage coral and prevent its regrowth, destroying crucial marine habitats for feeding and reproduction (Veron and others 2009, Hoegh-Guldberg and others 2007, Lumsden and others 2007).

Ecological shifts to algal overgrowth, and decreased species diversity, sometimes follow coral disturbances, creating new ecosystem states that are stable but dominated by herbivores and less commercially valuable species.Ocean acidification

has been implicated in similar ecological shifts, from corals and other calcifying organisms to seagrasses and algae, in communities where pH levels are decreasing (Norström and others 2009, Wootton and others 2008, Hoegh-Guldberg and others 2007).

Initial concerns about ocean acidification focused on reduced calcification in coral reefs and other calcareous organisms, but other concerns are emerging. Elevated concentrations of dissolved CO_2 may impose a physiological strain on marine animals, impairing their performance and requiring energy that would otherwise be used for locomotion, predation, reproduction, or coping with other environmental stresses such as warming oceans or oxygen depletion (Brewer and Peltzer 2009, Guinotte and others 2008).

To identify the best response to these changes, the degree to which ocean acidification influences critical physiological or developmental processes needs to be better understood. These processes are drivers of calcification, ecosystem structure

Box 3: An international observation network for ocean acidification

A new international and interdisciplinary programme to determine large-scale changes in the properties of ocean water and associated biological responses to ocean acidification has been proposed by scientists. This programme would consist of ship-based hydrography, time-series moorings, floats and gliders with a carbon system, pH and oxygen sensors, and ecological surveys. By coordinating future research plans of the ocean carbon and biological communities, and adding additional sensors and moorings where needed, many requirements for research on ocean acidification could be met in open ocean regions. In coastal environments, a large network of new hydrographic and ecological surveys, moorings, and floats would be required to provide a coastal observing system for ocean acidification.

These activities would necessitate a coordinated international research effort, closely linked with other international carbon research programmes such as the Global Carbon Cycle Project. Many data syntheses, data archiving, and international data management activities could be shared with other ocean programmes. A number of countries are taking part in ocean acidification research and monitoring activities. The total cost of current observational efforts related to ocean acidification is estimated at about US$10 million per year. Cost estimates for an expanded international programme, such as the one proposed, reach approximately US$50 million per year.

Source: EPOCA (2009)

and functioning, biodiversity, and ultimately ecosystem health. Research is urgently needed on the synergistic effects that ocean acidification and other human-induced environmental changes have with respect to marine food webs, and on the potential transformative effects these changes could have on marine ecosystems (Guinotte and others 2008) (**Box 3**).

Ocean acidification is progressing at rates that far exceed models and projections. While the ocean's capacity to absorb carbon has buffered the effects of 150 years of emissions to the atmosphere, this is now taking its toll on marine health. The problem of ocean acidification cannot be solved by addressing radiative forcing through geo-engineering, as some have suggested (see the Resource Efficiency chapter). Ocean acidification is therefore perceived by some as the 'other' CO_2 problem (Robock and others 2009).

EXPANDING TROPICS AND REGIONAL VARIABILITY

Direct observations and modelling indicate that since the 1970s the tropical belt, which roughly encompasses the equatorial regions, is expanding. Observation-based evidence indicates that there has been an estimated 1.0 degree of latitude, ~110 kilometres, widening per decade over the recent four to five decades (Reichler 2009). Expansion of the tropical belt results in poleward displacements of wind and pressure systems throughout the global atmosphere. This phenomenon has been attributed to increases in radiative forcing (Lu and others 2009). The associated trends, which are important indicators of climate change, are likely to have significant influences on ecosystems and societies (Isaac and Turton 2009, Reichler 2009, Seidel and others 2008). These trends will affect the climate regimes that have traditionally characterized latitudinal bands, with a modified intertropical convergence zone and shifting subtropical and temperate zones (Isaac and Turton 2009, Reichler 2009, Sachs and others 2009). The observed rate of expansion over the last ten years has already exceeded climate model projections for the entire 21st century (IPCC 2007). Widening of the tropics will have a cascading effect, not only on large-scale circulation systems but also on precipitation patterns that determine ecosystem types, agricultural productivity, and availability of water resources for domestic and industrial purposes. Expansion of the tropical zone will lead to poleward displacement of the subtropical zones, where most deserts are located, to higher latitudes. The shift may currently be underway (Isaac and Turton 2009, Johanson and Fu 2009, Lu and others 2009, Reichler 2009, Sachs and others 2009, Seidel and others 2008, Seager and others 2007).

Water is already scarce in many parts of the world. Pressures from agriculture and urban expansion will be exacerbated by expected changes in temperature and in precipitation patterns, brought about by global changes in climate. In many tropical regions, more than 90 per cent of the inhabitants work in agriculture. Since water dominates tropical agriculture, climate

variability may be responsible for lack of economic resilience in such areas (Isaac and Turton 2009). Thus, in response to worsening drought, large-scale human migrations could occur, leading to overcrowding, violence, outbreaks of disease, and pressures on resources in neighbouring areas (Matthew 2008). Water shortages faced by communities around the world are creating major food security issues (Battisti and Naylor 2009, World Bank 2009, Lobell and others 2008) (**Figure 4**).

Southeastern Australia has been short of water for nearly a decade (Isaac and Turton 2009, Murphy and Timbal 2008). The southwestern part of North America may already have undergone the transition from a sporadic to a perennial drought climate (MacDonald and others 2008). Other regions projected to suffer persistent drought and water scarcity in coming

years include southern and northern Africa, the Mediterranean basin, much of West Asia, and a broad band running through Central Asia and the Indian subcontinent. This distribution is similar to that of currently water-stressed regions (Isaac and Turton 2009, Solomon and others 2009, IPCC 2007).

Southwestern North America

In southwestern North America, intensified aridity and a sustained drier climate, already predicted by modelling, are becoming a reality. Some researchers have suggested that the transition to a more arid climate may already be underway. As the transition progresses, persistent drought is likely to become this region's new climate (Seager and others 2007).

Unlike the multi-year droughts of the 1950s in western North America, which have been attributed to variations in sea surface temperatures or to La Niña effects, this projected intensified aridity will be the result of increased divergence of large-scale moisture regimes and other changes in atmospheric circulation linked to the poleward expansion of the subtropical dry zones (Seager and others 2007). The 21st century drying of subtropical areas in this region is expected to be unlike any other in the instrumental record. The severest droughts will continue to occur during persistent La Niña events, but the impacts will be worse than current extremes because La Niña conditions will be affecting a drier base state (Barnett and others 2008, MacDonald and others 2008, Seager and others 2007).

Mediterranean region

New research suggests that, by the end of the 21st century, the Mediterranean region will experience more severe aridity than previously estimated (Gao and Giorgi 2008, IPCC 2007). The entire region, particularly the southern Mediterranean, will suffer increasing water stress and desertification. Using the highest resolution projections, researchers have projected a substantial northward expansion of dry and semi-arid regimes in the region (Gao and Giorgi 2008) (**Figure 5**). This implies a corresponding retreat of temperate oceanic and continental climate regimes and a likely shift in vegetation cover, with significant implications for agriculture (Iglesias and others 2007).

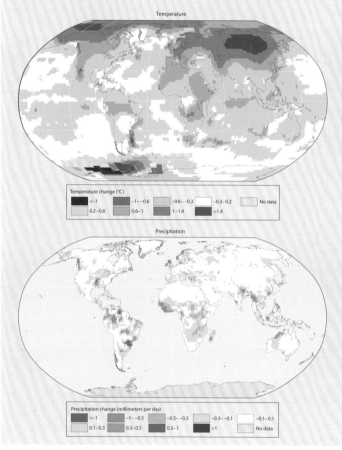

Figure 4: Regional variation in climate over the last 30 years

The top figure shows average increases in temperatures (°C) from 1980 to the present compared with the period 1950-1980. Warming has been greatest at higher latitudes, as shown by the darker orange shading, especially in the northern hemisphere. The bottom figure shows Orange denotes increased precipitation in millimetres per day, and blue decreases from 1980 to the present compared with the previous three decades. Drying has been greatest in continental interiors, while rainfall has become more intense in many coastal areas.

Source: World Bank (2009)

Figure 5: Two scenarios for precipitation changes in the Mediterranean region

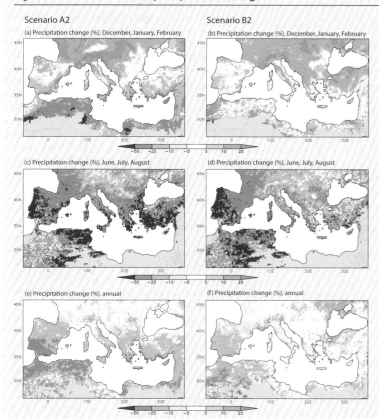

Scenario A2
(a) Precipitation change (%), December, January, February
(c) Precipitation change (%), June, July, August
(e) Precipitation change (%), annual

Scenario B2
(b) Precipitation change (%), December, January, February
(d) Precipitation change (%), June, July, August
(f) Precipitation change (%), annual

The maps show mean precipitation change scenarios for the Mediterranean region for the period 2071-2100, based on IPCC (2000) GHG emission scenarios. Scenario A2 is a high emission scenario, with CO_2 concentrations of about 850 ppm by 2100. Scenario B2 is a lower emission scenario, with CO_2 concentrations of about 570 ppm by 2100. a) DJF (December-January-February), A2 scenario; b) DJF, B2 scenario; c) JJA (June-July-August), A2 scenario; d) JJA, B2 scenario; e) annual, A2 scenario; f) annual, B2 scenario. Units are percentage of reference precipitation. Areas with <0.1 mm per day precipitation are coloured grey.

Source: Gao and Giorgi (2008)

Andean cloud forests may become drier as temperatures rise, threatening endemic species.
Credit: Brian Gross

The severe effects of higher temperatures on the human population in this region have been modelled, extrapolating from observations of heat stress during the record-breaking 2003 heat wave (Diffenbaugh and others 2007). Local topography and landscape features will affect microclimate variations. However, occurrences of what are now considered high-temperature extremes could increase by 200-500 per cent by the end of the century (Diffenbaugh and others 2007).

Amazonia

Amazonian ecosystems face the dual threats of deforestation and climate change (see the Ecosystem Management chapter). While deforestation remains the most visible threat, there is widespread concern about the impacts of climate change, particularly drought (Phillips and others 2009, Malhi and others 2008). Climate change in the Amazon forest ecosystem will likely be associated with lower precipitation during the already dry season (Betts and others 2008). The Andean flank of the Amazon is especially vulnerable. Adjoining the most biodiverse parts of lowland Amazonia, it contains numerous sheltered wet spots in otherwise dry areas. Andean cloud forests at 1 500 to 3 000 metres are susceptible to drying, as cloud levels rise in response to warmer temperatures. Higher elevation-restricted endemic species will be vulnerable, since the cloud levels could rise more quickly than species are able to respond—or the cloud cover could disappear entirely (Malhi and others 2008).

Observations suggest that lower-elevation Amazon basin forests are also vulnerable to increasing dryness. Damage to these forests could potentially result in large carbon losses, creating positive feedbacks to climate change. According to some researchers, the exceptional rise in global atmospheric CO_2 concentrations in 2005 may have been partially caused by Amazon die-off following regional drought (Phillips and others 2009, Cox and others 2008).

A recent study examined how climate change-induced dieback of the Amazon rainforest might advance. The findings suggest that it is more likely that the region will become a seasonal forest than a savanna (Malhi and others 2009). While a seasonal forest could cope with drought, it is likely to be vulnerable to water stress caused by higher temperatures. This leaves forests susceptible to fires, which are still rare in much of Amazonia today. Advancing deforestation, logging, and fragmentation facilitate the start of fires, which can lead to the development of fire-dominated, low-biomass forests (Malhi and others 2009, Thompson and others 2009).

The potential costs and benefits of maintaining a healthy and expanding Amazon carbon sink are substantial. An annual increase of only 0.4 per cent in Amazon forest biomass would roughly offset Western Europe's total fossil fuel emissions. Transition from a moderate carbon sink to even a neutral state or moderate carbon source would have significant implications for the build-up of CO_2 concentrations in the atmosphere. Average growth at the stand level is about 2.0 per cent per year and the mortality rate is about 1.6 per cent; therefore, a small decrease in growth or small increase in mortality could shut the sink down (Phillips and others 2009).

Wetlands, peatlands, and thawing permafrost regions

Wetlands cover about 6 per cent of the surface of the planet (see the Ecosystem Management chapter). They include tidal marshes, estuaries, coastal lagoons, inland deltas and lakes, oases, tundra, and peatland. The water layer in wetlands is usually shallow and easily affected by evaporation. Wetlands are particularly vulnerable to shifting climatic patterns that increase aridity (Wetlands International 2009). Peatlands, a category that includes moors, bogs, mires, peat swamp forests, and permafrost tundra, have a thick soil layer of organic matter which is defined by its carbon content. The world's peatlands contain nearly 30 per cent of all terrestrial carbon (Schuur and others 2008).

Peatlands are formed by the accumulation of dead vegetation over hundreds to thousands of years. When they are drained, the organic matter decomposes and part of the carbon is released

Céide Fields archaeological site in County Mayo, Ireland, where the remains of a Stone Age landscape lie beneath a growing blanket bog.
Credit: Céide Fields Visitor Centre

to the atmosphere as CO_2 (Wetlands International 2009).

Forested tropical peatlands in South East Asia store about 3 per cent of the planet's soil carbon. Human activity and climate change continue to threaten the stability of this important sink, which has been rapidly disappearing over the last several decades as a result of deforestation, drainage, and fire. Since 1985, about 47 per cent of South East Asia's peatlands have been deforested. Most of these peatlands were drained by 2006 (Hooijer and others 2009). Ironically, some of this region's carbon sink is being destroyed to produce biofuels. Recent estimates indicate that 1.3-3.1 per cent of current global CO_2 emissions come from the decomposition of drained peatlands in South East Asia (Hooijer and others 2009). These areas are likely to become more arid during this century, affecting carbon storage in the remaining peatlands and the depth of those peatlands that have been partially drained (Hooijer and others 2009).

Mountain regions

As climates change, habitats change, and plants and animals move inland and upslope. This trend is already being observed in some species (Kelly and Goulden 2008, Lenoir and others 2008, Rosenzweig and others 2008). As these species adapt to higher altitudes, they may be classified as non-native or even invasive. Features that confer advantages of adaptability in the face of climate change are the same ones that characterize weeds and invasive species.

Traditionally, in the lowland regions where most of the relevant studies have been carried out, biological invasions have been recognized as a major driver of biodiversity loss and altered ecosystem functioning (Pauchard and others 2009). In contrast, high-elevation environments appear to be less affected by invasions, an assumption based on their harsher climatic conditions and comparatively low human population densities. However, it was recently estimated that more than a thousand non-native species have become established in natural areas at high elevations worldwide. Many are not considered invasive, but some may threaten native mountain ecosystems (Pauchard and others 2009).

Rapid and significant shifts in plant distribution to higher altitudes have been documented, confirming

a strong correlation between observed changes in the distributional margins of these plant species and in regional climate conditions. Comparing surveys of plant cover from 1977 and 2007 along a 16-kilometre transect that reaches an altitude of 2 314 metres in California's Santa Rosa Mountains, researchers found that the average elevation of the dominant plant species had shifted upward 65 metres over 30 years (Kelly and Goulden 2008). In the same period, southern California experienced surface warming, increased precipitation variability, and decreased snow cover. Upward shifts were uniform across elevation, suggesting that the vegetation responded to a uniformly distributed causal factor. Vegetation shifts also resulted in part from mortality during two distinct periods of drought. Following these lines of evidence, the researchers attributed these shifts to climate change rather than to air pollution or fire (Kelly and Goulden 2008).

Another recent study of the temperate and Mediterranean mountain forests of Western Europe indicates a similar upward shift in forest plant species. Researchers compared the altitudinal distribution of 171 plant species from 0 to 2 600 metres above sea level. The results show a significant upward shift of 29 metres per decade in the optimum elevation of species over the 20th century (Lenoir and others 2008). As ecosystems shift, native species may adapt in ways that have similar effects to those of invasive species.

Among insects, in particular, changing conditions may provide advantages that disturb relationships evolved over millennia. Many insects in temperate zones are just surviving at temperatures that inhibit their optimal metabolic capabilities (Deutsch and others 2008). With warmer temperatures, reproductive seasons and rates increase, resulting in population increases. In northwestern North America, the mountain pine bark beetle has been ravaging US and Canadian forest stands for nearly a decade. Active populations persist because warmer winters have fewer and less extreme freezing episodes, and more beetle larvae survive to breed in spring. Longer summers support more reproduction every year; larger populations are surviving the warmer winters and produce more offspring that weaken trees (Kurz and others 2008). The damaged forests are losing their capacity to sustain water tables and avert soil erosion. Most recently, they have started to become carbon sources instead of carbon sinks as more of the trees succumb to the pest and begin to decompose (Kurz and others 2008).

Reasons for concern

To moderate or possibly avoid the effects of worsening climate change, innovative and perhaps even unorthodox approaches may be necessary, incorporating concepts such as thresholds and cumulative effects in risk assessments. In addition, minimizing the importance of what cannot be quantified while focusing on parameters that are already well-defined should be avoided. The development of tools to help comprehend the scale and duration of the changes ahead, and the climate change commitment that already exists, would contribute to optimal management strategies.

One of the most difficult factors to include accurately in estimates of radiative forcing at the global, regional, and local levels is the effect of aerosols–suspended particles that absorb solar radiation but can also reflect it. Aerosols that reflect radiation are more common; they function as a mask that prevents the full effect of radiative forcing to warm the planet. These aerosols form brown clouds in the atmosphere, causing health problems through pollution at the planet's surface. As they are addressed because of growing concerns about ground-level pollution, their climate change masking function will be affected and temperatures may increase beyond what has been projected (Hill and others 2009, Paytan and others 2009, Shindell and Faluvegi 2009).

Recent analyses have quantified potential thresholds in different ways. In one analysis, 1-5°C is estimated to be the range of global mean temperature increase over pre-industrial levels that would determine 'tipping elements' (Lenton and others 2008). In another, 0-5°C above 1990 levels is treated as 'reason for concern' (Smith and others 2009). Despite variations in the estimated numbers required for various effects, scientists are concluding that the planet *will* experience significant long-term environmental changes from the commitment we have already made by emitting GHGs (Rockström and others 2009, Smith and others 2009, Solomon and others 2009, Lenton and others 2008, Ramanathan and Feng 2008).

Figure 6: Probability distribution for committed warming associated with GHG emissions between 1750 and 2005

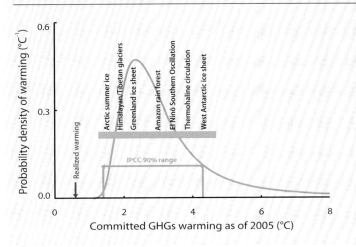

The figure shows the probability distribution for committed warming associated with GHG emissions between 1750 and 2005, and different climate-tipping elements including the temperature threshold range that initiates tipping.

Source: Ramanathan and Feng (2008)

According to one study, a range of 1.4-4.3°C for committed warming before 2005 overlaps and surpasses the currently perceived threshold range for dangerous anthropogenic interference, incorporating a number of tipping elements such as disappearance of summer Arctic sea-ice, and disintegration of the Greenland ice sheet (Ramanathan and Feng 2008) (**Figure 6**).

An estimated warming of 2.4°C is already committed to, and 0.6°C of the warming has occurred so far. Most of the rest of the total warming is expected to take place in the next 50 years and on through to the end of the 21st century (Ramanathan and Feng 2008). The accompanying sea-level rise could continue for several centuries (Solomon and others 2009). Even the most aggressive CO_2 mitigation measures so far envisioned can only limit further warming: they cannot reduce the already committed warming of 2.4°C (Ramanathan and Feng 2008).

Because GHG emissions have been accelerating since 2005 and seem unlikely to stop immediately, some scientists are suggesting that climate change adaptation efforts should assume a commitment to 4°C warming (Parry and others 2009).

A number of proposals are emerging that would require differentiated responsibilities, to be assumed over the next decade (Meinshausen and others 2009, Moore and MacCracken 2009,

Vaughan and others 2009, Elzen and Höhne 2008, Mignon and others 2008, Ramanathan and Feng 2008). These responsibilities would have to be accepted by all governments, the private sector, and civil society organizations. Immediate decisions are required that would take effect in the next few years.

LOOKING AHEAD

Despite the disappointment felt by many at the conclusion of the UN Climate Change Conference in Copenhagen, progress has been made in the areas of forestry, oceans, and terrestrial carbon sequestration (see the Environmental Governance and Ecosystem Management chapters). It will also be possible to move ahead with some confidence on projects and programmes concerned with adaptation to climate change. Monitoring technologies and approaches will continue to be refined, in anticipation of greater scrutiny becoming feasible.

Successful collaborations such as the Global Carbon Project and the International Polar Year serve as models for new areas of focus. The proposed ocean acidification observational network could coordinate the research and analysis urgently needed to formulate a managed response to that aspect of higher CO_2 concentrations.

REFERENCES

Bamber, J.L., Riva, R.E.M., Vermeersen, B.L.A. and LeBrocq, A.M. (2009). Reassessment of the Potential Sea-Level Rise from a Collapse of the West Antarctic Ice Sheet. *Science*, 324(5929), 901-903

Barnett, T., Pierce, D., Hidalgo, H., Bonfils, C., Santer, B. and others (2008). Human-induced changes in the hydrology of the western United States. *Science*, 319(5866), 1080-1083

Battisti, D.S. and Naylor, R.L. (2009). Historical warnings of future food insecurity with unprecedented seasonal heat. *Science*, 323(5911), 240-244

Bell, R.E. (2008). The role of subglacial water in ice-sheet mass balance. *Nature Geoscience*, 1(5), 297-304

Betts, R., Sanderson, M. and Woodward, S. (2008). Effects of large-scale Amazon forest degradation on climate and air quality through fluxes of carbon dioxide, water, energy, mineral dust and isoprene. *Philosophical Transactions of the Royal Society B*, 363(1498), 1873-1880

Brewer, P.G. and Peltzer, E.T. (2009). Limits to Marine Life. *Science*, 324(5925), 347-348

Briner, J.P., Bini, A.C. and Anderson, R.S. (2009). Rapid early Holocene retreat of a Laurentide outlet glacier through an Arctic fjord. *Nature Geoscience*, 2, 496-49

Broeke, M. van den, Bamber, J., Ettema, J., Rignot, E., Schrama, E. and others (2009). Partitioning Recent Greenland Mass Loss. *Science*, 326(5763), 984-986

Cazenave, A., Dominh, K., Guinehut, Berthier, E., Lovel, W. and others (2009). 2003-2008. Global *and Planetary Change*, 65(1-2), 83-88

Cohen, A.L., McCorkle, D.C., Putron, S., Gaetani, G.A. and Rose, K.A. (2009). Morphological and compositional changes in the skeletons of new coral recruits reared in acidified seawater. *Geochemistry Geophysics Geosystems*, 10, Q07005

Cooley, S.R. and Doney, S.C. (2009). Anticipating ocean acidification's economic consequences for commercial fisheries. *Environmental Research Letters*, 4, 024007

Cox, P.M., Harris, P.P., Huntingford, C., Betts, R.A., Collins, M. and others (2008). Increasing risk of Amazonian drought due to decreasing aerosol pollution. *Nature*, 453(7192), 212-215

Deutsch, C.A., Tewksbury, J.J., Huey, R.B., Sheldon, K.S., Ghalambor, C.K. and others (2008). Impacts of climate warming on terrestrial ectotherms across latitude. *Proceedings of the National Academy of Sciences*, 105(18), 6668-6672

Diffenbaugh, N.S., Pal, J.S., Giorgi, F. and Gao, X. (2007). Heat stress intensification in the Mediterranean climate change hotspot. *Geophysical Research Letters*, 34, L11706

Domingues, C.M., Church, J.A., White, N.J., Gleckler, P.J., Wijffels, S.E. and others (2008). Improved estimates of upper-ocean warming and multi-decadal sea-level rise. *Nature*, 453, 1090-1093

Doney, S.C, (2009). The consequences of human-driven ocean acidification for marine life. *F1000 Biology Reports*, 1, 36

Doney, S.C., Fabry, V.J., Feely, R.A. and Kleypas, J.A. (2009). Ocean Acidification: The Other CO_2 Problem. *Annual Review of Marine Science*, 1, 169-192

Elzen, M. and Höhne, N. (2008). Reductions of greenhouse gas emissions in Annex I and non-Annex I countries for meeting concentration stabilisation targets. Climatic Change, 91, 249–274

EPOCA (2009). Ocean acidification observational network. European Project on Ocean Acidification. http://oceanacidification.wordpress.com/2009/12/24/ocean-acidification-observational-network/

Fabry, V.J., Seibel, B.A., Feely, R.A. and Orr, J.C. (2008). Impacts of ocean acidification on marine fauna and ecosystem processes. *ICES Journal of Marine Science*, 65(3), 414-432

Feely, R.A., Fabry, V.J., Dickson, A., Gattuso, J.P., Bijma, J. and others (2009). An International Observational Network For Ocean Acidification, Oceanobs 2009, community white paper

Fletcher, C. (2009). Sea level by the end of the 21st century: A review. *Shore & Beach*, 77(4), 1-9

Francis, J.A., Chan, W., Leathers, D.J., Miller, J.R. and Veron, D.E. (2009). Winter Northern Hemisphere weather patterns remember summer Arctic sea-ice extent. *Geophysical Research Letters*, 36, L07503

Gao, X. and Giorgi, F. (2008). Increased aridity in the Mediterranean region under greenhouse gas forcing estimated from high resolution regional climate projections. *Global and Planetary Change*, 62(3-4), 195-209

Gillett, N.P., Stone, D.A., Stott, P.A., Nozawa, T., Karpechko, A.Y., Hegerl, G.C., Wehner, M.F. and Jones, P.D. (2008a). Attribution of polar warming to human influence. *Nature Geoscience*, 1, 864-869

Gillett, N.P., Stott, P.A. and Santer, B.D. (2008b). Attribution of cyclogenesis region sea surface temperature change to anthropogenic influence. *Geophysical Research Letters*, 35, L09707

GISS (Goddard Institute for Space Studies) (2009a). 2009: Second Warmest Year on Record; End of Warmest Decade. http://www.giss.nasa.gov/research/news/20100121/

GISS (Goddard Institute for Space Studies)(2009b) GISS Surface Temperature Analysis: Analysis Graphs and Plots. http://data.giss.nasa.gov/gistemp/graphs/

Guinotte, J.M., Fabry, V.J. and Ann, N.Y. (2008). Ocean Acidification and Its Potential Effects on Marine Ecosystems. *Proceedings of the National Academy of Sciences*, 1134(1), 320-342

Haas, C., Pfaffling, A., Hendricks, S., Rabenstein, L., Etienne, J.L. and Rigor, I. (2008). Reduced ice thickness in Arctic Transpolar Drift favors rapid ice retreat. *Geophysical Research Letters*, 35, L17501

Hill, J., Polasky, S., Nelson, E., Tilman, D., Huo, H. and others. (2009). Climate change and health costs of air emissions from biofuels and gasoline. *Proceedings of the National Academy of Sciences*, 106(6), 2077-2082

Hoegh-Guldberg, O., Mumby, P.J., Hooten, A.J., Steneck, R.S., Greenfield, P. and others (2007). Coral Reefs Under Rapid Climate Change and Ocean Acidification. *Science*, 318 (5857), 1737-1742

Holland, D.M., Thomas, R.H., de Young, B., Ribergaard, M.H. and Lyberth, B. (2008). Acceleration of Jakobshavn Isbrae triggered by warm subsurface ocean waters. *Nature Geoscience*, 1(10), 659-664

Hooijer, A., Page, S., Canadell, J.G., Silvius, M., Kwadijk J. and others (2009). Current and future CO_2 emissions from drained peatlands in Southeast Asia. *Biogeosciences-Discuss*, 6(4), 7207-7230

Howat, I.M., Smith, B.E., Joughin, I. and Scambos, T.A. (2008). Rates of Southeast Greenland Ice Volume Loss from Combined ICESat and ASTER Observations. *Geophysical Research Letters*, 35, L17505

Iglesias, A., Garrote, L., Flores, F. and Moneo, M. (2007). Challenges to Manage the Risk of Water Scarcity and Climate Change in the Mediterranean. *Water Resources Management*, 21(5), 775-788

IJIS (2010) IARC-JAXA Information System (IJIS) Data of Sea Ice Extent. http://www.ijis.iarc.uaf.edu/en/home/seaice_extent.htm

IPCC (Intergovernmental Panel on Climate Change) (1990, 1995, 2001, 2007). All Working Group 1 Reports are available at the IPCC website, as well as Reports of Working Groups 2 and 3 and Supplementary Reports: http://www.ipcc.ch/publications_and_data/publications_and_data_reports.htm

IPY (2009). International Polar Year web site. www.antarctica.ac.uk/indepth/ipy/index.php

Isaac, J. and Turton, S. (2009). Expansion of the tropics: Evidence and implications. http://www.jcu.edu.au/idc/groups/public/documents/media_release/jcuprd_048832.pdf [Accessed 1 November 2009]

Johanson, C.M. and Fu, Q. (2009). Hadley Cell Widening: Model Simulations versus Observations. *Journal of Climate*, 22(10), 2713-2725

Jones, C., Lowe, J., Spencer, L. and Betts, R. (2009). Committed terrestrial ecosystem changes due to climate change. *Nature Geoscience*, 2, 484-486

Karl, T.R., Melillo, J.M., and Peterson, T.C. (2009). *Global Climate Change Impacts in the United States*. U.S. Climate Change Science Program and the Subcommittee on Global Change Research, Washington, D.C.

Kelly, A.E. and Goulden, M.L. (2008). Rapid shifts in plant distribution with recent climate change. *Proceedings of the National Academy of Sciences*, 105(33), 11823-11826

Khatiwala, S., Primeau, F. and Hall, T. (2009) Reconstruction of the history of anthropogenic CO_2 concentrations in the ocean. *Nature*, 462, 346-349

Kurihara, H., Asai, T., Kato, S. and Ishimatsu, A. (2009). Effects of elevated CO_2 on early development in the mussel *Mytilus galloprovincialis*. *Aquatic Biology*, 4, 225–33

Kurz, W.A., Dymond, C.C., Stinson, G., Rampley, G.J., Neilson, E.T., Carroll, A.L., Ebata, T. and Safranyik, L. (2008). Mountain pine beetle and forest carbon feedback to climate change. *Nature*, 452, 987-990

Lawrence, D.M., Slater, A.G., Tomas, R.A., Holland, M.M. and Deser, C. (2009). Accelerated Arctic land warming and permafrost degradation during rapid sea ice loss. *Geophysical Research Letters*, 35, L11506

Lenoir, J., Gegout, J.C., Marquet, P.A., de Ruffray, P. and Brisse, H. (2008). A Significant Upward Shift in Plant Species Optimum Elevation During the 20th Century. *Science*, 320(5884), 1768-1771

Lenton, T.M., Held, H., Kriegler, E., Hall, J.W., Lucht, W., Rahmstorf, S. and Schellnhuber, H.J. (2008). Tipping elements in the Earth's climate system. *Proceedings of the National Academy of Sciences*, 105(6), 1786-1793

Le Quéré, C., Raupach, M.R., Canadell, J.G., Marland, G., Bopp and others. (2009). Trends in the sources and sinks of carbon dioxide. *Nature Geoscience*, 2, 831-836

Lobell, D., Burke, M.B., Tebaldi, C., Mastrandrea, M.D., Falcon, W.P. and Naylor, R.L. (2008). Prioritizing Climate Change Adaptation Needs for Food Security in 2030. *Science*, 319 (5863), 607-610

Lu, J., Deser, C. and Reichler, T. (2009). Cause of the widening of the tropical belt since 1958. *Geophysical Research Letters*, 36, L03803

Lumsden, S.E., Hourigan, T.F., Bruckner, A.W. and Dorr, G. (eds.) (2007). *The State of Deep Coral Ecosystems of the United States. National Oceanic and Atmospheric Administration (NOAA) Technical Memorandum CRCP-3*

MacDonald, G.M., Bennett, K.D., Jackson, S.T., Parducci, L., Smith, F.A., Smol, J.P. and Willis, K.J. (2008). Impacts of climate change on species, populations and communities: palaeobiogeographical insights and frontiers. *Progress in Physical Geography*, 32(2), 139-172

Malhi, Y., Aragão, L., Galbraith, D., Huntingford, C., Fisher, R. and others. (2009). Exploring the likelihood and mechanism of a climate-change-induced dieback of the Amazon rainforest. *Proceedings of the National Academy of Sciences*, 106(49), 20610-20615

Malhi, Y., Roberts, J.T., Betts, R.A., Killeen, T.J., Li, W. and Nobre, C.A. (2008). Climate change, deforestation, and the fate of the Amazon. *Science*, 319(5860), 169-172

Mars, J.C. and Houseknecht, D.W. (2007). Quantitative remote sensing study indicates doubling of coastal erosion rate in past 50 yr along a segment of the Arctic coast of Alaska. *Geology*, 35(7), 583-586

Maslanik, J., Fowler, A.C., Stroeve, J., Drobot, S., Zwally, J., Yi, D. and Emery, W. (2007). A younger, thinner Arctic ice cover: Increased potential for rapid, extensive sea-ice loss. *Geophysical Research Letters*, 34, L24501

Matthew, R. (2008). Threat Assessment. In: *Global Climate Change National Security Implications* (ed. Carolyn Pumphrey). The Strategic Studies Institute, U.S. Army War College

Meier, M.F, Dyurgerov, M.B., Rick, U.K., O'Neel, S., Pfeffer, W.T and others (2007). Glaciers Dominate Eustatic Sea-Level Rise in the 21st Century. *Science*, 317(5841), 1064-1067

Meinshausen, M., Meinshausen, N., Hare, W., Raper, S.C.B., Frieler, K., Knutti, R., Frame, D.J. and Allen, M.R. (2009). Greenhouse-gas emission targets for limiting global warming to 2°C. *Nature*, 458, 1158-1162

Mignon, B.K., Socolow, R.H., Sarmiento, J.L. and Oppenheimer, M. (2008). Atmospheric stabilization and the timing of carbon mitigation. *Climatic Change*, 88, 251-265

Milne, G.A., Gehrels, W.R., Hughes, C.W. and Tamisiea, M.E. (2009.) Identifying the causes of sea-level change. *Nature Geoscience*, 2, 471-478

Moore, F. C. and MacCracken, M.C. (2009). Lifetime-leveraging. *International Journal of Climate Change Strategies and Management*, 1(1), 42-62.

Murphy, B.F. and Timbal, B. (2008). A review of recent climate variability and climate change in southeastern Australia. *International Journal of Climatology*, 28(7), 859-879

NCDC (2009) National Climatic Data Center State of the Climate Report. http://www.ncdc.noaa.gov/sotc/ [Accessed 1 November 2009]

NOAA (2009) National Oceanic and Atmospheric Administration Climate Attribution. http://www.esrl.noaa.gov/psd/csi/ [Accessed 28 October 2009]

Norström, A., Nyström, M., Lokrantz, J. and Folke, C. (2009). Alternative states of coral reefs: beyond coral-macroalgal phase shifts. *Marine Ecology Progress Series*, 376, 295-306

NSIDC (2009). Arctic sea ice news and analysis. National Snow and Ice Data Center. http://nsidc.org/arcticseaicenews

Parry, M., Lowe, J, and Hansen C. (2009). Overshoot, adapt and recover, *Nature*, 458, 1102

Pauchard, A., Kueffer, C., Dietz, H, Daehler, C.C., Alexander, J. and others. (2009). Ain't no mountain high enough: plant invasions reaching new elevations. *Frontiers in Ecology and the Environment*, 7(9), 479-486

Paytan, A., Mackey, K.R.M., Chen, Y., Lima, I.D., Doney, S.C., Mahowald, N., Labiosa, R. and Post, A.F. (2009). Toxicity of atmospheric aerosols on marine phytoplankton. *Proceedings of the National Academy of Sciences*, 106(12), 4601-4605

Perovich, D. and Richter-Menge, J. (2009) Loss of Sea Ice in the Arctic. *Annual Review of Marine Science*, 1, 417-441

Pfeffer, W.T., Harper, J.T. and O'Neel, S. (2008). Kinematic constraints on glacier contributions to 21st century sea-level rise. *Science*, 32(5894),1340-1343

Phillips, O.L., Aragão, L.E., Lewis, S.L., Fisher, J.B., Lloyd and others. (2009). Drought Sensitivity of the Amazon Rainforest. *Science*, 323(5919), 1344-1347

Pritchard, H.D., Arthern, R., Vaughan, D. and Edwards, L. (2009) Extensive dynamic thinning on the margins of the Greenland and Antarctic ice sheets. *Nature*, 461, 961-975

Ramanathan, V. and Feng, Y. (2008). On avoiding dangerous anthropogenic interference with the climate system: Formidable challenges ahead. *Proceedings of the National Academy of Sciences*, 105(38), 14245-14250

Raupach, M.R., Marland, G., Ciais, P., Le Quéré, C., Canadell, J.G., Klepper, G. and Field, C.B. (2007). Global and regional drivers of accelerating CO_2 emissions. *Proceedings of the National Academy of Sciences*, 104(24), 10288-10293

Reichler, T. (2009) Changes in the Atmospheric Circulation as Indicator of Climate Change. In: *Climate Change: Observed Impacts on Planet Earth* (ed. T.M. Letcher). Elsevier, Amsterdam, 145-164

Rignot, E., Bamber, J., van den Broeke, M., Davis, C., Li, Y. and others (2008). Recent Antarctic ice mass loss from radar interferometry and regional climate modelling. *Nature Geoscience*, 1, 106-110

Robock, A., Marquardt, A., Kravitz, B. and Stenchikov, G. (2009). The Benefits, Risks, and Costs of Stratospheric Geoengineering. *Geophysical Research Letters*, 36, L19703

Rockström, J., Steffen, W., Noone, K., Persson, Å, Chapin, F.S. and others. (2009). A safe operating space for humanity. *Nature*, 461, 472-475.

Rosenzweig, C., Karoly, D., Vicarelli, M., Neofotis, P., Wu, Q. and others (2008). Attributing physical and biological impacts to anthropogenic climate change. *Nature*, 453, 353-357

Sachs, J.P., Sachse, D., Smittenberg, R.H., Zhang, Z., Battisti, D.S. and Golubic, S. (2009). Southward movement of the Pacific intertropical convergence zone AD 1400-1850. *Nature Geoscience*, 2, 519-525

Schuur, E.A.G., Bockheim, J., Canadell, J.G., Euskirchen, E., Field, C.B. and others. (2008). Vulnerability of permafrost carbon to climate change: implications for the global carbon cycle. *BioSciences*, 58(8), 701-714

Seager, R., Ting, M., Held, I., Kushnir, Y., Lu, J. and others (2007). Model Projections of an Imminent Transition to a More Arid Climate in Southwestern North America. *Science*, 316(5828), 1181-1184

Seidel, D.J., Fu, Q., Randel, W.J. and Reichler, T.J. (2008). Widening of the tropical belt in a changing climate. *Nature Geoscience*, 1, 21-24

Serreze, M.C., Holland, M.M. and Stroeve, J.C. (2007). Perspectives on the Arctic's shrinking sea-ice cover. *Science*, 315(5818), 1533-1536

Shindell, D.T. and Faluvegi, G. (2009). Climate response to regional radiative forcing during the twentieth century. *Nature Geoscience* 2, 294-300

Simmonds, I. and Keay, K. (2009). Extraordinary September Arctic sea ice reductions and their relationships with storm behavior over 1979-2008. *Geophysical Research Letters*, 36, L19715

Smith, J.B., Schneider, S.H., Oppenheimer, M., Yohee, W. and others (2009). Assessing dangerous climate change through an update of the Intergovernmental Panel on Climate Change (IPCC) "reasons for concern". *Proceedings of the National Academy of Sciences*, 106(11), 4133-4137

Solomon, S., Plattner, G.-K., Knutti, R. and Friedlingstein, P. (2009). Irreversible climate change due to carbon dioxide emissions. *Proceedings of the National Academy of Sciences*, 106(6), 1704-1709

Steig, E.J., Schneider, D.P., Scott, D.R., Mann, M.E., Josefino, C.C., and Shindell, D.T. (2009). Warming of the Antarctic ice-sheet surface since the 1957 International Geophysical Year. *Nature*, 457, 459-462

Steinacher, M., Joos, F., Frolicher, T., Plattner, G.-K. and Doney, S. (2009). Imminent ocean acidification in the Arctic projected with the NCAR global coupled carbon cycle-climate model. *Biogeosciences*, 6, 515-533

Tarnocai, C., Canadell, J.G., Mazhitova, G., Schuur, E.A.G., Kuhry P. and Zimov, S. (2009). Soil organic carbon stocks in the northern circumpolar permafrost region. *Global Biogeochemical Cycles*, 23, GB2023

Thompson, I., Mackey, B., McNulty, S. and Mosseler, A. (2009). Forest Resilience, Biodiversity, and Climate Change. *Technical Series No. 43* Secretariat of the Convention on Biological Diversity, Montreal

Vaughan, N.E., Lenton, T.M., Shepherd, J.G. (2009). Climate change mitigation. *Climatic Change*, 96(1-2), 29-43

Velicogna, I. (2009). Increasing rates of ice mass loss from the Greenland and Antarctic ice sheets revealed by GRACE. *Geophysical Research Letters*, 36, L19503

Veron, J., Hoegh-Guldberg, O., Lenton, T.M., Lough, J.M., Obura, D.O. and others (2009). The coral reef crisis. *Marine Pollution Bulletin*, 58(10), 1428-1436

Walter, K.M., Smith, L.C. and Chapin III, F.S. (2007). Methane bubbling from northern lakes. *Philosophical Transactions of the Royal Society A*, 365(1856), 1657-1676

Westbrook, G.K., Thatcher, K.E., Rohling, E.J., Piotrowski, A.M., Pälike, H. and others (2009). Escape of methane gas from the seabed along the West Spitsbergen continental margin. *Geophysical Research Letters*, 36, L15608

Wetlands International (2009) What are wetlands?. http://www.wetlands.org/Whatarewetlands/tabid/202/Default.aspx

WMO (2009). 2000-2009, The Warmest Decade. World Meteorological Organization. http://www.wmo.int/pages/mediacentre/press_releases/pr_869_en.html

Wood, H.L., Spicer, J.I. and Widdicombe, S. (2008). Ocean acidification may increase calcification rates, but at a cost. *Proceedings of the Royal Society*, 275, 1767-1773

Wootton, J.T., Pfister, C.A. and Forester, J.D. (2009). Dynamic patterns and ecological impacts of declining ocean pH in a high-resolution multi-year dataset. *Proceedings of the National Academy of Sciences*, 105(48), 18848-18853

World Bank (2009). *World Development Report 2010: Development and Climate Change*. World Bank, Washington, D.C.

Disasters and Conflicts

In 2009, progress was made towards understanding how climate change, environmental degradation, and mismanagement of natural resources increase vulnerability to both disasters and conflicts—and how sustainable natural resource management may reduce vulnerability to disasters and conflict while supporting peacebuilding.

Flood defences on the island of Padma Pakur, Bangladesh. Between the village and the water, trees have been planted to prevent erosion and act as a shield against the wind.
Credit: Espen Rasmussen/Panos

INTRODUCTION

In the field of disaster risk reduction, there is growing recognition of the need to consider the effects of climate change along with underlying factors that contribute to disasters, such as ecosystem degradation, rural poverty, vulnerable livelihoods, and unplanned or badly managed urban growth. At the June 2009 session of the Global Platform for Disaster Risk Reduction in Geneva, the United Nations Secretary-General Ban Ki-moon emphasized the links between disaster risk reduction, adaptation to climate change, and development. "Risk reduction is an investment," the Secretary-General told the Global Platform. "It is our first line of defence in adapting to climate change." By linking implementation of the 2005-2015 Hyogo Framework for Action with

a new climate agreement in Copenhagen "we can achieve a triple win—against poverty, against disasters, and against climate change" (Ban 2009). Representatives of 152 governments and 135 NGOs unanimously agreed at the Global Platform session that the underlying factors responsible for increases in disaster risk should be addressed with greater urgency (GPDRR 2009).

Increasing attention is also being given to natural resources in conflict prevention and peacebuilding. Important aspects of human security are directly related to access to natural resources and vulnerability to environmental change. Conversely, much environmental change results from human activities and conflict, directly or indirectly. Former Assistant UN Secretary-General Carolyn McAskie

has stated that "War-torn countries rich in natural resources face particular challenges in the stabilization and reconstruction of their societies, despite the apparent promise that natural resource wealth holds for peacebuilding and development. Where resource exploitation has triggered war, or served to impede peace, improving governance capacity to manage natural resources is a critical element of peacebuilding" (UNEP 2009a). This point of view is reflected in the Secretary-General's report on peacebuilding in the immediate aftermath of a conflict, which calls for more international and regional expertise to help identify natural resource-related risks and opportunities in order to strengthen and rebuild governance structures (UN 2009a). Disasters and conflicts destroy development gains and undermine achievement of the Millennium Development Goals (MDGs). Preventing disasters and conflicts, and reducing their impacts when they occur, is therefore at the top of the international agenda.

For a number of reasons, the links between disasters and conflicts on one hand, and poverty on the other, are especially strong in the developing world. Massive disaster risks are concentrated in developing countries, and the negative impacts of climate change tend to affect people who live in these countries disproportionately. Moreover, the risks of disasters and conflicts threaten current and future development gains in countries whose economic growth largely depends upon sustainable management of natural resources (ISDR 2009a).

Tools and methodologies to reduce disaster risks and support peacebuilding continue to be developed. If used wisely, they can generate enormous savings compared to the costs of conflicts and disasters, including humanitarian response. Measures proven to reduce disaster risk, such as sustainable natural resource management and effective use of early warning systems, often contribute to peacebuilding, development, and adaptation to climate change.

ENVIRONMENTAL DRIVERS OF DISASTER RISK

Disasters are linked to the environment in two important ways. First, environmental degradation often results in the loss of natural defences and environmental services, increasing communities' vulnerability to environmental hazards and weakening their resilience. Second, climate change is expected to exacerbate environmental degradation and increase disaster risk as storms, floods, and droughts become more frequent and more intense (Allison and others 2009, ISDR 2009a).

The rural poor, who are heavily dependent on natural resources, are those most severely affected by deteriorating environmental conditions. Sustainable natural resource management may reduce communities' vulnerability to disasters by mitigating the negative effects of environmental hazards and of climate change, while increasing resilience through the creation of livelihoods. For example, in Madagascar the economic benefits of protecting crops from annual floods using reforestation are valued at up to US$100 000 per year; in Viet Nam 12 000 hectares of mangroves cost only US$1 million to plant and protect, but will reduce the costs of sea-dyke maintenance by more than US$7 million per year (ISDR 2009a). The mangroves are expected to help cope with climate change impacts, such as rising sea level and storm surges, as well as stimulate employment (PaCFA 2009). Not only does sustainable natural resource management reduce the risk of disasters, it also provides significant co-benefits in terms of climate change adaptation and meeting the MDGs.

Climate change: reconfiguring disaster risk

In 2009, progress in linking disaster risk reduction and climate change adaptation through sustainable natural resource management was made at the international policy level. Five years after its adoption, the Hyogo Framework for Action forms part of a growing number of international declarations and agreements that recognize the links between disaster risk reduction, poverty alleviation, and climate change adaptation (ISDR 2009a). Scientists and others are engaged in assessing the relative benefits of various financial instruments and determining the best ways to scale up local initiatives to reduce disaster risk. There is already a consensus among policy-makers and scientists that an effective way for governments to reduce the risk of disasters is to incorporate disaster risk reduction into development and climate change adaptation planning.

The Intergovernmental Panel on Climate Change (IPCC) Fourth Assessment Report, released in 2007, concluded that many observed changes in extremes, such as more frequent heavy precipitation events and longer, more intense droughts, are consistent with warming of the climate system (IPCC 2007). More recently, research appears to confirm that changes have occurred even faster than predicted by some climate models, raising the possibility that future changes will be more severe than previously thought. It is predicted that there will be more very heavy precipitation in wet regions, and more frequent and severe droughts in dry ones, due to the intensification of the global hydrological cycle associated with climate change (Allison and others 2009, UNEP 2009b).

Speaking at the African Union summit in Kampala, Uganda, in October 2009, John Holmes, the UN Under-Secretary-General for Humanitarian Affairs and Emergency Relief Coordination, observed that "climate change is already increasing the frequency and intensity of extreme hazard events, particularly floods, storms, and droughts" (IRIN 2009b). He pointed out that Africa has been, and is expected to continue to be, disproportionately affected by climate change, and that climate change could potentially be responsible for millions of new refugees and internally displaced persons (IDPs) in the next 12 years. According to the International Disaster Database (EM-DAT) maintained by the World Health Organization Collaborating Centre for Research on the Epidemiology of Disasters, 99 per cent of its

Hurricane Ida swept through El Salvador in November 2009, killing 184 people, displacing 14 000, and damaging 25 000 hectares of crops. In San Salvador, the capital, people look at damage to their homes.
Credit: Reuters/ William Bonilla

104 internationally reported disasters in 2008 were climate-related (EM-DAT 2009, IRIN 2009b).

Globally, the impact of increases in hydro-meteorological hazards as a result of climate change will vary, reflecting the uneven distribution of risk. Developing countries, where most of the risk is concentrated, will continue to be affected disproportionately (Peduzzi and Deichmann 2009). A study on the vulnerability to storms of 577 coastal cities in 84 developing countries predicted that climate change will increase the risk of storm surges in three of these cities in particular: Manila (the Philippines), Alexandria (Egypt), and Lagos (Nigeria) (Dasgupta and others 2009).

Adapting to climate change by reducing disaster risk

Synergies have been identified between disaster risk reduction and adaptation to climate change across a wide range of policy frameworks and practical methodologies. Drought-tolerant crop varieties and hydroponic aquaculture can reduce communities' vulnerability to environmental hazards such as droughts, and floods. Disaster reduction measures are being introduced to help communities adapt to gradual climate change, for example by improving water storage infrastructure in the Andes and the Himalayas, where people are threatened by both floods and droughts as glaciers melt (UNFCCC 2008a) (**Box 1**). If adaptation and disaster risk reduction measures are to be more effective, however, they should be integrated into national policies through sustainable development initiatives; establishment of transparent and effective governing structures; promotion of cross-sectoral dialogue and cooperation; expansion of existing and indigenous knowledge and tools; budget integration; and institutional capacity building (UNFCCC 2008a).

The IPCC is preparing a special report on synergies between disaster risk reduction and climate change adaptation. This report, *Managing the Risks of Extreme Events and Disasters to Advance Climate Change Adaptation*, will be published in late 2011. Preliminary findings indicate that climate-related disasters represent a major source of risk for the poor in developing countries, and that losses due to these disasters are a major threat to achievement of the MDGs. Although the range of risks covered by climate change adaptation is not restricted to disasters, disaster risk reduction can be considered a first line of defense in adapting to climate change. This is especially true in the most vulnerable countries in Africa and other parts of the world, including least developed countries (LDCs) and small island developing states (SIDS), which are experiencing drought, desertification, and floods (Nassef 2009). A scoping study for the forthcoming IPCC report stresses that successful integration of climate change adaptation, disaster risk reduction, and development will require collaboration among experts in each of these fields, as well as new systems with which to share experiences and link knowledge (Nassef 2009).

Risks compounded by societal factors and geographic exposure

Global disaster risk is increasing due to environmental hazards such as storms and floods, and resulting in an increasing economic loss risk. Disaster-related economic loss risk has grown much more rapidly than the disaster-related mortality risk (ISDR 2009a). In many instances, these losses stem from development in vulnerable areas. They are often a result of poor land use management or poor enforcement of building regulations.

Box 1: Securing Peru's glacier-fed water resources in a changing climate

Many of the glaciers in the Andes are already affected by a changing climate. The Cusco and Apurimac regions of Peru's Andean highlands are particularly vulnerable to climate change. Communities are struggling to cope with climate variability, drought, changes in the quality and quantity of glacier-fed water resources, and extreme cold. In these regions 40 per cent of the population suffers from malnutrition, while the basic needs of more than 75 per cent are not being met.

In 2009, regional and national authorities, overseas development agencies, and NGOs began implementing the Climate Change Adaptation Programme (PACC), which integrates water management, disaster prevention, and food security. This programme relies on a combination of local and scientific knowledge. Examples of suitable adaptation measures include increasing the number and size of water storage reserves to take account of glacier loss, introducing different crop varieties capable of withstanding extreme weather conditions, and integrating specific disaster prevention measures in regional planning. In addition, new information systems designed for regional and local users will raise communities' awareness of climate hazards and the measures being taken to address them.

Sources: Salzmann and others (2009), SDC (2009), Vergara, W. and others (2009), Huggel and others (2008)

The Puca Glacier in Peru's Andean highlands.

Credit: Steve Schmidt

Extreme water-related environmental events 2009

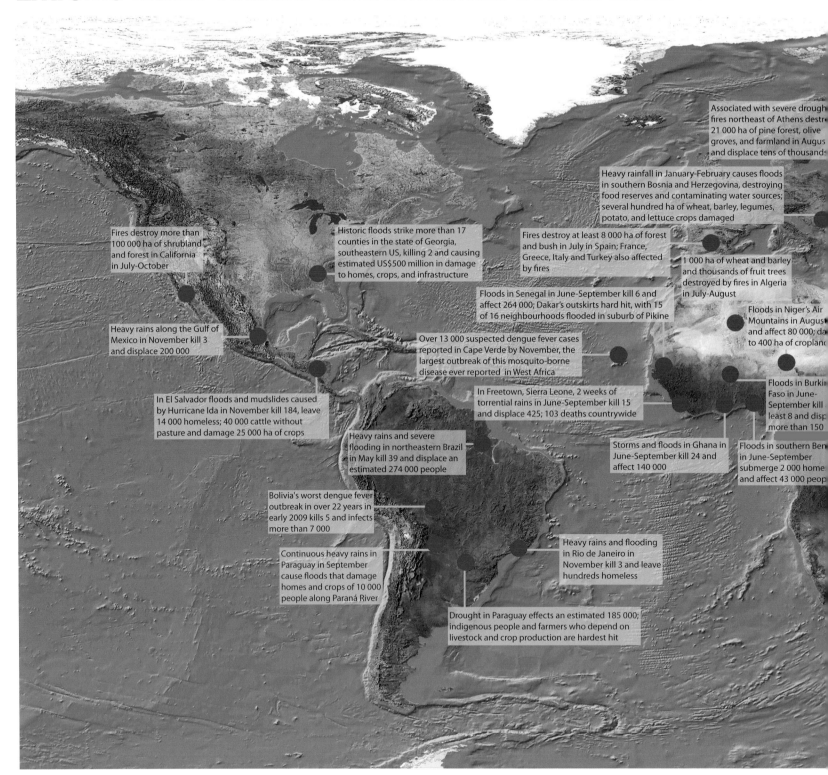

Fires destroy more than 100 000 ha of shrubland and forest in California in July-October

Historic floods strike more than 17 counties in the state of Georgia, southeastern US, killing 2 and causing estimated US$500 million in damage to homes, crops, and infrastructure

Fires destroy at least 8 000 ha of forest and bush in July in Spain; France, Greece, Italy and Turkey also affected by fires

Associated with severe drough fires northeast of Athens destr 21 000 ha of pine forest, olive groves, and farmland in Augus and displace tens of thousand

Heavy rainfall in January-February causes floods in southern Bosnia and Herzegovina, destroying food reserves and contaminating water sources; several hundred ha of wheat, barley, legumes, potato, and lettuce crops damaged

1 000 ha of wheat and barley and thousands of fruit trees destroyed by fires in Algeria in July-August

Floods in Senegal in June-September kill 6 and affect 264 000; Dakar's outskirts hard hit, with 15 of 16 neighbourhoods flooded in suburb of Pikine

Floods in Niger's Air Mountains in Augus and affect 80 000; da to 400 ha of croplan

Heavy rains along the Gulf of Mexico in November kill 3 and displace 200 000

Over 13 000 suspected dengue fever cases reported in Cape Verde by November, the largest outbreak of this mosquito-borne disease ever reported in West Africa

Floods in Burki Faso in June-September kill least 8 and disp more than 150

In El Salvador floods and mudslides caused by Hurricane Ida in November kill 184, leave 14 000 homeless; 40 000 cattle without pasture and damage 25 000 ha of crops

In Freetown, Sierra Leone, 2 weeks of torrential rains in June-September kill 15 and displace 425; 103 deaths countrywide

Heavy rains and severe flooding in northeastern Brazil in May kill 39 and displace an estimated 274 000 people

Storms and floods in Ghana in June-September kill 24 and affect 140 000

Floods in southern Ben in June-September submerge 2 000 home and affect 43 000 peop

Bolivia's worst dengue fever outbreak in over 22 years in early 2009 kills 5 and infects more than 7 000

Continuous heavy rains in Paraguay in September cause floods that damage homes and crops of 10 000 people along Paraná River

Heavy rains and flooding in Rio de Janeiro in November kill 3 and leave hundreds homeless

Drought in Paraguay effects an estimated 185 000; indigenous people and farmers who depend on livestock and crop production are hardest hit

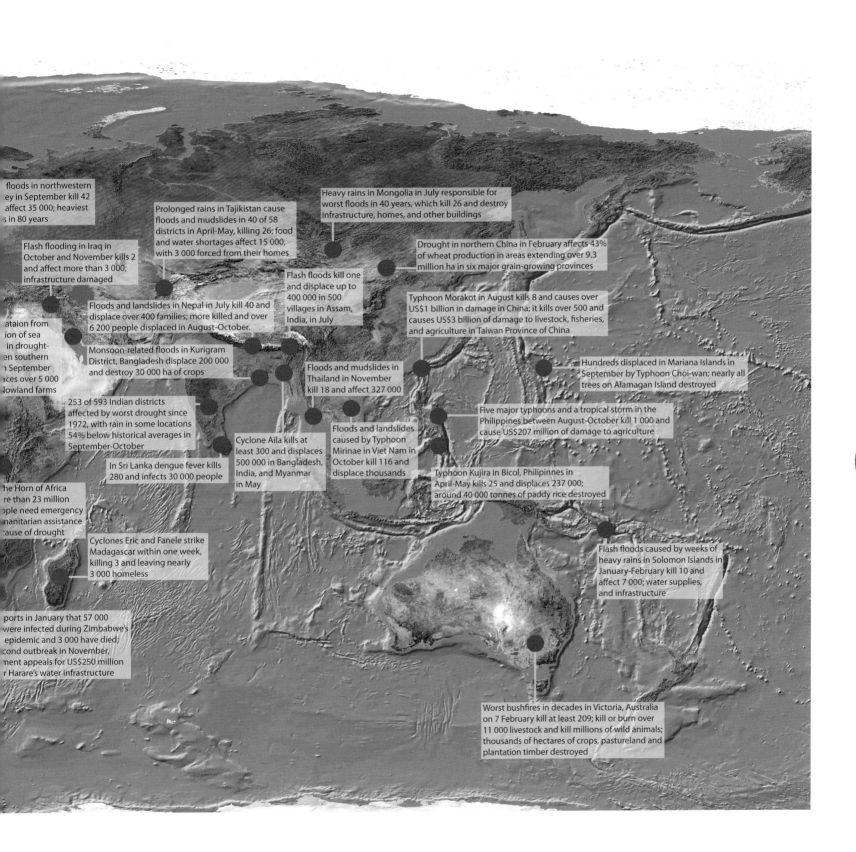

floods in northwestern
... y in September kill 42
... affect 35 000; heaviest
... s in 80 years

Flash flooding in Iraq in
October and November kills 2
and affect more than 3 000;
infrastructure damaged

Prolonged rains in Tajikistan cause
floods and mudslides in 40 of 58
districts in April-May, killing 26; food
and water shortages affect 15 000,
with 3 000 forced from their homes

Heavy rains in Mongolia in July responsible for
worst floods in 40 years, which kill 26 and destroy
infrastructure, homes, and other buildings

Drought in northern China in February affects 43%
of wheat production in areas extending over 9.3
million ha in six major grain-growing provinces

Flash floods kill one
and displace up to
400 000 in 500
villages in Assam,
India, in July

Floods and landslides in Nepal in July kill 40 and
displace over 400 families; more killed and over
6 200 people displaced in August-October.

... ataion from
... ion of sea
... in drought-
... n southern
... September
... ces over 5 000
... lowland farms

Monsoon-related floods in Kurigram
District, Bangladesh displace 200 000
and destroy 30 000 ha of crops

Typhoon Morakot in August kills 8 and causes over
US$1 billion in damage in China; it kills over 500 and
causes US$3 billion of damage to livestock, fisheries,
and agriculture in Taiwan Province of China

Floods and mudslides in
Thailand in November
kill 18 and affect 327 000

Hundreds displaced in Mariana Islands in
September by Typhoon Choi-wan; nearly all
trees on Alamagan Island destroyed

253 of 593 Indian districts
affected by worst drought since
1972, with rain in some locations
54% below historical averages in
September-October

Cyclone Aila kills at
least 300 and displaces
500 000 in Bangladesh,
India, and Myanmar
in May

Floods and landslides
caused by Typhoon
Mirinae in Viet Nam in
October kill 116 and
displace thousands

Five major typhoons and a tropical storm in the
Philippines between August-October kill 1 000 and
cause US$207 million of damage to agriculture

In Sri Lanka dengue fever kills
280 and infects 30 000 people

Typhoon Kujira in Bicol, Philipinnes in
April-May kills 25 and displaces 237 000;
around 40 000 tonnes of paddy rice destroyed

... he Horn of Africa
... re than 23 million
... ple need emergency
... manitarian assistance
... cause of drought

Cyclones Eric and Fanele strike
Madagascar within one week,
killing 3 and leaving nearly
3 000 homeless

Flash floods caused by weeks of
heavy rains in Solomon Islands in
January-February kill 10 and
affect 7 000; water supplies,
and infrastructure

... ports in January that 57 000
... were infected during Zimbabwe's
... epidemic and 3 000 have died;
... cond outbreak in November,
... ment appeals for US$250 million
... r Harare's water infrastructure

Worst bushfires in decades in Victoria, Australia
on 7 February kill at least 209; kill or burn over
11 000 livestock and kill millions of wild animals;
thousands of hectares of crops, pastureland and
plantation timber destroyed

For example, landslide risk can be heightened when trees are removed from hillsides (Bathurst and others 2009, Karsli and others 2009, Mafian and others 2009). Some have argued that a lack of appropriate land use regulations contributed to the large number of landslide-related casualties in Taiwan Province of China caused by Typhoon Morakot in October 2009 (Yeh 2009).

New research has attempted to quantify the economic costs of disasters in terms of human capital. The findings reveal that impacts on 'intangible assets' may be even more important to a country's long-term growth prospects than those on tangible assets. Certain types of low-intensity disasters could theoretically benefit a country's economy if they increased incentives to invest in human capital (López 2009). However, repeated exposure to even low-intensity disasters has been shown to undermine communities' resilience (ISDR 2009a).

A World Bank study has demonstrated that severe disasters never have positive economic impacts (Fomby and others 2009). Extreme events may erase development gains, as the poorest communities are frequently exposed to climate risks due to their physical location, their exposure to multiple environmental hazards, and prevailing socio-economic conditions (Fomby and others 2009). Women, who make up 67 per cent of the world's poor, are disproportionately affected by extreme events. During the September-October 2009 floods in the Philippines, an estimated 14 000 pregnant women were exposed to septic conditions in evacuation camps (IRIN 2009a). One reason women have a higher flood mortality risk than men is that fewer of them know how to swim (UNFCCC 2008a).

Countries with higher incomes and more advanced economies tend to have lower mortality and sustain smaller losses, measured against their total wealth, than countries with lower incomes (Peduzzi and Deichmann 2009). High-income countries account for 39 per cent of exposure to tropical cyclones, but only 1 per cent of the mortality risk; low-income countries account for 13 per cent of exposure to these storms and 81 per cent of the mortality risk. Thus, if Japan and the Philippines experience cyclones of the same magnitude, mortality in the Philippines is likely to be 17 times higher than in Japan although 1.4 times as many

people are exposed in Japan (ISDR 2009a).

The relatively higher risk of disasters affecting poorer communities is confirmed by disaster trend analyses of decades of data. A review of 8 866 'mega-disasters' worldwide found that 0.26 per cent of these events accounted for 78.2 per cent of disaster-related mortalities, mainly in developing countries (ISDR 2009a). This finding is consistent with other disaster trend analyses, which indicate that high mortality and economic losses are concentrated geographically and are associated with a relatively small number of disasters (Peduzzi and Deichmann 2009). However, an analysis of 38 years of data from 12 low- and middle-income countries—Argentina, Bolivia, Colombia, Costa Rica, Ecuador, India (States of Orissa and Tamil Nadu), Iran, Mexico, Nepal, Peru, Sri Lanka, and Venezuela—shows that vulnerable communities' exposure to climate-related hazards of moderate intensity is expanding rapidly (ISDR 2009a).

ENVIRONMENTAL DRIVERS OF ARMED CONFLICT
Although there is still some debate concerning the significance of resource scarcity versus resource abundance, 40 per cent of intra-state armed

conflicts have been shown to be directly linked to competition over natural resources (Binningsbø and Rustad 2009, HIIK 2009). In recent years, changes in the nature of armed conflicts—including intra-state conflicts over natural resources in countries such as Afghanistan, Sri Lanka, and Sudan—have given rise to more frequent complex emergencies in conflict zones (**Table 1**).

A wide range of research approaches, from game theory models to statistics, and micro- and macroeconomics, have focused on the potential role of various factors in conflict and peacebuilding. While gaps and biases have been identified in both the empirical data and case studies (Collier and others 2008), researchers have discovered new trends and challenged conventional wisdom by focusing on the drivers of conflict.

Resource scarcity and high-value resources
Many of the risks that environmental change poses to human security have been identified, but because of poor natural resource management these risks have not been adequately managed. The scale of consumption and pollution in modern, energy-intensive societies has contributed to

Table 1: Intra-state armed conflicts over resources

COUNTRY	DURATION	RESOURCES
Afghanistan	1978-2001	Gems, timber, opium
Angola	1975-2002	Oil, diamonds
Burma	1949-	Timber, tin, gems, opium
Cambodia	1978-1997	Timber, gems
Colombia	1984-	Oil, gold, coca, timber, emeralds
Congo, Dem Rep. of the	1996-1998, 1998-2003, 2003-2008	Copper, coltan, diamonds, gold, cobalt, timber, tin
Congo, Rep. of	1997-	Oil
Côte d'Ivoire	2002-2007	Diamonds, cocoa, cotton
Indonesia – Aceh	1975-2006	Timber, natural gas
Indonesia – West Papua	1969-	Copper, gold, timber
Liberia	1989-2003	Timber, diamonds, iron, palm oil, cocoa, coffee, rubber, gold
Nepal	1996-2007	Yarsa gumba (medicinal fungus)
Papua New Guinea – Bougainville	1989-1998	Copper, gold
Peru	1980-1995	Coca
Senegal – Casamance	1982-	Timber, cashew nuts
Sierra Leone	1991-2000	Diamonds, cocoa, coffee
Somalia	1991	Fish, charcoal
Sudan	1983-2005	Oil

The table shows the duration of resource-related intra-state armed conflicts between 1975 and 2008. These 20 conflicts occurred in 18 countries and involved resources such as oil, crops, timber, gems, and minerals.
Source: Adapted from UNEP (2009a)

deforestation, biodiversity loss, depletion of fish stocks, land degradation, water pollution and scarcity, degradation of coastal and marine ecosystems, and contamination of people, plants, and animals by chemicals and radioactive substances (Matthew and others 2009).

Conflict-prone societies tend to become more dependent on natural resources when low-level violence and the threat of armed conflict discourage investment, for example in manufacturing (Lujala 2009). Societies characterized by diverse livelihoods and strong economic growth are less likely to enter into conflict (Brunnschweiler and Bulte 2009).

Recent findings confirm that both resource scarcity and resource abundance can lead to conflicts (Brunnschweiler and Bulte 2009, Buhaug and others 2008). Statistical analyses of intra-state conflicts and types of resources, such as gemstones, oil, gas, and crops used in making illegal drugs, suggest that the location and type of resources within a country strongly affect these conflicts' intensity and duration. Even if gemstones, oil, or gas are not being extracted, their presence within a conflict zone can significantly increase the conflict's duration and can nearly double the number of conflict-related deaths. When the same resources are located outside the conflict zone, their impact on the conflict has been found to be negligible (Lujala 2010, Lujala 2009).

Ultimately, research suggests that resource allocation, especially resource scarcity, is only one of many factors that may lead to intra-state conflicts (Matthew and others 2009, Buhaug and others 2008, Theisen 2008). A household's economic status and exposure to violence may explain participation in intra-state armed conflicts. The poorer a household is at the start of the conflict, the more likely it is that household members will support an armed rebellion; the greater the risk of violence, the more likely it is that a household will support the rebels (Justino 2009). A large body of empirical research has linked low per capita income and inequitable distribution of power and resources to conflict because of the way these factors impact people's incentives to support, or even join, rebel factions (Justino 2009).

State and institutional capacity to manage natural resources is fundamentally linked to conflict risk. Since this capacity is often measured indirectly using proxy data, links between governance capacity, resources, and conflict can be difficult to quantify. To account for the impact of state capacity and political processes on post-conflict peace, experts rely upon factors such as per capita GDP, the degree of a country's democracy, the timing of post-conflict elections, and the degree of regional autonomy granted in constitutions (Polity IV Project 2009, Collier and others 2008). It is also difficult to separate state capacity from natural resource endowment, as a state's capacity may be affected by its natural resource base and rents captured from resource extraction (Lujala 2010). An oil-exporting state with a strong central government may reap the majority of the profits from its oil production and then use them to increase its institutional capacity.

Conservation, conflict, and peacebuilding

Depending on the context, conservation programmes may spark, sustain, or be interrupted by conflict (Hammill and others 2009). They may unintentionally engender conflict if they aggravate prevailing social or economic tensions stemming from political marginalization, equity issues, or ethnic tensions. Conservation programmes may also unintentionally sustain an ongoing conflict when they deprive people of their livelihoods or are manipulated by conflict participants. In the eastern Democratic Republic of the Congo, for example, armed groups have been known to target conservation beneficiaries who receive compensation in the form of cash or food. Violent conflicts often interrupt existing conservation activities both directly and indirectly–directly by destroying habitats, killing animals, and overexploiting natural resources, and indirectly by making conservation work too dangerous and scaring off sources of funding (Hammill and others 2009).

Conservation activities can be used to support peacebuilding when they address the underlying causes of conflict, or when they repair ecosystems and strengthen livelihoods. It has been suggested that the presence of scarce water resources, if successfully managed, can prevent conflict since economic interdependence gives countries a vested interest in each other's future and encourages a level of mutual trust (Hammill and others 2009, Tir and Ackerman 2009). Because global climate change and population pressure are expected to increase the strain on water resources in the coming decades, countries have a strong incentive to address transboundary water disputes before they escalate (Tir and Ackerman 2009, Buhaug and others 2008).

Armed conflict as a threat to the environment

An emerging field of study, 'warfare ecology', considers the complex and cascading effects of conflicts on the environment from pre-conflict through post-conflict reconstruction. A better understanding of the impacts of conflict-related activities on ecosystems would benefit policy-makers in several ways. For example, it could be used to incorporate ecosystem protection measures into weapons manufacturing, live fire training, tactical planning, monitoring of the movement of refugees and internally displaced persons, and rehabilitation projects (Machlis and Hanson 2008) (**Box 2**).

Box 2: The 'greening' of peacekeeping operations

Credit: UN DPKO

The United Nations Department of Peacekeeping Operations (DPKO) has designated staff at its headquarters and field bases to examine ways to reduce its environmental footprint. In addition, recognizing the protective role of ecosystems, UN peacekeeping troops have undertaken reforestation and ecological rehabilitation projects. They have also drilled water wells, taken part in environmental clean-up, and responded to disasters. Critics insist that these troops are already stretched thin, often experience difficulty in protecting civilians, and should not be used for environmental projects. Supporters argue that such activities create closer ties with local communities and help protect these communities from environmental hazards.

Source: Gronewald (2009)

The knowledge acquired from warfare ecology may also strengthen the implementation of international environmental agreements during conflicts. Due to gaps in existing legal structures and weak enforcement of legal instruments designed to protect the environment, ecosystems continue to sustain heavy damage during conflicts. This damage could have lasting impacts on societies. Depredation of ecosystem services during conflicts may hinder post-conflict peacebuilding and delay economic recovery (UNEP 2009b, Machlis and Hanson 2008).

Historical analysis of conflict trends suggests that stronger enforcement of international environmental laws, more effective governance, and environmental advocacy are badly needed. In the second half of the 20th century, more than 90 per cent of major armed conflicts took place in countries that contained biodiversity hotspots and more than 80 per cent occurred directly within a hotspot area (Hanson and others 2009). Hotspots, which cover a mere 2.3 per cent of the planet's surface, are sensitive to human disturbance and harbour at least 50 per cent of known vascular plants and 42 per cent of vertebrate animal species. Conflicts therefore present a very real threat to biodiversity (Hanson and others 2009).

More research is needed on the application of international environmental law during armed conflicts. Much existing research dates to the 1990s, following the 1990-1991 Gulf War. Since then, changes in international environmental law and conflict trends, including the increase in the number of intra-state conflicts, have made it necessary to clarify when and how international environmental law applies in this new context (UNEP 2009c). For example, Articles 35(3) and 55(1) of the Additional Protocol I to the 1949 Geneva Conventions (1977) prohibit "widespread, long-term and severe damage to the natural environment," but new research has shown that this prohibition has failed to protect the environment during conflicts due to the lack of well-defined and stringent thresholds for environmental damage (UNEP 2009c).

Environment and peacebuilding

Emerging trends in insecurity blur the lines between armed conflict and crime, and between community, national, and global security. Recent analyses have confirmed that societies emerging from conflict are more prone to armed violence than others, and more likely to suffer from escalating armed violence in rapidly urbanizing cities and towns. State actors are also more likely to collude with non-state criminal groups and enterprises in post-conflict societies (OECD 2009). These conditions, in turn, explain why roughly 40 per cent of these societies revert to conflict within a decade (Collier and others 2008). The short-term priorities of post-conflict resource management are likely to differ from peacetime objectives. Time horizons tend to be shorter, and the approaches that normally apply in sustainable natural resource management are frequently unfeasible in post-conflict situations (Bruch and others 2009). Actors and funding sources are also different, while government capacity tends to be especially weak. Given these distinctions, the effective management of natural resources during peacebuilding requires governments, NGOs, and conflict-affected communities to take account of the ways in which post-conflict and peacetime resource management activities differ (Bruch and others 2009).

Quantitative research on the reversion to conflict in post-conflict societies has found that peace often depends on an external military presence supporting a gradual economic recovery, rather than on strictly political solutions (Collier and others 2008). In many post-conflict countries, such as Liberia and the Central African Republic, economic growth is tied to management of resources like timber or oil. Researchers have also found a strong relationship between the magnitude of post-conflict risk and the extent of economic inequality within communities. They therefore suggest that resources be allocated in inverse proportion to people's incomes at the end of a conflict (Collier and others 2008).

The importance to peacebuilding of equity in the allocation, access to, and ownership of natural resources raises a number of governance and transparency issues, such as how to manage official and informal concessions. It also emphasizes the role of sustainable natural resource management. Intra-state conflicts over natural resources are twice as likely to relapse into conflict as those that are not. Only 25 per cent of peace negotiations incorporate resource management mechanisms, although studies indicate that the parties may achieve a more durable peace if sustainable natural resource management is explicitly addressed in negotiated settlements (Binningsbø and Rustad 2009) (**Box 3**).

Natural resources have proven crucial in effective post-conflict peacebuilding and recovery. In any given context, they may play a role in one or more of the following: negotiation of peace agreements; disarmament, demobilization, and reintegration (DDR) programmes; sustaining the livelihoods of refugees and IDPs; supporting governance, economic growth, and revenue generation; and establishing confidence among formerly warring parties (Bruch and others 2009, Conca and others 2009). The Government of Rwanda, for example, has embarked upon an ecotourism venture with the Governments of Uganda and the Democratic Republic of the Congo which allows tourists to view mountain gorillas in protected zones within each country. These countries formalized their cooperation by signing the Declaration of Goma in 2005 and the Rubavu Ministerial Declaration for Greater Virunga Transboundary Collaboration in 2008, demonstrating that transboundary resource management can serve as a vehicle for regional confidence-building (UNEP 2009a).

Although cooperative resource management can contribute to peacebuilding by building trust between conflicting parties, this approach is used too infrequently or without proper understanding (Binningsbø and Rustad 2009, Conca and others 2009). Most legal and policy institutions have yet to incorporate sustainable natural resource management into their operational policies or guidance material. Despite decades of experience using natural resources to facilitate disarmament, demobilization, and reintegration, the UN's *Operational Guide* for DDR does not yet address natural resources (Bruch and others 2009).

NEW TOOLS FOR DEALING WITH DISASTERS AND CONFLICTS

To mitigate disaster and conflict risks, the most promising tools are integrated into existing policy and institutional structures. Several factors and approaches that are common to disaster risk reduction, conflict prevention, and peacebuilding deserve closer attention because they are examples of policy breakthroughs or innovative use of new technologies and methodologies.

Box 3: Liberia's forest concessions

Sustainable natural resource management can strengthen governance and justice in post-conflict societies. Following Liberia's civil war, the National Transitional Government established the independent Forest Concession Review Committee (FCRC). In an effort to uncover corruption, its oversight has been expanded to examining past forest concessions. A partnership of government, international organizations, and NGOs, the FCRC was established to support the rehabilitation and reform of Liberia's forestry sector and enhance cooperation and coordination of activities in Liberia for the promotion of sustainable forest management. The FCRC has been at the forefront of efforts to reintroduce the rule of law in Liberia. Because of its initial success, it has been cited by experts as a model for reviews of other concessions and for similar activities in other countries.

Source: Bruch and others (2009)
Credit: The Goldman Environmental Prize/ Silas Siakor

New governance paradigms for sustainable natural resource management

The most effective way for countries to reduce disaster risk is to incorporate a disaster risk reduction platform into their development and climate change adaptation strategies (ISDR 2009a). Such a platform should recognize and build upon the fact that natural systems like floodplains, forests, mangroves, and coral reefs can reduce the adverse impacts of natural hazards. Although natural systems cannot provide total protection, they play a role in reducing the number of lives lost and the economic costs of hydro-meteorological hazards. Many indigenous communities understand the link between declining environmental quality and their increasing vulnerability to hazards, and therefore use ecosystem management to reduce their disaster risk. Often these links have not been made explicit in local planning, or governments have not effectively controlled the causes of environmental decline (Randall and others 2010, Mumba 2008).

Equitable and transparent governance can be a deterrent to conflict, and instruments that give state actors the proper incentives deserve closer inspection. For example, the Extractive Industries Transparency Initiative (EITI) and the Kimberly Process certification scheme, adopted to prevent trade in conflict diamonds, have induced greater transparency in participating governments. Involvement in these programmes by governments has allowed greater participation by civil society organizations that serve as watchdogs, monitor enforcement, and identify opportunities for stronger compliance (Global Witness 2009).

Programmes such as EITI also require participating governments—often those of post-conflict countries—to undertake reform and implement regulations. Such measures, in turn, may generate co-benefits by strengthening state institutions and supporting sustainable management policies. These programmes do not work in isolation, but they demonstrate how civil society and the private sector can complement peacebuilding (EC 2005, EITI 2009a). A more recent example of integrated peacebuilding is the plan for the Central African Republic, adopted in 2009, which calls for natural resources to be managed within a protected environment in a manner that benefits local communities. This plan incorporates sound, transparent management of energy and natural resources with the support of the UN Peacebuilding Commission, which will provide training and technical assistance and support government efforts to establish environmental protection agencies and to respect international standards such as those of EITI (UN 2009b).

Protecting vulnerable livelihoods by managing financial risk

Droughts, floods, and other climate-related hazards have always presented a challenge to communities whose livelihoods depend on sustainable natural resource management, such as farmers, herders, or fishermen. Particularly in the developing world, where droughts or floods may cause widespread defaults, farmers often do not have access to the credit they need to purchase improved seeds and fertilizers. Index-based insurance schemes—typically based on rainfall, temperature, humidity, or average crop yields rather than damages—and other risk-transfer instruments may protect farmers from such losses and strengthen vulnerable rural livelihoods in the face of climate change (Hellmuth and others 2009).

At the Thirteenth Conference of the Parties to the United Nations Framework Convention on Climate Change (UNFCCC) in December 2007, countries agreed on the Bali Action Plan, which identifies risk sharing and risk transfer as means of adapting to climate change. Since then, studies have analysed new and existing instruments. Risk sharing and risk transfer can reduce the risk of disasters under certain conditions, but these approaches are only part of the solution. They are most effective when implemented along with other disaster risk reduction measures (Warner and others 2009, UNFCCC 2008b).

Risk-transfer instruments have limitations. They do not prevent the loss of lives or assets, and they are not always the most appropriate means of managing risks in terms of cost-effectiveness or affordability (Warner and others 2009). Furthermore, most experts agree that, thus far, there has been too little experience to determine how to use risk-transfer instruments effectively (Hellmuth and others 2009, Warner and others 2009).

Where there is coordinated public and private action, and international support, insurance can provide a layer of security to vulnerable people and countries. Index-based micro-insurance has extended financial coverage for disaster risks to low-income households in Bolivia, Ethiopia, India, Malawi, Mongolia, Sudan, and Viet Nam (Hellmuth and others 2009, Warner and others 2009). Experience with the world's first multi-country, index-based catastrophe insurance pool, the Caribbean Catastrophe Risk Insurance Facility (CCRIF), launched in 2007, suggests that substantial improvements in disaster risk reduction are possible, but it will take time for them to be realized and to meet the needs of local communities. By 2009, member countries had paid more than US$21 million into the pool, supported by an additional US$65 million from donor countries (CCRIF 2009, Christian Aid 2009).

New technologies for early warning

New research suggests that early warning systems for disasters and conflicts could be improved if they were combined (Meier 2010). In particular, conflict early warning systems could provide reliable early warning more effectively if they incorporated relevant environmental indicators such as vegetation and natural resource use into their regular reporting. By adding this information to existing data for countries in the Horn of Africa, one pilot study has found that available vegetation is directly proportional to social triggers of conflict among pastoral communities (Meier 2010).

New research confirms the value of geographic information systems (GIS) in analysing and preventing intra-state conflicts where subnational environmental, socio-economic, and demographic factors play a key role (Stephenne and others 2009). GIS platforms are especially useful for integrating multidisciplinary data sets (**Figure 1**).

Basic geographic concepts such as contiguity, proximity, and diffusion in space and time are beginning to be used to shed new light on relationships among conflict drivers. Satellite imagery, for example, can be incorporated to monitor illicit revenue-generating activities such as diamond extraction in Sierra Leone or timber harvesting in Liberia, or population movements,

Figure 1: Using GIS to map multiple hazards

Regional distribution of multiple hazards mortality risk

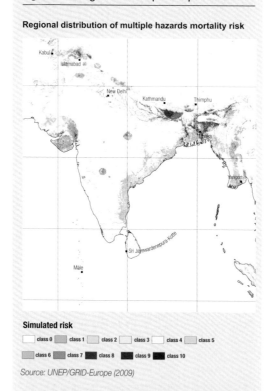

Simulated risk

class 0   class 1   class 2   class 3   class 4   class 5

class 6   class 7   class 8   class 9   class 10

Source: UNEP/GRID-Europe (2009)

This map is a close-up of the multiple global mortality risk analysis produced by UNEP for the *Global Assessment Report on Disaster Risk Reduction*. It is based on GIS hazards modelling of floods, tropical cyclones, landslides, and earthquakes, using geophysical and meteorological data and an intersecting population distribution model at 1 x 1 km resolution. Simulated risk categories range from lowest risk (class 0) to highest risk (class 10). The vulnerability analysis includes parameters such as governance, poverty, and urban growth identified using multiple regression statistical analysis.

Sources: ISDR (2009a), Peduzzi and others (2009)

land cover, and changes in rainfall patterns (Stephenne and others 2009, UNEP 2009d).

Multi-hazard GIS analysis can also incorporate data from climate models to develop future risk profiles. This knowledge can be used to inform the design of key infrastructure or help insurers assign a price to low-probability risks associated with high loss potential (UNFCCC 2008b). New studies incorporating climate model predictions into GIS have warned of potential food security crises in the coming decades (Battisti and Naylor 2009, Liu and others 2008).

Despite proposed improvements to early warning systems, practitioners warn that such tools need to be made more user-friendly (Nerlander 2009). Disaster preparedness and planning should consider the requirements of the target audience, so that warnings captured by satellites, computer models, or other technologies are received by the appropriate communities and then acted upon (IFRC 2009b) (**Box 4**). Citing the failure of early warnings to produce adequate humanitarian response to slow-onset disasters, both recent, such as the Niger food crisis in 2004-2006, and less recent, such as the drought and famine in the Sahel in 1972-1974, some of the research suggests that early warning systems are calibrated to meet the demands of donors rather than those of disaster-affected communities (Glenzer 2007). As a result of inherent structural flaws that dilute and displace authority and accountability, early warning systems have had only partial success. Too often, too little aid has been delivered too late to help disaster-affected communities (Glenzer 2007).

Use of local knowledge

One promising development in early warning systems, and in approaches to climate change adaptation generally, results from the integration of new technology, indigenous knowledge, and communications systems. Researchers supporting the African Monsoon Multidisciplinary Analysis project are collaborating with farmers to improve their adaptive capacity through combining the farmers' knowledge with improved regional climate models and modifying agricultural strategies (Mertz and others 2009). A follow-up analysis of the earthquake and tsunami that struck the Solomon Islands in 2007 found that the indigenous community of Tapurai suffered fewer casualties

Box 4: Threat and risk mapping and analysis project in Sudan

In July 2009, the United Nations Development Programme's (UNDP) Threat and Risk Mapping and Analysis project expanded its operations to all the states of Southern Sudan, after successfully establishing operations in all those of Eastern Sudan together with the Transitional Areas and Darfur. Launched in December 2007, with funding from the UK's Department for International Development and UNDP's Bureau for Crisis Prevention and Recovery, it supports development and recovery projects and has established an information management unit that shares data among state governments, NGOs, and 12 UN agencies. By the summer of 2009, state governments in Sudan had begun using the project's analyses to implement evidence-based and conflict-sensitive planning in war-affected communities that had previously been neglected. Examples of initiatives include the Early Recovery Strategy for Darfur, Reduction of Resource-based Conflict in the Three Areas, and numerous disaster risk reduction measures in East Sudan and the Three Areas.

The Threat and Risk Mapping and Analysis project invites stakeholders from all levels of society to participate in the mapping process through two-day focus groups at the community and state levels. Focus group participants identify and map the most important crisis-related factors in their area, such as the location of key natural resources. Then the project team collects real-time data using mobile phone technology and compares the changes to initial baseline maps. Maps are once again shared with the initial participants and analysed for hidden conflict patterns, which can serve as early warning signals in the future.

Stakeholders participate in a threat and risk mapping and analysis project workshop in Sudan.
Credit: UNDP

Sources: Meier (2009), UNDP (2009a), UNDP (2009b)

---

than immigrant settlements, although the wave at Tapurai was more powerful. The community fared better, chiefly because it quickly recognized natural indicators such as water rushing out of the lagoon and took appropriate action. Tapurai children were also more likely to know how to swim (McAdoo and others 2009). Indigenous knowledge and understanding of the environment could potentially reduce disaster risk if integrated into tsunami early warning systems (McAdoo and others 2009).

LOOKING AHEAD

In 2009, much was learned about the environmental drivers of disaster and conflict risks, and about managing or reducing those risks. However, a number of important questions need further research. For example, what is the environmental cost of disasters? How should damage to ecosystems due to a disaster be valued? There is currently little agreement on how to measure the value of ecosystem services (see the Ecosystem Management chapter). This lack of consensus makes it difficult to answer questions about the true environmental costs of disasters, or the protective value of ecosystem services in reducing disaster risks.

The UNFCCC has created a database of local coping strategies for adaptation to climate change,

as well as a compendium of methods and tools (UNFCCC 2009a, UNFCCC 2008c). There is still a need to analyse concrete case studies in order to identify best practices and determine the most effective means of using natural resources to reduce disaster risk, prevent conflicts, and support peacebuilding processes.

In 2010, the World Bank will release its comprehensive *Assessment on the Economics of Disaster Risk Reduction*, which should provide a normative framework that will facilitate attempts to calculate the costs of disasters and the value of ecosystems goods and services. Among the crucial issues it will address, is the true value of 'ex ante' measures to reduce disasters, compared with disaster response costs. This eagerly anticipated report will likely serve as an analytic and policy tool for practitioners and for developing country governments seeking adaptation funds.

In December 2009, the Parties to the UNFCCC adopted the Copenhagen Accord. According to this agreement, developed countries are to provide US$30 billion between 2010 and 2012, roughly half of which will fund adaptation measures in the most vulnerable developing countries (UNFCCC 2009b). As these new adaptation funds become available, governments will begin to scale up pilots and local initiatives, most of which address existing

environmental hazards by carefully managing natural resources.

Aid practitioners in 2010 also expect the publication of a revised Sphere *Humanitarian Charter and Minimum Standards in Disaster Response* handbook that will guide the provision of humanitarian assistance to disaster- and conflict-affected communities (Sphere 2010).

In 2010, the largest research programme of its kind on natural resource management and peacebuilding will present its findings. Based on 130 case studies from 40 post-conflict countries, this programme, coordinated by the Environmental Law Institute, the International Union for Conservation of Nature, UNEP, the International Peace Research Institute, Oslo, and the Universities of McGill and Tokyo, will identify best practices and lessons learned over the past 40 years in terms of minimizing conflict risks related to natural resources while maximizing opportunities for economic development and livelihoods.

REFERENCES

Allison, I., Bindoff, N.L., Bindschadler, R.A., Cox, P.M., de Noblet, N., England, M.H., Francis, J.E., Gruber, N., Haywood, A.M., Karoly, D.J., Kaser, G., Le Quéré, C., Lenton, T.M., Mann, M.E., McNeil, B.I., Pitman, A.J., Rahmstorf, S., Rignot, E., Schellnhuber, H.J., Schneider, S.H., Sherwood, S.C., Somerville, R.C.J., Steffen, K., Steig, E.J., Visbeck, M. and Weaver, A.J. (2009). *The Copenhagen Diagnosis: Updating the World on the Latest Climate Science*. The University of New South Wales Climate Change Research Centre (CCRC), Sydney

Ban, K.-M. (2009). Video Message for the Second Global Platform for Disaster Risk Reduction, Geneva, 16 June 2009. United Nations, Geneva

Bathurst, J.C., Bovolo, C.I. and Cisneros, F. (2009). Modelling the effect of forest cover on shallow landslides at river basin scale. *Ecological Engineering*, 9 July 2009

Battisti, D.S. and Naylor, R.L. (2009). Historical Warnings of Future Food Insecurity with Unprecedented Seasonal Heat. *Science,* 323(5911), 240-244

Binningsbø, H.M. and Rustad, S.A. (2009). *Resource Conflicts, Wealth Sharing and Postconflict Peace*. Background paper for the UNEP Expert Advisory Group on Environment, Conflict and Peacebuilding prepared by the Norwegian University of Science and Technology and the Centre for the Study of Civil War. International Peace Research Institute (PRIO), Oslo

Bruch, C., Jensen, D., Nakayama, M., Unruh, J., Gruby, R. and Wolfarth, R. (2009). Post-Conflict Peace Building and Natural Resources. In: *Yearbook of International Environmental Law* 2008 (eds. O.K. Fauchald, D. Hunter and W. Xi). Oxford University Press, UK

Brunnschweiler, C.N. and Bulte, E.H. (2009) Natural resources and violent conflict: resource abundance, dependence, and the onset of civil wars. *Oxford Economic Papers,* 61(2009), 651-674

Buhaug, H., Gleditsch, N.P. and Theisen, O.M. (2008). *Implications of Climate Change for Armed Conflict*. Paper commissioned by the World Bank Group for the "Social Dimensions of Climate Change" workshop 5-6 March 2008. World Bank, Washington, D.C.

CCRIF (2009). The Caribbean Catastrophe Risk Insurance Facility web site. http://www.ccrif.org

Christian Aid (2009). *The potential role of the Caribbean Catastrophe Risk Insurance Facility (CCRIF) as a tool for Social Protection, Disaster Risk Reduction and Climate Change Adaptation: A civil society perspective*. Christian Aid, London

Collier, P., Hoeffler, A. and Söderbom, M. (2008). Post-Conflict Risks. *Journal of Peace Research,* 45(4), 461-478

Conca, K., Dabelko, G.D. and Weinthal, E. (2009). *Opportunities for Environmental Peacebuilding*. Prepared for the UNEP Post-Conflict and Disaster Management Branch under a grant to the International Institute for Sustainable Development

Dasgupta, S., Laplante, B., Murray, S. and Wheeler, D. (2009). *Climate Change and the Future Impacts of Storm-Surge Disasters in Developing Countries*. Working Paper 182. Center for Global Development, Washington, D.C.

EC (2005). Council Regulation (EC) No. 2173/2005 of 20 December 2005 on the establishment of a FLEGT licensing scheme for imports of timber into the European Community. European Commission. http://eur-lex.europa.eu/LexUriServ/LexUriServ.do?uri=CELEX:32005R2173:EN:HTML

EITI (2009a). *Case Study: Addressing the roots of Liberia's conflict through EITI*. Extractive Industries Transparency Initiative, Oslo

EM-DAT (2009). The International Disaster Database, Centre for Research on the Epidemiology of Disasters—CRED. http://www.emdat.be (Data set of "Natural Disasters" in Africa during 2008)

Fomby, T., Ikeda, Y. and Loayza, N. (2009). *The Growth Aftermath of Disasters*. Policy Research Working Paper 5002. The World Bank Development Research Group and Global Facility for Disaster Risk Reduction, Washington, D.C.

Glenzer, K. (2007). We Aren't the World: The Institutional Production of Partial Success. In: *Niger 2005 : Une catastrophe si naturelle* (eds. X. Crombé and J.-H. Jézéquel). Karthala, Paris

Global Witness (2009). Credibility of Liberia's forestry reform programme at point of collapse, warns Global Witness. Global Witness, London. http://www.globalwitness.org/media_library_detail.php/808/en/credibility_of_liberias_forestry_reform_programme_

GPDRR (2009). Outcome Document: Chair's Summary of the Second Session: Global Platform for Disaster Risk Reduction, Geneva

Gronewald, N. (2009). Environmental Demands Grow for U.N. Peacekeeping Troops. *The New York Times*, 11 August 2009. http://www.nytimes.com/gwire/2009/08/11/11greenwire-environmental-demands-grow-for-un-peacekeeping-40327.html

Hammill, A., Crawford, A., Craig, R., Malpas, R. and Matthew, R. (2009). *Conflict-Sensitive Conservation*. International Institute for Sustainable Development (IISD), Winnipeg

Hanson, T., Brooks, T.M., da Fonseca, G.A.B., Hoffmann, M., Lamoreux, J.F., Machlis, G., Mittermeier, C.G., Mittermeier, R.A. and Pilgrim, J.D. (2009). Warfare in Biodiversity Hotspots. *Conservation Biology,* 23(3), 578-587

Hellmuth, M.E., Osgood, D.E., Hess, U., Moorhead, A. and Bhojwani, H. (eds.) (2009). *Index insurance and climate risk: Prospects for development and disaster management*. International Research Institute for Climate and Society (IRI). Columbia University, New York

HIIK (2009). *Conflict Barometer 2009*. Heidelberg Institute for International Conflict Research, Heidelberg

Huggel, C., Encinas, C., Eugster, S. and Robledo, C. (2008). The SDC climate change adaptation programme in Peru: disaster risk reduction with an integrative climate change context. In: *Proceedings of the International Disaster and Risk Conference* (IDRC), Davos, Switzerland, 25-29 August 2008

IFRC (2009a). Italy: Earthquake DREF Operation No. MDRIT001, Update No. 3, International Federation of Red Cross and Red Crescent Societies, Geneva. http://www.reliefweb.int/rw/rwb.nsf/retrieveattachments?openagent&shortid=AMMF-7S6LPJ&file=Full_Report.pdf

IFRC (2009b). *World Disasters Report: Focus on early warning, early action*. International Federation of Red Cross and Red Crescent Societies, Geneva

IPCC (2007). *Climate Change 2007: The Physical Science Basis. Contribution of Working Group I to the Fourth Assessment Rerpot of the Intergovernmental Panel on Climate Change, 2007* (eds. S. Solomon, D. Qin, M. Manning, Z. Chen, M. Marquis, K.B. Aveyrt, M. Tignor and H.L. Miller). Cambridge University Press, UK

IRIN (2009a). Philippines: Pregnant women vulnerable in evacuation camps. Integrated Regional Information Networks, UN Office for the Coordination of Humanitarian Affairs. http://www.irinnews.org/Report.aspx?ReportId=86545

IRIN (2009b). Africa: Climate change could worsen displacement. Integrated Regional Information Networks, UN Office for the Coordination of Humanitarian Affairs. http://www.irinnews.org/report.aspx?ReportID=86716

ISDR (2009a). *Global Assessment Report on Disaster Risk Reduction: Risk and poverty in a changing climate*. United Nations International Strategy for Disaster Reduction, Geneva

Justino, P. (2009). Poverty and Violent Conflict: A Micro-Level Perspective on the Causes and Duration of Warfare. *Journal of Peace Research,* 46(3), 315-333

Karsli, F., Atasoy, M., Yalcin, A., Reis, S., Demir, O. and Gokceoglu, C. (2009). Effects of land-use changes on landslides in a landslide-prone area (Ardesen, Rize, NE Turkey). *Environmental Monitoring and Assessment,* 156(1-4), 241-255

Liu, J., Fritz, S., van Wesenbeeck, C.F.A., Fuchs, M., You, L., Obersteiner, M. and Yang, H. (2008). A spatially explicit assessment of current and future hotspots of hunger in Sub-Saharan Africa in the context of global change. *Global and Planetary Change,* 64(3-4), 222-235

López, R. (2009). *Natural Disasters and the Dynamics of Intangible Assets*. Policy Research Working Paper 4874. The World Bank Sustainable Development Network, Global Facility for Disaster Reduction and Recovery Unit, Washington, D.C.

Lujala, P. (2009). Deadly Conflict over Natural Resources: Gems, Petroleum, Drugs, and the Severity of Armed Civil Conflict. *Journal of Conflict Resolution,* 53(1), 50-71

Lujala, P. (2010) (forthcoming). The spoils of nature: armed civil conflict and rebel access to natural resources. *Journal of Peace Research*

Machlis, G.E. and Hanson, T. (2008). Warfare Ecology. *BioScience,* 58(8), 729-736

Mafian, S. Huat, B.B.K. and Ghiasi, V. (2009). Evaluation on Root Theories and Root Strength Properties in Slope Stability. *European Journal of Scientific Research,* 30(4), 594-607

Matthew, R.A., Barnett, J., McDonald, B. and O'Brien, K.L. (eds.) (2009). *Global Environmental Change and Human Security*. MIT Press, Cambridge, USA.

McAdoo, B.G., Moore, A. and Baumwoll, J. (2009). Indigenous knowledge and the near field population response during the 2007 Solomon Islands tsunami. *Natural Hazards,* 48(1), 73-82

Meier, P. (2009). Threat and Risk Mapping and Analysis in Sudan. iRevolution. http://irevolution.wordpress.com/2009/04/09/threat-and-risk-mapping-analysis-in-sudan/

Meier, P. (2010) (forthcoming). Networking Disaster and Conflict Early Warning Systems for Environmental Security. Accepted for publication in *Coping with Global Environmental Change, Disasters and Security—Threats, Challenges, Vulnerabilities and Risks* (eds. H.G. Brauch, J. Grin, P. Kameri-Mbote, B. Chourou, P. Dunay and J. Birkmann). Hexagon Series on Human and Environmental Security and Peace, Vol. 5. Springer-Verlag, Berlin-Heidelberg-New York

Mertz, O., Bouzou, I., Diouf, A., Dabi, D., Nielsen, J. Ø., Diallo, D., Mbow, C., Ka, A. and Malga, A. (2009). Perceptions of environmental stress by rural communities in the Sudan-Sahel zone of West Africa. *Earth and Environmental Science*, 6, 41302

Mumba, M. (2008). Adapting to climate change and why it matters for local communities and biodiversity—the case of Lake Bogoria catchment in Kenya. *Policy Matters,* 16, 157-162.

Nassef, Y. (2009). *UNFCCC Post-2012 Negotiations and the Nairobi Work Programme on Adaptation. Presentation for IPCC Working Group II Scoping Meeting: Possible Special Report on "Extreme Events and Disasters: Managing the Risks*." International Panel on Climate Change, Geneva

Nerlander, L. (2009). *Climate Change and Health*. The Commission on Climate Change and Development, Stockholm

OECD (2009). *Armed Violence Reduction*. Organisation for Economic Co-operation and Development, Paris

PaCFA (2009). Fisheries and Aquaculture in our Changing Climate. Global Partnership for Climate, Fisheries and Aquaculture. http://www.cnn.com/2009/WORLD/asiapcf/03/15/afghan.taliban.threat/index.html

Peduzzi, P., Dao, H., Herold, C. and Mouton, F. (2009) Assessing global exposure and vulnerability towards natural hazards: the Disaster Risk Index. *Natural Hazards and Earth System Sciences,* 9, 1149-1159

Peduzzi, P. and Deichmann, U. (2009). Global disaster risk: patterns, trends and drivers. In: *Global Assessment Report on Disaster Risk Reduction: Risk and poverty in a changing climate (2009)*. United Nations, Geneva

Polity IV Project (2009). Polity IV Individual Country Regime Trends, 1946-2008. http://www.systemicpeace.org/polity/polity4.htm

Randall, J., Stolton, S. and Dolcemascolo, G. (2010) (forthcoming). Natural Security: Protected areas and hazard mitigation. In: *Arguments for Protected Areas: Multiple benefits for conservation and use* (eds. S. Stolton and N. Dudley). Earthscan, London

Salzmann, N., Huggel, C., Calanca, P., Díaz, A., Jonas, T., Jurt, C., Konzelmann, T., Lagos, P., Rohrer, M., Silverio, W. and Zappa, M. (2009). Integrated assessment and adaptation to climate change impacts in the Peruvian Andes. *Advances in Geosciences,* 22, 35-39

SDC (2009). Climate change in Peru: Maximising resilience to minimise vulnerability. Swiss Development Corporation, Berne. http://www.sdc.admin.ch/en/Home/Projects/Climate_change_in_Peru

Sphere (2010). Humanitarian Charter and Minimum Standards in Disaster Response. www.sphereproject.org

Stephenne, N., Burnley, C. and Ehrlich, D. (2009). Analyzing Spatial Drivers in Quantitative Conflict Studies: The Potential and Challenges of Geographic Information Systems. *International Studies Review,* 11, 502-522

Theisen, O.M. (2008) Blood and Soil? Resource Scarcity and Internal Armed Conflict Revisited. *Journal of Peace Research,* 45(6), 801-818

Tir, J. and Ackerman, J.T. (2009). Politics of Formalized River Cooperation. *Journal of Peace Research,* 46(5), 623-640

UN (2009a). *Report of the Secretary-General on peacebuilding in the immediate aftermath of conflict*. United Nations General Assembly/Security Council, New York. Document A/63/881–S/2009/304

UN (2009b). *Strategic framework for peacebuilding in the Central African Republic 2009-2011*. United Nations General Assembly/Peacebuilding Commission, New York. Document PBC/3/CAF/7

UNDP (2009a). Enhancing National Capacities for Conflict Mapping, Analysis and Transformation in Sudan, United Nations Development Programme Sudan. http://www.sd.undp.org/projects/dg13.htm

UNDP (2009b). Sudan Threat and Risk Mapping and Analysis Project, United Nations Development Programme Sudan. http://www.sd.undp.org/projects/crisis/documents/TRMA%20brief%20June%202009. doc

UNEP (2009a). *From Conflict to Peacebuilding: The Role of Natural Resources and the Environment*. United Nations Environment Programme, Nairobi

UNEP (2009b). *Climate Change Science Compendium 2009*. United Nations Environment Programme, Nairobi

UNEP (2009c). *Protection of the Environment During Armed Conflict: An Inventory and Analysis of International Law*. United Nations Environment Programme, Nairobi

UNEP (2009d). *Mapping Environment and Security Issues in the Southern Mediterranean Region*. United Nations Environment Programme, Geneva

UNFCCC (2008a). *Integrating practices, tools and systems for climate risk assessment and management and strategies for disaster risk reduction into national policies and programmes. A technical paper prepared for the Subsidiary Body for Scientific and Technological Advice (SBSTA) under the Nairobi work programme on impacts, vulnerability and adaptation to climate change*. FCCC/TP/2008/4. 21 November 2008. United Nations Framework Convention on Climate Change secretariat, Bonn

UNFCCC (2008b). *Mechanisms to manage financial risks from direct impacts of climate change in developing countries. A technical paper prepared for the Ad Hoc Working Group on Long-term Cooperative Action under the Convention*. FCCC/TP/2008/9. 21 November 2008. United Nations Framework Convention on Climate Change secretariat, Bonn

UNFCCC (2008c). Compendium on methods and tools to evaluate impacts of, and vulnerability and adaptation to, climate change. United Nations Framework Convention on Climate Change secretariat, Bonn. http://unfccc.int/adaptation/nairobi_work_programme/knowledge_resources_and_publications/items/2674. php

UNFCCC (2009a). Database on local coping strategies. United Nations Framework Convention on Climate Change secretariat, Bonn. http://maindb.unfccc.int/public/adaptation/

UNFCCC (2009b). Copenhagen Accord. United Nations Framework Convention on Climate Change secretariat, Bonn. http://unfccc.int/files/meetings/cop_15/application/pdf/cop15_cph_auv.pdf

Vergana, W., Deeb, A., Valencia, A., Haeussling, S., Zarzar, A., Bradley, R. S. and Francou, B. (2009). The Potential Consequences of Rapid Glacier Retreat in the Northern Andes. In:: *Assessing the Potential Consequences of Climate Destablization in Latin America* (ed. W. Vergara). Latin America and Caribbean Region Sustainable Development Working Paper 32, The World Bank, Washington D.C.

Warner, K., Ranger, N., Surminski, S., Arnold, M., Linnnerooth-Bayer, J., Michel-Kerjan, E., Kovacs, P. and Herweijer, C. (2009). *Adaptation to Climate Change: Linking Disaster Risk Reduction and Insurance*. United Nations International Strategy for Disaster Reduction Secretariat, Geneva

Yeh, B. (2009). Taiwan rethinks land use after killer Typhoon. Agence France-Presse, 24 November 2009. http://reliefweb.int/rw/rwb.nsf/db900SID/SNAA-7Y58FL?OpenDocument&rc=3&emid=TC-2009-000150-TWN

Resource Efficiency

Tracking production and consumption patterns is the first step in management aimed at optimizing resource efficiency. A better understanding of material and energy flows will help meet the challenges associated with economic growth, habitat destruction, pollution, and climate change.

Valuable raw materials extracted in mines throughout the world, including those in the Democratic Republic of the Congo, are used to make electronic products such as mobile phones, MP3 players, digital cameras, and laptop computers.
Credit: Mark Craemer

INTRODUCTION

In the last few decades, awareness that our growth-oriented society may be over-reaching the planet's carrying capacity has been increasing. Through the development of interdisciplinary perspectives such as sustainability science and Earth system science, the cumulative environmental effects of human activities are becoming more evident.

The fundamental issue addressed by resource efficiency is how to improve the management of both production and consumption. Poor management contributes to natural resource depletion, ecosystem destruction, pollution, climate change, and waste of materials. Resource efficiency employs a variety of approaches to reduce resource use and environmental impacts

per unit of production, trade, or consumption over the entire life cycle of goods, services, and materials.

Industrial ecologists and material chain analysts examine processes on many different scales. Some compare the delivery and consumption of industrial materials, and the accumulation of by-products, to the metabolism of living entities (Krausmann and others 2009). Evolving analytical perspectives on the human appropriation of net primary productivity (HANPP), and on the ecological footprints of products, individuals, businesses, countries, and our globalized civilization, use the concept of metabolism in such a way (Ayres 2008, Haberl and others 2008). According to this approach, growth in

industrial metabolism is a major driver of global environmental change (Ayres and Warr 2009).

MATERIALS USE

A recent assessment of global use of materials since the beginning of the 20th century was based on the conceptual and methodological principles of material flow accounting (MFA). This assessment produced a quantitative estimate of the annual global extraction of biomass, fossil fuels, metal ores, industrial minerals, and construction minerals for the period 1900-2005 (Krausmann and others 2009) (**Figure 1**).

During the 20th century, global materials use increased eight-fold. The amount of all types of materials used per year is currently almost 60 billion metric tonnes (or gigatonnes, Gt). The level of anthropogenic materials consumption is now comparable to major global material flows in ecosystems, such as the amount of biomass produced annually by green plants (Krausmann and others 2009).

The period since the Second World War has been characterized by rapid physical infrastructure growth, driven by economic and population growth. In this period there has been a relative shift from the dominance of renewable biomass towards the use of mineral materials. There is no evidence that the growth of materials use is slowing down or might eventually do so (Krausmann and others 2009).

Global materials use in the 20th century was partially driven by population growth. A large share of consumption and production resulted from rising, and then stabilizing, per-capita materials use in developed countries. However, over the last decade or so, per-capita resource use and associated environmental impacts

Figure 1: Global materials use, 1900-2005

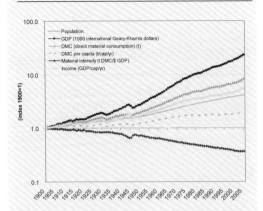

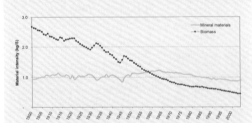

The graphs show, from top to bottom: the development of materials use (DMC), DMC per capita, population, and income; total primary energy supply (TPES), metabolic rates (materials use and TPES per capita and per year); material and energy intensity; and material intensity for biomass and mineral materials (fossil energy carriers, metal ores and industrial minerals, and construction minerals).

Source: Adapted from Krausmann and others (2009)

have increased in emerging economies such as Brazil, China, India, and Mexico (SERI 2008). Less developed countries, too, are beginning the transition towards higher levels of per-capita resource use. With future global economic development continuing in a business as usual mode, and projected population growth of 15-51 per cent by 2050, another sharp rise in the level of global material extraction can be expected (Krausmann and others 2009, UN 2009, SERI 2008).

Managing projected supply and demand is the objective of sustainable consumption and production, and of resource efficiency strategies (Jackson 2009). Reducing global materials use, or at least stabilizing it at the current level, will require major reductions of metabolic rates, above all in industrialized countries. Gains in the efficiency of materials use could contribute to a decoupling of economic growth from the use of both materials and energy, but this would require effective and innovative management strategies to avoid rebound effects (Bleischwitz and others 2009, Jackson 2009, Krausmann and others 2009, OECD 2009, Lutz and others 2004) (**Box 1**).

ENERGY ISSUES

In particular, innovations are being sought to reduce energy consumption and the use of fossil fuels (**Box 2**). Dependence on fossil fuels is associated with health and environmental problems, such as the effects of high carbon dioxide (CO_2) concentrations in the atmosphere, leading to climate change and ocean acidification.

Box 1: The rebound effect

The energy savings to be achieved through improved efficiency are commonly estimated using basic engineering principles and models. However, the predicted energy savings are seldom realized. A generally accepted explanation is that improvements in energy efficiency encourage greater use of the services the energy helps to provide. For example, if lighting comes at a lower cost due to increased energy efficiency, more of it is likely to be used. This behavioural response is called the 'rebound effect'. While the rebound effect varies widely in extent, it may lead to an overall increase in energy consumption, an outcome referred to as 'backfiring'.

Source: Herring and Cleveland (2008), Sorrell (2007)

Box 2: World Energy Outlook 2009

The International Energy Agency's (IEA) *World Energy Outlook 2009*, released in November, confirmed earlier projections that energy consumption would continue to track economic output.

The economic and financial crisis has had a considerable impact on the energy sector worldwide. CO_2 emissions in 2009 may have fallen by as much as 3 per cent. The crisis has been responsible for a deferral of investment in polluting technologies. With good environmental governance, the investment hiatus could present an opportunity to forestall the construction or expansion of carbon-intensive installations, and to meet the demand targeted by these installations with renewable energy sources.

Despite the impact of this crisis, energy related CO_2 emissions for the business as usual path are predicted to rise from 28.8 billion tonnes in 2007 to 34.5 billion in 2020 and 40.2 billion in 2030. World greenhouse gas emissions, including those of non-energy related CO_2 and all other greenhouse gases (GHGs), are projected to increase by one-third between 2005 and 2030, from 42.4 billion tonnes of CO_2-equivalent to 56.5 billion tonnes.

World Energy Outlook 2009 presents a 450 parts per million (ppm) of CO_2-equivalent scenario in which it is assumed that end-user efficiencies would account for 50 per cent of projected emissions reductions, with other measures including sectoral agreements and national measures. To achieve this, global energy related CO_2 emissions would need to peak before 2020 at 30.9 billion tonnes and decline to 26.4 billion tonnes in 2030. Beyond efficiency improvements, this projection assumes early retirement of old, inefficient coal plants and their replacement by more efficient power plants, producing an additional 5 per cent global emissions reduction. Greater deployment of renewable energy would account for 20 per cent of CO_2 savings, while increased use of biofuels in the transport sector would account for 3 per cent. Finally, in the IEA's 450 ppm scenario, carbon capture and storage (CCS) installations and nuclear energy would each represent 10 per cent of emission decreases in 2030 relative to the business as usual path.

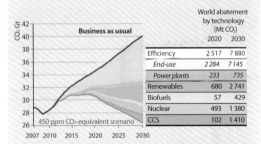

In the 450 ppm CO_2-equivalent scenairo, efficiency measures will account for two-thirds of the 3.8 Gt of CO_2 abatement in 2020, with renewables contributing close to one-fifth.

Sources: GCP (2009), IEA (2009a), Le Quéré and others (2009), IEA (2008)

Solar power

Solar power, the most abundant energy source, is the basis of the world's fastest growing renewable energy industry. Solar is even becoming competitive with coal (Carr 2009). There are two main solar power technologies. The most familiar uses photovoltaic systems, which convert solar energy directly into electricity at efficiency rates ranging from 12 to 18 per cent. By comparison, naturally photosynthesizing plants utilize sunlight at a 1 per cent efficiency rate (US DOE 2009, Schiermeier and others 2008).

An alternative system, concentrated solar power, uses mirrors to focus sunlight onto a fluid that generates steam to drive conventional turbines. While concentrated solar power is less expensive and has the greatest potential to produce large-scale baseload power and replace fossil fuel-burning power plants, it requires significant amounts of cooling water. This is a constraint in the arid regions where solar installations tend to be built (World Bank 2009a, Schiermeier and others 2008).

A technology developed more than a decade ago, but temporarily discarded when fossil fuel prices were comparatively low, uses molten salt as fluid. The turbines are driven by the steam produced when the salt is heated. This system requires only one-tenth as much cooling water as other types. The salt stores solar energy and continues to drive the turbine at night or when there is cloud cover (AE 2009, Woody 2009).

While the large mirrors that focus the solar beam are expensive, a thin, inexpensive reflective film has been developed that can decrease the weight and mass of the installation (Economist 2009).

Solar photovoltaic systems can be customized to meet specific needs, are quickly built, and are suitable for generating distributed electricity and for off-grid applications. Solar water heaters, in particular, can reduce the need to use grid power or gas for this purpose. China dominates the solar water heater market, producing more than 60 per cent of global capacity (REN21 2009, World Bank 2009b).

Hydropower

With a global generating capacity of 800 GW, hydroelectric power plants supply nearly 20 per cent of all electricity consumed worldwide. Large hydropower installations can respond quickly to changing power demands, independently of weather conditions, and are used to back up other renewable energy sources. One advantage of large hydroelectric installations is their capacity to store energy produced elsewhere by pumping water uphill into reservoirs when energy is abundant. The reservoirs can supply water for irrigation and flood control (Schiermeier and others 2008).

Small-scale hydropower is increasingly used to supply local grids. In China, it has spread quickly for several reasons: short construction periods; limited impacts in terms of population displacement and environmental damage; short distances to reach users; low costs for transmission lines; and low levels of electricity loss. In 2007, China built 45 317 small hydropower stations whose total installed capacity represented about 32 per cent of the country's hydropower capacity built that year. This approximately equalled all the small hydropower capacity installed in the rest of world (REN21 2009).

Large dams and reservoirs require lengthy and costly planning and construction, as well as the relocation of those living in the reservoir area. Over the last few decades in China and India, millions of people have been relocated to make way for large dam complexes (Schiermeier and others 2008, WCD 2000). Dams have an impact on ecosystems up- and downstream. Among these impacts, they are a barrier to migrating fish and they disrupt the delivery of sediment to agricultural areas downstream and to deltas (see the Ecosystem Management chapter). In some tropical and subtropical locations, biomass decomposing in reservoirs releases methane and CO_2 in amounts roughly equivalent to the carbon emissions avoided through not burning fossil fuels. Many large hydropower operations are threatened by the effects of climate change, including decreasing discharges from glaciers and flooding following glacier outbursts (World Bank 2009a, Schiermeier and others 2008).

Wind power

Wind power is renewable, widely available, and produces little pollution. In 2000, global wind energy potential was estimated at up to 72 000 GW, nearly five times the total energy demand, under perfect wind conditions at 80 metres and with a wind speed of 6.9 metres per second (**Figure 2**). Probably 20 per cent of this energy potential could be captured in the future, representing almost 15 000 GW (Archer and Jacobson 2005).

In Spain, new solar panel plant PS20 is under construction next to plant PS10. At a height of 115 metres, PS10 is powered by 624 mirrored heliostats. At 165 metres, PS20 is powered by 1 255 of them. PS20 has been designed to produce twice the energy of its smaller, 11 MW neighbour. Although not the world's first 'power towers', these are the first such plants conceived on such a scale.
Credit: Abengoa Solar

Figure 2: Average annual wind speeds

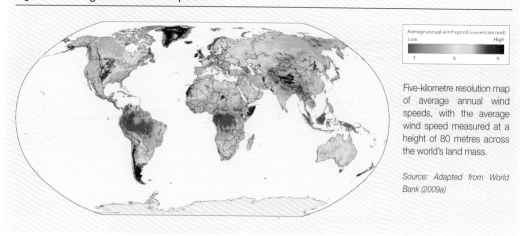

Average annual wind speed (meters/second)
Low   High

3   6   9

Five-kilometre resolution map of average annual wind speeds, with the average wind speed measured at a height of 80 metres across the world's land mass.

Source: Adapted from World Bank (2009a)

In the past five years, global installed wind power generation capacity has grown at a rate of 25 per cent per year. It totalled 120 GW in 2008. In Europe, more wind generation capacity was installed in that year than that for any other type of electricity-generating technology (World Bank 2009a). Installed capacity in the United States was estimated at 31 GW in late 2009. More wind generation capacity is planned in the United States than coal and gas plant capacity combined (AWEA 2009, Schiermeier and others 2008).

In China, which has one of the world's largest wind power programmes, installed capacity has nearly doubled every year since 2004. China is the fourth largest wind power producer after the US, Germany, and Spain, with capacity by the end of 2010 expected to be about 20 GW. Its goal is 100 GW of installed capacity by 2020. Assuming a guaranteed-into-the-future price per kilowatt hour for delivery of electricity to the grid over an agreed initial average period of ten years, electricity generated by wind power could displace 23 per cent of that generated by China's coal-fired power stations (Carr 2009, McElroy and others 2009, World Bank 2009b).

Bioenergy

Into the 20th century, trees and grass were humanity's most important energy sources. Today biomass is still second in importance only to fossil fuels. Wood, crop residues, and other forms of

biomass are important energy sources for more than two billion people. Although biomass is mainly burned on fires and in cooking stoves, in recent years it has become a source of electricity generation in combined heat and power plants (Hackstock 2008).

Advanced wood combustion, which has helped meet energy needs in Scandinavia for decades, is expanding in Austria, France, Germany, and other European countries. Solid wood fuel in advanced combustion facilities can supply a significant proportion of heat and electricity needs from locally grown renewable resources. Community-scale wood energy combustion can add financial value to local forest stands, support forest restoration and improvement through selective harvesting, and provide local employment. Careful monitoring of sustainable use of local forests is necessary to ensure that forest-energy outputs enhance rather than deplete ecosystems. Ideally, technical advances in wood-energy development should control combustion and pollution. Austria's thousand advanced wood combustion facilities produce minimal pollutant emissions owing to high-quality combustion control, combined with wood's low pollutant content compared with most fossil fuels (Richter and others 2009, Hackstock 2008).

The power generating capacity of biomass may be as much as 40 GW. Biomass use in co-generation plants can capture 85-90 per cent of available energy, using waste heat as well as electric power (Schiermeier and others 2008).

The greatest problem for new biomass power plants is finding a reliable concentrated feedstock that is available locally. Keeping transport costs down means making sure plants can be supplied with locally available fuel and are therefore relatively small, which increases capital cost per megawatt (World Bank 2009a). Serving local grids can help ensure their security, together with local control of energy supplies.

Use of waste and residues may remove carbon from the soil that would otherwise enrich it. In addition, the poor, who often have traditional rights to residues, could be deprived of an important fuel source, leaving them no alternative but to destroy standing woodlots (UNEP 2008). Large-scale dependence on bioenergy can lead to over-extraction of water resources or insect infestations, while land use changes often have climate effects of their own. For example, clearing land for energy crops can produce greenhouse gas emissions at a rate that would be difficult to offset through the use of these crops as biofuels. Again, the best use of biomass energy sources could be in small-scale systems serving local needs (Schiermeier and others 2008, UNEP 2008).

The production and global supply of large quantities of biofuels is widely considered to be a option to substitute fossil fuel use in transport (**Box 3**). In 2009, however, a number of reports on biofuels cautioned against overly enthusiastic support for this energy source. One comprehensive report, based on a comparatively rapid assessment by scientists working with the Scientific Committee on Problems of the Environment (SCOPE), attempted to present the many facets of the biofuels issue without making any judgments (Howarth and Bringezu 2009).

Another report, published by UNEP and based on a thorough literature review, encouraged further research and development for some crop-based fuels, based on analyses of environmental costs and benefits. The use of other crop-based fuels was dismissed. For example, the report supported production of ethanol from sugar cane when the benefits of sequestering CO_2 from the atmosphere are optimized. Using the same analytical approach, full consideration was given to palm oil from cleared tropical forest areas; in this case, the net effect found was an increase in greenhouse gas emissions, especially if the cleared land had been peatland (Bringezu and others 2009) (see the Climate Change chapter).

Box 3: A radical change in transport

Growth in biofuel production has been driven by the need to reduce GHG emissions in the transport sector. Transport accounts for about 19 per cent of global energy use and 23 per cent of global energy related CO_2 emissions. Based on current trends, transport energy use and CO_2 emissions from transport are projected to increase nearly 50 per cent by 2030 and more than 80 per cent by 2050.

A major transport study by the International Energy Agency (IEA), published in 2009, describes possible paths to 2050 under different scenarios. This study indicates that, if the transition to more efficient transport began now, real progress could be made towards reducing the growth of transport emissions over the next four decades. To significantly reduce CO_2 emissions from transport, however, radical changes would be necessary.

The IEA study found that by shifting travel to the most efficient modes, improving vehicle fuel efficiency by up to 50 per cent, using cost-effective, incremental technologies, and moving towards use of electricity, hydrogen, and advanced biofuels, growth in CO_2 emissions from transport could be reduced far below current levels by 2050 at lower costs than many have assumed. Under this scenario, strong governmental policy implementation would be required.

The reductions achieved under such a scenario would require slow growth in vehicle travel and stabilization of CO_2 emission levels. To halve CO_2 emissions by 2050, and then cut transport sector emissions to below 1990 levels, radical technological changes would be required, based on the use of electricity, biofuels, and hydrogen. There are considerable obstacles in the way of these changes being made on the necessary scales. These include infrastructure requirements, costs, and the need for sustainable feedstocks.

A radical technology transition would necessitate both a drastic shift in policies by governments and unprecedented investment in new technologies, including support for infrastructure such as electricity recharging systems. Countries would need to work together with a range of stakeholders to ensure that all decision-making bodies move in the same direction. Since much of the growth in travel, energy use, and CO_2 emissions will occur in developing countries, these countries must be part of a global effort to achieve a sustainable, low carbon emissions transport future.

Sources: IEA (2009b), Jackson (2009), IEA (2008)

Perhaps most importantly, the report showed that calculating and comparing greenhouse gas emissions alone does not address how the environmental burden can be shifted. Assessments of biofuel costs and benefits generally do not consider the effects of acidification and nutrient loading of waterways, and they seldom look at potential impacts on, for example, air quality, ozone depletion, or even biodiversity (Bringezu and others 2009).

Another recent study looked at water resource requirements for biofuel production (**Figure 3**). The authors, who examined the effects of irrigation, fertilizer use, transport, and other agricultural production factors, warned that maximizing the resource efficiency of biofuel production requires specific management skills that have not yet been fully developed. Of particular concern is potential damage to surface and groundwater bodies from fertilizer and pesticide run-off (Dominguez-Faus and others 2009).

ACCOUNTING FOR FRESHWATER
Freshwater is becoming scarcer in many parts of the world. Population growth, climate change, pollution, lack of investment in sanitation, and management failures all have negative impacts on the amount of water that is available relative to demand. Today, 2.8 billion people live under conditions of water stress; almost half the world population will live under these conditions by 2030 if effective new policies are not introduced and implemented (UNESCO 2009a, Bates and others 2008, OECD 2008).

The 'water footprint' concept, introduced in 2002, draws on the well-known concept of the ecological footprint. An ecological footprint indicates the bioproductive area needed to sustain a population. A water footprint represents the freshwater volume required. In elaborating the water footprint concept into a well-defined quantifiable indicator, a number of methodological issues are being addressed, similar to those addressed for the ecological footprint (Hoekstra 2009).

Water footprints take into account the source of products and circumstances related to their production. They assess actual water use rather than looking at global averages. Thus, the spatial distribution of a country's water footprint can be localized. Food consumption contributes significantly to both the ecological and the water footprint. Mobility and associated energy use is very important only for the ecological footprint. From a sustainability perspective, the water footprint tells another story and at times places particular development strategies in a different perspective (Hoekstra 2009). In 2009, the International Organization for Standardization (ISO) began to develop a water footprint standard for products (ISO 2009).

The water footprint of a product, in the form of goods or services, is the volume of freshwater used at all stages of the product chain. Water use is measured in terms of water volumes consumed and/or polluted. A water footprint is a geographically explicit indicator that provides

Figure 3: Water requirements for energy production

	litres per MWh
Petroleum extraction	10-40
Oil refining	80-150
Oil shale surface retort	170-681
NGCC power plant,* closed loop cooling	230-30 300
Coal integrated gasification, combined cycle	~900
Nuclear power plant, closed loop cooling	~950
Geothermal power plant, closed loop tower	1900-4200
Enhanced oil recovery	~7600
NGCC,* open loop cooling	28 400-75 700
Nuclear power plant, open loop cooling	94 600-227 100
Corn ethanol irrigation	2 270 000-8 670 000
Soybean biodiesel irrigation	13 900 000-27 900 000
*Natural gas combined cycle	

Some crops yield more biofuel energy than others and require less cropland, fertilizer, and water. Consumptive water (evapotranspiration) requirements tend to increase with land requirements. Large volumes of water are used to produce energy from other sources, for example to pump petroleum out of the ground, generate steam to turn turbines, or cool nuclear power plants. However, the volume of water required to produce an equivalent amount of energy from biofuels is comparatively large and water use is more consumptive.

Source: Dominguez-Faus and others (2009)

Figure 4: Components of a water footprint

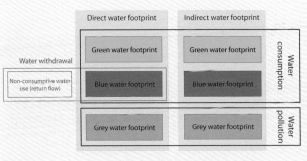

Schematic representation of the components of a water footprint. The direct water footprint of a consumer or product refers to the freshwater consumption and pollution associated with use of the water. The indirect water footprint refers to water consumption and pollution associated with goods and services consumed by the consumer or during production. 'Green' water refers to rainwater stored in the soil as soil moisture or on vegetation. 'Blue' water is surface and groundwater. 'Grey' water is polluted freshwater, and includes the amount needed to dilute pollutants emitted to the natural water system. The non-consumptive part of water use, the return flow, is not part of the water footprint.

Source: Hoekstra (2009)

information not only about water use and pollution, but also about the locations and timing of water use (**Figure 4**).

'Virtual water' is another concept used in assessing the amount of water needed to produce a consumable or tradable good. Countries can conserve their own water if they import products such as foodstuffs with a large virtual water component rather than producing them domestically. For example, Jordan's imports, which include wheat and rice from the United States, have a virtual water content of some 5-7 billion cubic metres per year compared with domestic water use of some 1 billion cubic metres. This import policy produces enormous water savings, but it also increases food dependency. Most countries in North and South America, Asia, and Central Africa, as well as Australia, are not exporters of virtual water. Most countries in Europe, northern and southern Africa, and the Middle East, as well as Indonesia, Japan, and Mexico, are net importers (Chapagain and Hoekstra 2008).

Methods of accounting for water and managing its distribution and use, in the context of resource efficiency and sustainable development, include traditional conservation and distribution methods. There is growing interest in the possibilities of upscaling local and indigenous water management methods and technologies and applying modern efficiency techniques. Water management systems in India, the rice terraces of the Philippine Cordilleras, and the karez or qanat systems of the North African and Eurasian arid belt are examples (UNESCO 2009b, Walther 2009, Jacob 2008) (**Box 4**).

Box 4: Ancient technologies with new applications

Innovative approaches to address water shortages include a renewed interest in karezes, or qanats. The karez system, used in arid regions, delivers groundwater through an underground tunnel, or series of tunnels, from a cliff face or talus slope at the base of a mountainous area. The tunnel system follows a water-bearing formation and emerges at some distance to provide water, for example to an oasis. Through a series of such tunnel systems, large areas can be supplied with water for irrigation and domestic purposes

The gravity-based karez system harvests groundwater without any need of mechanical devices. A vertical well is dug to tap into groundwater some 30 metres underground. Instead of bringing water to the surface at the well site, a horizontal tunnel with a gentle downward slope can bring it to the surface several kilometres away.

It is important to ensure that the angle of a tunnel is not too steep. Otherwise, the flow can be impeded, creating pools where the walls could be in danger of collapsing. If the angle is not steep enough, the water will stagnate. Karez tunnels are about 1.5 metres high and 0.75 metres wide, with vertical shafts facilitating maintenance. The deepest known tunnel was 60 metres below the surface, and the longest reported tunnels extended for 70 kilometres.

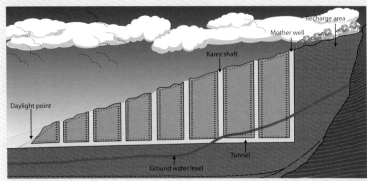

Karez systems are generally operated and maintained collectively. Intricate relationships have evolved over time for managing and distributing karez water, according to individual shareholders' inputs of land, labour, tools, and money; and numerous laws have been developed to regulate their construction, maintenance, and use.

In parts of West Asia, these systems are called qanats. They are also found on Cyprus, where a proposal has been made to construct a new qanat to meet water needs on the island's northeast coast.

Revival of the use and maintenance of karez and qanat systems throughout the region and in other arid regions has been established as a new initiative by UNESCO and FAO. There is a training centre in Yazd, Iran.

A karez consists of a tunnel on an incline, with vertical wells and shafts that allow activities such as excavation and dredging to be carried out.
Source: Hussain and others (2008)

Sources: Walther (2009), Endreny and Gokcekus (2008), Hussain and others (2008)

Qanat supplying water to a garden.
Credit: Livius.org

MODIFYING NATURAL SYSTEMS

Lack of adequate political response to the threat posed by atmospheric concentrations of greenhouse gases has prompted some scientists, and others, to consider the possibility of intervening in Earth systems to forestall or postpone the worsening impacts of climate change (Blackstock and others 2009, Lenton and Vaughan 2009, Robock and others 2009, Royal Society 2009, Lunt and others 2008, Robock 2008a, Robock 2008b, Tilmes and others 2008, Matthews and Caldeira 2007, Trenbeth and Dai 2007).

Interventions to counter the effects of GHG overload range from a great many local-scale activities, such as planting and maintaining forest ecosystems, to proposals for large-scale technological interventions, which are generally referred to as 'geo-engineering'.

Large-scale 'technological fixes' fall into two categories. Carbon dioxide removal (CDR) techniques are designed to extract CO_2 from the atmosphere. Solar radiation management (SRM) techniques are intended to reflect a portion of the sun's light back into space. CDR is based on biological or geological carbon sequestration. SRM is based on natural effects observed in the atmosphere following volcanic eruptions (Lenton and Vaughan 2009, Robock and others 2009, Royal Society 2009, Robock 2008a) (**Figure 5**).

Carbon dioxide removal

One proposed method of removing CO_2 from the atmosphere is nutrient fertilization. This method would exploit the CO_2 sequestration potential of parts of the ocean, which are nutrient rich, but do not support plankton growth because a particular nutrient such as iron is lacking. For decades it has been suggested that supplying large amounts of iron to these areas could stimulate plankton blooms, binding carbon molecules and eventually sequestering them on the deep seabed. Many small-scale experiments have been conducted, using iron filings and other nutrient sources, and have shown some success in producing plankton blooms. The most serious concern about this approach is the possible disruption of the nutrient cycles through which ocean life is sustained (see the Ecosystem Management, and Harmful Substances and Hazardous Waste chapters).

Marine ecosystems are already overexploited and endangered by human activities. The Convention on the Prevention of Marine Pollution released a statement in November 2007 that plans for "large-scale fertilization operations using micro-nutrients—for example, iron—to sequester carbon dioxide are currently not justified" (UNEP 2008, IMO 2007).

Another potential ocean-based approach to CO_2 removal is manipulation of the oceans' overturning circulation to increase the rate of sequestration of atmospheric carbon in the deep sea. Vertical pipes would be used to pump deep seawater to the surface, enhancing upwelling rates and promoting downwelling of dense water in the subpolar oceans (Lovelock and Rapley 2007). The possible effects on the overall carbon balance of altering natural circulation patterns are unknown. This upwelling could lead to carbon release rather than sequestration (Royal Society 2009).

A land-based approach would involve artificial CO_2 collectors that emulate the sequestration capability of green plants. Based on a technology used in fish tank filters and developed by scientists at Columbia University's Earth Institute, this process, called 'air capture', would remove CO_2 from the air or from smokestacks and inject it in specific geological formations. The goal is to reproduce the effects of two natural processes in combination: the pulling of CO_2 from the air as done through photosynthesis by plants, and the formation of calcite and dolomite deposits to bind the carbon molecules for millions of years. These formation types are common in every part of the world (Lackner and Liu 2008, Gislason and others 2007, Morton 2007) Other methods are storage of carbon in reservoirs or the deep sea (**Box 5**).

Large-scale ecosystems seen as potential carbon sinks can be enhanced through 'biosphere carbon stock management' (Fahey and others 2009, Read 2008). This sustainable management technique aims at long-term sequestration capacity, while maintaining ecosystem service cycles in the shorter term to support local communities and their interactions. As noted by some researchers, sustainable forest management practices can maximize carbon sequestration rates and then provide harvests, as the amount of

accumulated carbon for exploitation as low GHG fuel decreases, through advanced combustion or as long-term construction material replacing carbon-intensive concrete and steel (Fahey and others 2009, Liu and Han 2009, Canadell and Raupach 2008, Read 2008). Innovative soil sequestration approaches can keep carbon out of the atmosphere for millennia, while locally mitigating the soil degradation problems that affect 84 per cent of the world's arable land (Bruun and others 2009, UNEP 2009a, Montgomery 2008). An intensive reforestation effort with the objective of long-term carbon sequestration in ecosystems could be up and running within a decade, and could optimally be sequestering four times the current land sink by mid-century (Lenton and Vaughan 2009, Canadell and Raupach 2008).

Biochar may offer a low-risk and efficient way to mitigate climate change and improve soil fertility. This approach involves producing charcoal (the 'biochar') and incorporating it into soils. Biochar is essentially the product of burning biomass at low temperature in the absence of oxygen, so that it

Box 5: Carbon capture and storage

Carbon capture and storage (CCS) is a method of geological CO_2 sequestration. CCS systems are designed to capture emissions where they are most concentrated, at industrial point sources such as coal power generation plants, and transport them to storage reservoirs.

In theory, the captured CO_2 would be compressed, and then pumped through a pipeline, or transported on a vessel or vehicle to a site where it would be injected into the target reservoir. The injection technology, which already exists, is used in oil fields to optimize production of crude oil. Depleted oil and gas reservoirs have been suggested as suitable CO_2 destinations, as have deep saline formations and unexploitable coal seams.

Other storage methods being investigated include direct injection of CO_2 into the deep ocean, where it is assumed that high pressure would keep any CO_2 from leaking to the surface, or into the ocean itself, which would contribute to ocean acidification and result in marine ecosystem crises or upwelling to the surface. All these methods are considered experimental in regard to storing large amounts of CO_2. Their effectiveness is unknown and possible environmental impacts have not been determined.

Source: Blackford and others (2009)

turns into charcoal. Early research suggests that biochar sequestration could not only keep CO_2 from reaching the atmosphere, but also extract it *from* the atmosphere (Bruun and others 2009, Gaunt and Lehmann 2009, McHenry 2009). Moreover, the prolonged decomposition of biochar, which would take from centuries to millennia, would enhance soil fertility and have other benefits, including increasing water retention and ion exchange capacities (Bruun and others 2009).

Recent studies have improved understanding of the biochar mechanisms for mineralizing carbon. The rates of subsequent demineralization through chemical breakdown are not yet thoroughly understood (Bruun and others 2009, Gaunt and Lehmann 2008). However, farmers are moving ahead with biochar use because it can reinvigorate degraded soils. Biochar made in Australia using a patented pyrolysis process has been marketed globally as a soil amendment product.

According to a study which examined the viability of 17 carbon management and geo-engineering options, biochar has the potential to sequester nearly 400 billion tonnes of carbon over the 21st century, reducing atmospheric CO_2 concentrations by 37 parts per million (Lenton and Vaughan 2009). Some researchers caution that these figures are likely to be on the high side, but even the most conservative estimates of 20 billion tonnes of carbon sequestered by 2030 could have a significant impact on atmospheric greenhouse gas concentrations (Kleiner 2009, Lehmann 2007).

Solar radiation management

Solar radiation management is a very different approach to the climate change issue compared to carbon dioxide removal. Aerosol injection schemes are designed to increase aerosol levels in the stratosphere artificially, causing an overall increase in planetary reflectivity. A method using sulphate aerosols simulates the effect of large volcanic eruptions on the global climate by reducing incoming solar radiation. This method has been the subject of climate geo-engineering proposals for some time (Royal Society 2009, Robock and others 2009, Robock 2008a).

Proposed means of delivering the required amount of sulphate aerosols to the stratosphere include aircraft, aircraft/rocket combinations, artillery, and balloons. The annual cost could be in the tens of billions of dollars (Blackstock and others 2009). The environmental impacts of the delivery system would need to be factored into feasibility analyses of such schemes (Robock and others 2009, Royal Society 2009).

The increased reflectivity of the stratosphere following the eruption of Mt. Pinatubo in the Philippines in 1991 affected the hydrological cycle, resulting in droughts after a drop in global

Figure 5: Geo-engineering proposals

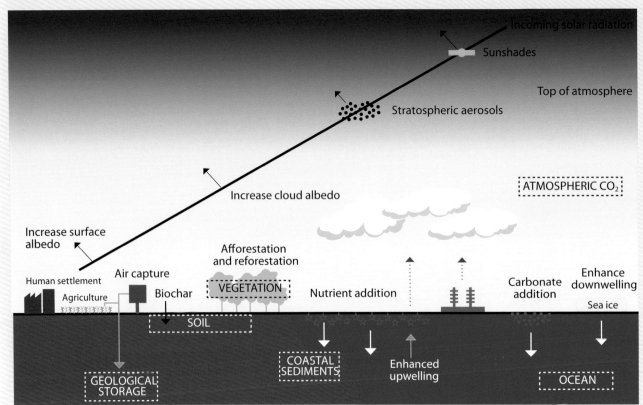

Schematic overview of geo-engineering proposals. Black arrowheads indicate shortwave radiation; white arrowheads indicate enhancement of natural flows of carbon; grey downward arrow indicates engineered flow of carbon; grey upward arrow indicates engineered flow of water; dotted vertical arrows illustrate source of cloud condensed nuclei; dashed boxes indicate carbon storage.

Source: Adapted from Lenton and Vaughan (2009)

precipitation levels in 1992 (Trenberth and Dai 2007). Detailed ocean-atmosphere modelling indicates that enhancing stratospheric sulphate aerosols would reduce precipitation during the Asian and African summer monsoons, potentially affecting more than a billion people (Robock and others 2009). An enhanced layer of sulphate aerosols would also reduce stratospheric ozone levels. Global ozone levels were about 2 per cent below expected values following the Mt. Pinatubo eruption (Robock and others 2009). Use of stratospheric sulphate aerosols could cause substantial depletion of Arctic ozone, possibly delaying the recovery of this layer by up to 70 years (Tilmes and others 2008).

A proposal for 'sunshade' geo-engineering consists in the installation of space-based sunshields, or reflective mirrors, to deflect a proportion of incoming solar radiation before it reaches the atmosphere. Sunlight deflectors would be placed in near-Earth orbits or near the Lagrange point, about 1.5 million kilometres above the planet, where the gravitational pull of Earth and the sun are equal. An array of sunshades in this position would pose less threat to orbiting satellites than would near-Earth objects. Recent modelling has demonstrated that sunshade engineering could be successful (Lunt and others 2008).

Relatively modest schemes to increase reflectivity at the planet's surface include covering deserts with reflective film, painting roofs white, or generating low-level cloud cover over oceans have been proposed. Most of these ideas have risky side effects or only local effects (Royal Society 2009).

Although implementing any of the solar radiation management proposals could take decades, the cooling effect they are designed to achieve would be relatively rapid, with atmospheric temperatures responding within a few years (Matthews and Caldeira 2007). SRM methods could therefore be useful in reducing global temperatures should catastrophic climate change begin. Such systems would require a huge commitment of resources, given the need for constant upkeep over the period of their implementation. Any failure or 'switching off' of an SRM scheme could result in rapid warming (Robock 2008a). Without a reduction of emissions to the atmosphere, other direct effects of increasing CO_2 concentrations— particularly ocean acidification and the collapse of marine ecosystems—would remain unaddressed. The logistical and technical difficulties of space-based geo-engineering render these proposals unfeasible as solutions to dangerous climate change in the short term. Moreover, there are many unknowns related to costs, risks, effectiveness, and time required for implementation (Royal Society 2009).

Given the complexities of Earth systems and uncertainties about interactions among the components that are constrained by 'planetary boundaries' (see the Ecosystem Management chapter), there is widespread concern that further interference with biophysical cycles using large-scale technological fixes to partially address GHG overload in the atmosphere could be unwise (Rockström and others 2009).

Thorough technology assessment and environmental impact assessment should indicate possibilities for environmental burden shifting as a result of proposed technological fixes. Shifts of the environmental burden have been documented over the last decade, from industrialized to developing countries, through globalization (Schutz and others 2004). Shifts of the burden from one environmental system to another are only beginning to be appreciated (Bringezu and others 2009). Potential shifts from the burden of radiative forcing to those that could delay ozone layer recovery, reduce precipitation levels, or alter Asian and African raining seasons—without addressing ocean acidification threats at all—are not real solutions to global environmental problems. Launching large-scale reforestation activities, and efforts to sequester carbon in biomass land stocks, appear to be approaches that would produce quick results and offer good opportunities for adaptive management—an essential advantage under changing conditions (Lenton and Vaughan 2009, Read 2008).

LOOKING AHEAD

Improved resource efficiency, which supports sustainable consumption and production, has become an increasingly accepted objective for management decisions, from the household to the international environmental governance levels.

Developed countries recognize that pursuing resource efficiency, and innovating to minimize waste of materials and energy use, present opportunities to lower costs and to share relevant technologies with developing countries (Jackson 2009, OECD 2009).

2009 saw the launch of the Global Market Transformation for Efficient Lighting initiative, which will accelerate a global market transformation towards energy-efficient lighting technologies and development of a worldwide strategy to phase out incandescent bulbs, thereby reducing global greenhouse gas emissions (UNEP 2009b).

In 2010, nine countries on the North Sea will establish an electrical grid designed for large-scale integration of renewable electricity. This will be made possible by new high-voltage, direct-current cables which lose significantly less energy during transmission than previous types (EWEA 2009).

Governments, civil society, and the private sector could all take advantage of the global economic slowdown to reorient their business plans and economic objectives towards sustainable development, and to accelerate the transformation towards a green economy and sustainable prosperity. To achieve a transition in the energy and transport sectors towards the comparatively radical shifts in consumption and production patterns that many experts consider necessary, implementation efforts need to begin now (IEA 2009a, IEA 2009b).

Scientists working in a number of fields warn that we risk crossing the thresholds that define 'planetary boundaries' (Rockström and others 2009). Understanding the significance of these boundaries, and how to pull back and operate within safe limits, will require continual refinement of analytical tools, drawing on the lessons of the past, and the development of sustainable solutions to environmental challenges such as decoupling of resource use and environmental impacts from economic growth.

Accepting limitations on use of the planet's resources, and improving our understanding of interactions among Earth systems, would make it possible to implement solutions through sustainable resource management rather than geo-engineered technological fixes (Read 2008).

REFERENCES

AE (2009). Molten Salt Solar Plant. Alternative Energy. http://www.alternative-energy-news.info/molten-salt-solar-plant/

AWEA (2009). American Wind Energy Association web site. http:www.awea.org

Archer, C. and Jacobson, M. (2005) Evaluation of global wind power. *Journal of Geophysical Research*, 110, D12110

Ayers, R.U. (2008). Sustainability Economics: Where do we stand? *Ecological Economics*, 67, 2

Ayers, R.U. and Warr, B. (2009). *The Economic Growth Engine: How energy and work drive material prosperity*. Edward Elgar Publishing Ltd., UK

Bates, B.C., Kundzewicz, Z.W., Wu, S. and Palutikof, J.P. (eds.) (2008). *Climate Change and Water*. IPCC Secretariat, Geneva

Blackford, J., Jones, N., Proctor, R., Holt, J., Widdicombe, S., Lowe, D. and Rees, A. (2009). An initial assessment of the potential environmental impact of CO_2 escape from marine carbon capture and storage systems. Proceedings of the Institution of Mechanical Engineers, Part A. *Journal of Power and Energy*, 223(3), 269-280

Blackstock, J.J., Battisti, D.S., Caldeira, K., Eardley, D.M., Katz, J.I., Keith, D.W., Patrinos, A.A.N., Schrag, D.P., Socolow, R.H. and Koonin, S.E. (2009). Climate Engineering Responses to Climate Emergencies. Novim, archived online at http://arxiv.org/pdf/0907.5140

Bleischwitz, R., Giljum, S., Kuhndt, M. and Schmidt-Bleek, F. (2009). *Eco-innovation—putting the EU on the path to a resource and energy efficient economy*. Wuppertal Institute for Climate, Environment and Energy. European Parliament, Policy Department Economy and Science, Brussels

Bringezu, S., Schütz, H., O'Brien, M., Kauppi, L., Howarth, R. and McNeely, J. (2009). *Assessing Biofuels*. United Nations Environment Programme, Nairobi

Bruun, S., El-Zahery, T. and Jensen, L. (2009). Carbon sequestration with biochar—stability and effect on decomposition of soil organic matter. *IOP Conference Series: Earth and Environmental Science*, 6, 242010

Canadell, J.G. and Raupach, M.R. (2008). Managing Forests for Climate Change Mitigation. Science 320(5882), 1456-1457

Carr, G. (2009). The Coming Alternatives. The World in 2010. *The Economist*, 13 November 2009

Chapagain, A. and Hoekstra, A. (2008). The global component of freshwater demand and supply: an assessment of virtual water flows between nations as a result of trade in agricultural and industrial products. *Water International*, 33, 1,19-32

Dominguez-Faus, R., Powers, S., Burken, J. and Alvarez, A. (2009). The Water Footprint of Biofuels: A Drink or Drive Issues? *Environ. Sci. Technol.*, 43 (9), 3005-3010

Economist (2009). The other kind of solar power. *The Economist*, 4 June 2009

Endreny, T. and Gokcekus, H. (2008). Ancient eco-technology of qanats for engineering a sustainable water supply in the Mediterranean Island of Cyprus. *Environmental Geology*, 57, 2

EWEA (2009). Political declaration on the North Seas Countries Offshore Grid Initiative. European Wind Energy Association, Brussels

Fahey, T.J., Woodbury, P.B., Battles, J.J., Goodale, C.L., Hamburg, S., Ollinger, S., Woodall, C.W. (2009). Forest carbon storage: ecology, management, and policy. *Frontiers in Ecology and the Environment*. doi:10.1890/080169

Gaunt, L.J. and Lehmann, J. (2008). Energy Balance and Emissions Associated with Biochar Sequestration and Pyrolysis Bioenergy Production. *Environmental Science and Technology*, 42, 4152-4158

GCP (2009). Global Carbon Project web site. http://www.globalcarbonproject.org/

Gislason, S.R., Gunnlaugsson, E., Broecker, W.S., Oelkers, E.H., Matter, J.M., Stefánsson, A., Arnórsson, S., Björnsson, G., Fridriksson, T. and Lackner, K. (2007). Permanent CO_2 sequestration into basalt: the Hellisheidi, Iceland project. *Geophysical Research Abstracts*, 9, 07153

Haberl, H., Erb, K.-H. and Krausmann, F. (lead authors) and McGinley, M. (topic editor) (2008). Global human appropriation of net primary production (HANPP). In: *Encyclopedia of Earth*. Environmental Information Coalition, National Council for Science and the Environment, Washington, D.C.

Hackstock, R. (2008). Renewable Energy—The Way Forward for the Next Century. Austrian Energy Agency, Vienna. www.energyagency.at/(en)/projekte/res_overview.htm

Herring, H. (lead author) and Cleveland, C.J. (topic editor) (2008). Rebound effect. In: *Encyclopedia of Earth* (ed. C.J. Cleveland). Environmental Information Coalition, National Council for Science and the Environment, Washington, D.C.

Hoekstra, A. (2009). Human appropriation of natural capital: A comparison of ecological footprint and water footprint analysis. *Ecological Economics*, 68 (7), 1963-1974

Howarth, R.W. and Bringezu, S. (eds.) (2009) *Biofuels: Environmental Consequences and Interactions with Changing Land Use*. Report of the International SCOPE Biofuels Project. http://cip.cornell.edu/biofuels/

Hussain, I., Abu-Rizaiza, O.S., Habib, M.A.A and Ashfaq, M. (2008). Revitalizing a traditional dryland water supply system: the karezes in Afghanistan, Iran, Pakistan and the Kingdom of Saudi Arabia. *Water International*, 33 (3), 333-349

IEA (2008). *Energy Technology Perspectives 2008—Scenarios and Strategies to 2050*. International Energy Agency, Paris

IEA (2009a). *World Energy Outlook 2009*. International Energy Agency, Paris

IEA (2009b). *Transport, Energy and CO_2: Moving towards Sustainability*. International Energy Agency, Paris

IMO (2007). Large-scale ocean fertilization operations not currently justified. International Marine Organization, press briefing. http://www.imo.org

ISO (2009). International Organization for Standardization Technical Committee (TC) 207, Environmental Management, Subcommittee (SC) 5, Life Cycle Assessment. http://www.tc207.org/About207.asp

Jackson, T. (2009) *Prosperity without growth? The transition to a sustainable economy*. Sustainable Development Commission, UK

Jacob, N. (2008). *Jalyatra: Exploring India's Traditional Water Management Systems*. Penguin Books, India

Kleiner, K. (2009). The bright prospect of biochar. Nature Reports Climate Change. http://www.nature.com/climate/2009/0906/full/climate.2009.48.html

Krausmann, F., Fischer-Kowalski, M., Schandl, H. and Eisenmenger, N. (2008). The global socio-metabolic transition: past and present metabolic profiles and their future trajectories. *Journal of Industrial Ecology*, 12, 637-656

Krausmann, F., Gingrich, S., Eisenmenger, N., Erb, K-H., Haberl, H. and Fischer-Kowalski, M. (2009). Growth in global materials use, GDP and population during the 20th century. *Ecological Economics*, 68 (10), 2696-2705

Lackner, K. and Liu, P. (2008). *Removal of Carbon Dioxide from Air*. The International Bureau, The World Intellectual Property Organization

Lehmann, J. (2007). A handful of carbon. *Nature*, 447, 143-144

Lenton, T.M. and Vaughan, N.E. (2009). Radiative forcing potential of climate geoengineering. *Atmospheric Chemistry and Physics Discussions*, 9, 1-50

Le Quéré, C., Raupach, M.R., Canadell, J.G., Marland, G., Bopp, L., Ciais, P., Conway, T.J., Doney, S.C., Feely, R.A., Foster, P., Friedlingstein, P., Gurney, K., Houghton, R.A., House, J.I., Huntingford, C., Levy, P.E., Lomas, M.R., Majkut, J., Metzl, N., Ometto, J.P., Peters, G.P., Prentice, I.C., Randerson, J.T., Running, S.W., Sarmiento, J.L., Schuster, U., Sitch, S., Takahashi, T., Viovy, N., van der Werf, G.R. and Woodward, F.I. (2009). Trends in the sources and sinks of carbon dioxide. *Nature Geoscience*, 2, 831-836

Liu, G. and Han, S. (2009). Long-term forest management and timely transfer of carbon into wood products help reduce atmospheric carbon. *Ecological Modelling,* 220, 1719-1723

Lovelock, J.E. and Rapley, C.G. (2007). Ocean pipes could help the earth to cure itself. *Nature*, 449, 403

Lunt, D.J., Ridgwell, A., Valdes, P.J. and Seale, A. (2008). "Sunshade World": A fully coupled GCM evaluation of the climatic impacts of geoengineering. *Geophysical Research Letters*, 35, L12710

Lutz, W., Sanderson, W.C. and Scherbov, S. (2004). *The end of world population growth in the 21st century: New Challenges for Human Capital Formation and Sustainable Development*. Earthscan, London

Maddison, A., 2009. Historical Statistics for the World Economy: 1-2001 AD. http://www.ggdc.net/maddison/

Matthews, H.D. and Caldeira, K. (2007). Transient climate-carbon simulations of planetary geoengineering. *Proceedings of the National Academy of Sciences,* 104, 9949–9954

McElroy, M., Lu, X., Nielsen, C. and Wang, Y. (2009). Potential for Wind-Generated Electricity in China. *Science*, 325 (5946), 1378-1380

McHenry, M. (2009). Agricultural bio-char production, renewable energy generation and farm carbon sequestration in Western Australia: Certainty, uncertainty and risk. *Agriculture, Ecosystems and Environment*, 129, 1-7

Montgomery, R.D. (2008). Why We Need Another Agricultural Revolution. In: *Dirt: The Erosion of Civilizations*. University of California Press

Morton, O. (2007). Is this what it takes to save the world? *Nature*, 447, 132-136

OECD (2008). *Environmental Outlook to 2030*. Organisation for Economic Co-operation and Development, Paris

OECD (2009). *Sustainable Manufacturing and Eco-innovation: Framework, Practices and Measurement Synthesis Report*. Directorate for Science, Technology and Industry, Organisation for Economic Co-operation and Development, Paris

Read, P. (2008). Biosphere carbon stock management: Addressing the threat of abrupt climate change in the next few decades. *Climatic Change*, 87, 3-4

Reimann, C. and Banks, D. (2004). Setting action levels for drinking water: are we protecting our health or our economy (or our backs!)? *Science of the Total Environment*, 332,1-3

REN21 (2009). Background Paper: Chinese Renewables Status Report (English). Renewables Global Status Report 2009 Update. http://www.ren21.net/

Richter, D., McCreery, L.R., Nemestothy, K.P., Jenkins, D.H., Karakash, J.T. and Knight, J. (2009). Wood Energy in America. *Science*, 323 (5920), 1432-1433

Robock, A. (2008a). 20 reasons why geoengineering may be a bad idea. *Bulletin of the Atomic Scientists*, 64(2), 14-18

Robock, A. (2008b). Whither Geoengineering? *Science*, 320 (5880), 1166-1167

Robock, A., Marquardt, A., Kravitz, B. and Stenchikov, G. (2009). The Benefits, Risks, and Costs of Stratospheric Geoengineering, *Geophysical Research Letters*. 36

Rockström, J., Steffen, W., Noone, K., Persson, Å, Chapin, F.S., Lambin, E.F., Lenton, T.M., Scheffer, M., Folke, C., Schellnhuber, H.J., Nykvist, B., De Wit, C.A., Hughes, T., Van Der Leeuw, S., Rodhe, H., Sörlin, S., Snyder, P.K., Costanza, R., Svedin, U., Falkenmark, M., Karlberg, L., Corell, R.W., Fabry, V.J., Hansen, J., Walker, B., Liverman, D., Richardson, K., Crutzen, P. and Foley, J.A. (2009). A safe operating space for humanity. *Nature*, 461, 472-475

Royal Society (2009). *Geoengineering the climate: science, governance and uncertainty*. The Royal Society, London

Schiermeier, Q., Tollefson, J., Scully, T., Witze, A. and Morton, O. (2008). Electricity without Carbon. *Nature*, 454, 816-823

Schutz, H., Moll, S. and Bringezu, S. (2004). Globalisation and the shifting environmental burden: material trade flows of the European Union. Wuppertal Papers No. 134e. Wuppertal Institute, Wuppertal, Germany

SERI (2008). Global resource extraction 1980 to 2005. Online database. Sustainable Europe Research Institute, Vienna. http://www.materialflows.net/mfa/index2.php

Sorrell, S. (2007). *The Rebound Effect: an assessment of the evidence for economy-wide energy savings from improved energy efficiency*. UK Energy Research Centre

Tilmes, S., Müller, R. and Salawitch, R. (2008). The Sensitivity of Polar Ozone Depletion to Proposed Geoengineering Schemes. *Science*, 320(5880), 1201-1204

Trenberth, K.E. and Dai, A. (2007). Effects of Mount Pinatubo volcanic eruption on the hydrological cycle as an analog of geoengineering. *Geophysical Research Letters*, 34, L15702

UN (2009). World Population Prospects: the 2008 revision—United Nations Population Division—Population database. http://esa.un.org/unpp/

UNEP (2008). *United Nations Environment Programme Year Book Book 2008.* Nairobi

UNEP (2009a). *United Nations Environment Programme Year Book 2009*. Nairobi

UNEP (2009b). Global Phase Out of Old Bulbs Announced by UN, GEF, and Industry. *Press Release*. Washington D.C./Nairobi

UNESCO (2009a) *The United Nations World Water Development Report 3: Water in a Changing World*. World Water Assessment Programme. UNESCO, Paris, and Earthscan, London

UNESCO (2009b). World Heritage Site: Rice Terraces of the Philippine Cordilleras. http://www.worldheritagesite.org/sites/riceterracescordilleras.html

US DOE (2009). *International Energy Outlook 2009*. US Department of Energy, Washington, D.C.

Walther, C. (2009). Qanats of Iraq: Reviving traditional knowledge for sustainable management of natural resources, *UNESCO-UNEP Induction Training, World Heritage Nomination Process of the Iraqi Marshlands*

WCD (2000), *Dams and Development: A new framework for decision-making*. World Commission on Dams. Earthscan, London

Woody, T. (2009). Solar Power When the Sun Goes Down. *The New York Times*, 3 Nov. 2009. http://greeninc.blogs.nytimes.com/2009/11/03/solar-power-when-the-sun-goes-down/#more-30475

World Bank (2009a). *World Development Report 2010: Development and Climate Change*. Washington, D.C.

World Bank (2009b). RE Toolkit. http://web.worldbank.org/WBSITE/EXTERNAL/TOP-ICS/EXTENERGY2/EXTRENENERGYTK/0,,menuPK:5138378~pagePK:149018~piPK:149093~theSitePK:5138247,00.html

Yool, A., Shepherd, J.G., Bryden, H.L. and Oschlies, A. (2009). Low efficiency of nutrient translocation for enhancing oceanic uptake of carbon dioxide *Journal of Geophysical Research*, 114, C08009

Acronyms and Abbreviations

ACP-EU JPA — Africa Caribbean Pacific-European Union Joint Parliamentary Assembly
ADAM — ADaptation And Mitigation
AMSR-E — Advanced Microwave Scanning Radiometer-Earth Observing System
AoA — Assessment of Assessments
BFRs — brominated flame retardants
$CaCO_3$ — calcium carbonate
CAI — Computer Aid International
CBD — Convention on Biological Diversity
CCRC — Climate Change Research Centre
CCRIF — Caribbean Catastrophe Risk Insurance Facility
CCS — Carbon capture and storage
CDM — Clean Development Mechanism
CDR — Carbon dioxide removal
CEB — UN System Chief Executives Board for Coordination
CH_4 — methane
CITES — Convention on International Trade in Endangered Species of Wild Fauna and Flora
CLASLite — Carnegie Landsat Analysis System Lite
CMS — Convention on Migratory Species
CO_2 — carbon dioxide
COP — Conference of the Parties
CRCP — Coral Reef Conservation Program
CSD — Commission on Sustainable Development
DMC — Direct material consumption
DDR — Disarmament, demobilization, and reintegration
DDT — dichlorodiphenyltrichloroethane
deca-BDE — decabromodiphenyl ether
DPKO — UN Department of Peacekeeping Operations
ECOSOC — UN Economic and Social Council
EEA — European Environment Agency
EFSA — European Food Safety Authority
EM-DAT — International Disaster Database
EMG — Environment Management Group
ETS — EU Emission Trading Scheme
FAO — Food and Agriculture Organization of the UN
FCRC — Forest Concession Review Committee
GC/GMEF — Governing Council/ Global Ministerial Environment Forum
GEF — Global Environment Facility
GEO BON — Group on Earth Observations Biodiversity Observation Network
GEOSS — Global Earth Observation System of Systems
GHGs — Greenhouse gases
GIS — Geographic Information System
GISS — Goddard Institute for Space Studies
GMOs — Genetically modified organisms
GPDRR — Global Platform for Disaster Risk Reduction
GW — Gigawatt
HANPP — Human appropriation of net primary productivity
HBCD — hexabromocyclododecane
HFCs — hydrofluorocarbons
IAEA — International Atomic Energy Agency

IDP — Internally displaced person
IEA — International Energy Agency
IEG — International environmental governance
IFA — International Fertilizer Industry Association
IFAD — International Fund for Agricultural Development
IFRC — International Federation of Red Cross and Red Crescent Societies
IISD — International Institute for Sustainable Development
IJIS — IARC-JAXA Information System
ILRI — International Livestock Research Institute
IMO — International Maritime Organization
INI — International Nitrogen Initiative
IOC — Intergovernmental Oceanographic Commission
IPBES — Intergovernmental Platform on Biodiversity and Ecosystem Services
IPCC — Intergovernmental Panel on Climate Change
IPY — International Polar Year
IRIN — Integrated Regional Information Networks
ISDR — International Strategy for Disaster Reduction
ISO — International Organization for Standardization
IUCN — International Union for Conservation of Nature
IWG-IFR — Informal Working Group on Interim Finance for REDD+
IWMI — International Water Management Institute
JIU — Joint Inspection Unit
LDCs — Least developed countries
LIDAR — Light Detection And Ranging
MA — Millennium Ecosystem Assessment
MDGs — Millennium Development Goals
MEA — Multilateral environmental agreement
MFA — Material flow accounting
MODIS — Moderate Resolution Imaging Spectroradiometer
MOP — Meeting of the Parties
N_2O — nitrous oxide
NASA — National Aeronautics and Space Administration
NCDC — National Climatic Data Center
NGCC — Natural gas combined cycle
NGO — Non-governmental organization
NNI — National Nanotechnology Initiative
NOAA — National Oceanic and Atmospheric Administration
NRC — National Research Council
NSIDC — National Snow and Ice Data Center
ODA — Official development assistance
OECD — Organisation for Economic Co-operation and Development
PACC — Climate Change Adaptation Programme
PACE — Partnership for Action on Computing Equipment
PaCFA — Global Partnership Climate, Fisheries and Aquaculture
PBDD — polybrominated dibenzodioxin
PBDEs — polybrominated diphenyl ethers
PCBs — polychlorinated biphenyls
PEER — Partnership for European Environmental Research
PFCs — perfluorocarbons

POPs — Persistent organic pollutants
ppm — parts per million
PRODES — Amazon Deforestation Monitoring Project
R&D — Research and development
REDD — Reducing Emissions from Deforestation and Forest Degradation
REN21 — Renewable Energy Policy Network for the 21st Century
SBSTTA — Subsidiary Body on Scientific, Technical and Technological Advice
SCENIHR — Scientific Committee on Emerging and Newly Identified Health Risks
SCOPE — Scientific Committee on Problems of the Environment
SCP — Sustainable consumption and production
SF_6 — sulphur hexafluoride
SIDS — Small island developing states
SRM — Solar radiation management
TBBPA — tetrabromobisphenol A
TPES — Total primary energy supply
TSCA — US Toxic Substances Control Act
UAE — United Arab Emirates
UNCCD — UN Convention to Combat Desertification
UNCLOS — UN Convention on the Law of the Sea
UNCTAD — UN Conference on Trade and Development
UN DESA — UN Department of Social and Economic Affairs
UNDP — UN Development Programme
UNECE — UN Economic Commission for Europe
UNEP — UN Environment Programme
UNESCO — UN Educational, Scientific and Cultural Organization
UNFCCC — UN Framework Convention on Climate Change
UNGA — UN General Assembly
US EPA — US Environmental Protection Agency
WCMC — World Conservation Monitoring Centre
WCD — World Commission on Dams
WDR — World Development Report
WEEE — Waste Electrical and Electronic Equipment
WMO — World Meteorological Organization
WWDR — World Water Development Report
WWF — World Wildlife Fund
WSSD — World Summit on Sustainable Development

Acknowledgements

ENVIRONMENTAL GOVERNANCE

Science Writer:
Jörg Baloiger, Institute for Environmental Decisions, Swiss Federal Institute of Technology, Zürich, Switzerland

Reviewers:
Ivar Baste, Environment Management Group Secretariat, UNEP, Geneva, Switzerland
Theo A.M. Beckers, Institute for Globalization & Sustainable Development (GLOBUS), Tilburg, The Netherlands
Bradnee Chambers, DELC, UNEP, Nairobi, Kenya
Marion Cheatle, DEWA, UNEP, Nairobi, Kenya
Munyaradzi Chenje, UNEP New York Office, New York, United States
Ahmed Hassan Farghally, Accounting Department, Cairo University, Cairo, Egypt
Michael Flitner, Research Center for Sustainability Studies, University of Bremen, Bremen, Germany
Tessa Goverse, DEWA, UNEP, Nairobi, Kenya
Edgar E. Gutiérrez-Espeleta, School of Statistics, University of Costa Rica, San José, Costa Rica
Maria Ivanova, Global Environmental Governance Project, Yale University and College of William and Mary, Washington, D.C., United States
Matthias Kern, Secretariat of the Basel Convention, UNEP, Geneva, Switzerland
Clara Nobbe, Office for Policy and Inter-agency Affairs, UNEP, Nairobi, Kenya
Balakrishna Pisupati, DELC, UNEP, Nairobi, Kenya
Kilaparti Ramakrishna, DELC, UNEP, Nairobi, Kenya
John Scanlon, Office for Policy and Inter-agency Affairs, UNEP, Nairobi, Kenya
Suzanne M. Skevington, WHO Centre for the Study of Quality of Life, University of Bath, Bath, United Kingdom
Cecilia Vaverka, IISD Reporting Services, International Institute for Sustainable Development, New York, United States
Hugh Wilkins, Earth Negotiations Bulletin, International Institute for Sustainable Development, New York, United States

ECOSYSTEM MANAGEMENT

Science Writer:
Penny Park, freelance journalist, Montreal, Canada

Reviewers:
Joana Akrofi, DEWA, UNEP, Nairobi, Kenya
Sara Brogaard, Lund University Centre for Sustainability Studies, Lund, Sweden
Thierry de Oliveira, DEWA, UNEP, Nairobi, Kenya
Salif Diop, DEWA, UNEP, Nairobi, Kenya
Tessa Goverse, DEWA, UNEP, Nairobi, Kenya
Martin Kijazi, Faculty of Forestry, University of Toronto, Toronto, Canada
Marcus Lee, Finance, Economics and Urban Department, The World Bank, Washington, D.C., United States
Patrick Mmayi, DEWA, UNEP, Nairobi, Kenya
Dennis Ojima, Natural Resource Ecology Laboratory, Colorado State University, Fort Collins, Colorado, United States
Lennart Olsson, Lund University Centre for Sustainability Studies, Lund, Sweden
Neeyati Patel, DEWA, UNEP, Nairobi, Kenya
Danièle Perrot-Maître, DEPI, UNEP, Nairobi, Kenya
Ravi Prabhu, DEPI, UNEP, Nairobi, Kenya
Anthony A. Prato, Center for Applied Research and Environmental Systems, University of Missouri, Columbia, Missouri, United States
Elina Rautalahti, DEWA, UNEP, Nairobi, Kenya
Gemma Shepherd, DEWA, UNEP, Nairobi, Kenya
Stephen Twomlow, DGEF, UNEP, Nairobi, Kenya

HARMFUL SUBSTANCES AND HAZARDOUS WASTE

Science Writer:
Fred Pearce, freelance journalist, London, United Kingdom

Reviewers:
Nalini Basavaraj, Secretariat of the Basel Convention, UNEP, Geneva, Switzerland
Philippe Bourdeau, The Free University of Brussels, Royal Academies for Science and the Arts, Brussels, Belgium
Surya Chandak, International Environmental Technology Centre, DTIE, UNEP, Kusatsu City, Japan
Heidelore Fiedler, DTIE, UNEP, Geneva, Switzerland
Bernard Goldstein, Department of Environmental and Occupational Health, University of Pittsburgh, Pittsburgh, Pennsylvania, United States
Alastair Iles, Department of Environmental Science Policy and Management, College of Natural Resources, University of California, Berkeley, California, United States
Matthias Kern, Secretariat of the Basel Convention, UNEP, Geneva, Switzerland
Juliette Kohler, Secretariat of the Basel Convention, UNEP, Geneva, Switzerland
Gunilla Lindström, MTM Research Center, Örebro University, Örebro, Sweden
David Piper, DTIE, UNEP, Geneva, Switzerland
David Rickerby, Institute for Health and Consumer Protection, European Commission Joint Research Centre, Ispra, Italy
Nora Savage, National Center for Environmental Research, US Environmental Protection Agency, Washington, D.C., United States
Martin Scheringer, Institute for Chemical and Bioengineering, Swiss Federal Institute of Technology, Zürich, Switzerland
Suzanne M. Skevington, WHO Centre for the Study of Quality of Life, University of Bath, Bath, United Kingdom
Gang Yu, POPs Research Center, Tsinghua University, Beijing, China

CLIMATE CHANGE

Science Writer:
Catherine McMullen, Allophilia Consultants, Ottawa, Canada

Reviewers:
Grant Galland, Center for Marine Biodiversity and Conservation, Scripps Institution of Oceanography, La Jolla, California, United States
Joel Harper, Department of Geosciences, University of Montana, Missoula, Montana, United States
Seraphine Haeussling, DTIE, UNEP, Paris, France
Dorothee Herr, IUCN-US Multilateral Office, Washington, D.C., United States
Anna Kontorov, DEPI, Nairobi, Kenya
Marcus Lee, Finance, Economics and Urban Department, The World Bank, Washington, D.C., United States
James Maslanik, Colorado Center for Astrodynamics Research, University of Colorado, Boulder, Colorado, United States
W. Tad Pfeffer, Institute of Arctic and Alpine Research, Department of Civil, Environmental, and Architectural Engineering, University of Colorado, Boulder, Colorado, United States
Hans Martin Seip, Department of Chemistry, Oslo University, Oslo, Norway
Kaveh Zahedi, DTIE, UNEP, Paris, France

DISASTERS AND CONFLICTS

Science Writer:
Justin Ginnetti, Tufts University, Medford, Massachusetts, United States

Reviewers:
Marion Cheatle, DEWA, UNEP, Nairobi, Kenya
Salif Diop, DEWA, UNEP, Nairobi, Kenya
Marisol Estrella, DEPI, UNEP, Geneva, Switzerland
Silja Halle, DEPI, UNEP, Geneva, Switzerland
Stephanie Hodge, Education Division, UNICEF, New York, United States
Terry Jeggle, Center for Disaster Management, University of Pittsburgh, Pittsburgh, Pennsylvania, United States
David Jensen, DEPI, UNEP, Geneva, Switzerland
Allan Lavell, The Latin American Social Science Faculty, San Jose, Costa Rica
Richard Matthew, Center for Unconventional Security Affairs, University of California, Irvine, California, United States
Johannes Refisch, DEPI, UNEP, Nairobi, Kenya
Renard Sexton, DEPI, UNEP, Geneva, Switzerland
Susanne M. Skevington, WHO Centre for the Study of Quality of Life, University of Bath, Bath, United Kingdom
Henrik Slotte, DEPI, UNEP, Geneva, Switzerland
Suchitra Sugar, Education Division, UNICEF, New York, United States
Sonia Sukdeo, Education Division, UNICEF, New York, United States

RESOURCE EFFICIENCY

Science Writer:
Catherine McMullen, Allophilia Consultants, Ottawa, Canada

Reviewers:
Surya Chandak, International Environmental Technology Centre, DTIE, UNEP, Kusatsu City, Japan
Bas de Leeuw, Sustainability Institute, Hartland, Vermont, United States
Richard Fleming, Canadian Forest Service, Sault Ste. Marie, Canada
Tessa Goverse, DEWA, UNEP, Geneva, Switzerland
Bernard Jamet, DTIE, UNEP, Paris, France
Sylvia Karlsson-Vinkhuyzen, Finland Futures Research Centre, Turku School of Economics, Tampere, Finland
Michael Kuhndt, Wuppertal Institute, UNEP Collaborating Centre on Sustainable Consumption and Production, Wuppertal, Germany
Gustavo Mañez i Gomis, DTIE, UNEP, Paris, France
R.E. (Ted) Munn, Centre for Environment, University of Toronto, Toronto, Canada
Jon Samseth, SINTEF, Trondheim, Norway
Guido Sonnemann, DTIE, UNEP, Paris, France
Jaap van Woerden, DEWA, UNEP, Geneva, Switzerland

CONTRIBUTING EXPERTS OF THE SCIENTIFIC COMMITTEE ON PROBLEMS OF THE ENVIRONMENT

Ahmed Hassan Farghally, Accounting Department, Cairo University, Cairo, Egypt
Carla Gomez Wichtendahl, Institute of the Environment, University of Ottawa, Ottawa, Canada
Susan Greenwood Etienne, Scientific Committee on Problems of the Environment, Paris, France
Barbara Göbel, The Ibero-American Institute, Berlin, Germany
Guizhen He, Research Center for Eco-Environmental Sciences, Chinese Academy of Sciences, Beijing, China
Allan Lavell, The Latin American Social Science Faculty, San Jose, Costa Rica
Jérôme Payet, Federal Polytechnic School of Lausanne, Lausanne, Switzerland
W. Tad Pfeffer, Institute of Arctic and Alpine Research, University of Colorado, Boulder, Colorado, United States
Véronique Plocq-Fichelet, Scientific Committee on Problems of the Environment, Paris, France
Jon Samseth, SINTEF, Trondheim, Norway
Suzanne M. Skevington, WHO Centre for the Study of Quality of Life, University of Bath, Bath, United Kingdom
Gang Yu, POPs Research Center, Tsinghua University, Beijing, China

PRODUCTION:

Márton Bálint
Susanne Bech (Coordinator)
Jason Jabbour
John Smith (Copy editor)

SUPPORT:

Tessa Goverse
Beth Ingraham
Grace Kighenda
Stanley Kinyanjui
Kelvin Memia
Nick Nuttal
Audrey Ringler

Order form

Please send me the NEW! UNEP Year Book 2010 @ US$20.00 in the following languages/quantities:

Year Book 2010

Language	Quantity	Total price US$
English (ISBN: 978-92-807-3044-9)	_____	_____
French (ISBN: 978-92-807-3045-6)	_____	_____
Spanish (ISBN: 978-92-807-3046-3)	_____	_____
Russian (ISBN: 978-92-807-3047-0)	_____	_____
Arabic (ISBN: 978-92-807-3048-7)	_____	_____
Chinese (ISBN: 978-92-807-3049-4)	_____	_____

Purchase any of the previous Year Books (2009, 2008, 2007, 2006, 2004/05, and 2003) at a discounted rate of US$10.00 each. Please specify languages and quantites:

Previous Year Books

Language	Years	Quantity	Total price US$
English	_____	_____	_____
French	_____	_____	_____
Spanish	_____	_____	_____
Russian	_____	_____	_____
Arabic	_____	_____	_____
Chinese	_____	_____	_____

Discounted price is 50% for developing countries and 75% for least developed countries.
To order, please return this completed form to the address below.
You can also email us, or place your order online at our bookstore (www.earthprint.com).

EarthPrint Limited
P.O. Box 119, Stevenage, Hertfordshire SG14TP, England
Tel: +44 1438 748 111 • Fax: +44 1438 748 844 • Email: unep@earthprint.com

☐ Europe/UK postage: US$8.00 for first item, plus US$4.00 for each subsequent item.
☐ Rest of the world: US$12.00 for first item, plus US$6.00 for each subsequent item.
☐ Please find enclosed a cheque for US$_____ (made payable to EarthPrint Ltd.).
☐ Please invoice our institution/organization.
☐ Please charge my credit card (Amex/Visa/Mastercard).

Card No. ☐☐☐☐☐☐☐☐☐☐☐☐☐☐☐☐☐ Expiry date ☐☐/☐☐/☐☐

Name: _____ Organisation: _____

Address: _____ Country: _____

Email or fax: _____

For other UNEP publications, please visit www.earthprint.com

Questionnaire

Please take a few minutes to fill out this questionnaire and share your opinion of this publication - Thank you!

The UNEP Year Book 2010 is the most recent annual report on new science and recent developments in our changing environment produced by the United Nations Environment Programme, in collaboration with many world environmental experts

1. How would you rate the overall usefulness of the content of each chapter of the UNEP Year Book?

	Very useful	Useful	Not very useful	Not useful at all	No opinion
Environmental Governance					
Ecosystem Management					
Harmful Substances and Hazardous Waste					
Climate Change					
Disasters and Conflicts					
Resource Efficiency					

Please provide any additional comments on the content of the chapters:

2. How informative did you find the UNEP Year Book with respect to the following statements?

	Very informative	Informative	Not very informative	Not informative at all	No opinion
Environmental Governance					
Ecosystem Management					
Harmful Substances and Hazardous Waste					
Climate Change					
Disasters and Conflicts					
Resource Efficiency					

Please provide any additional comments on your intended use of the information in the chapters:

3. Please help us improve the next Year Book by suggesting new emerging issues that could be of interest to the readers of the Year Book.

4. About yourself

Please specify the type of organization you belong to:

Government	
Development organization	
Non-government/civil society	
Academic/research institution	
International organization	
Private sector	
Press or media	
Other (please specify):	

Your position:

Minister/director	
Manager	
Advisor	
Scientist	
Student	
Technical specialist	
Journalist	
Consultant	
Other (please specify):	

Please state the use of the information from the Year Book:

Private interest	
Commercial	
Research/academic	
Policy-makers	
Education/teaching	
Development work	
Other (please specify):	

Thank you!

Please mail your completed questionnaire to:

EarthPrint Limited
P.O. Box 119
Stevenage, Hertfordshire
SG14TP, England

You can also complete this questionnaire on-line at
www.unep.org/yearbook/2010